ADVOCACY AND ORGANIZATIONAL ENGAGEMENT

ADVOCACY AND ORGANIZATIONAL ENGAGEMENT

Redefining the Way Organizations Engage

BY

LUKASZ M. BOCHENEK
Leidar, Switzerland

emerald
PUBLISHING

United Kingdom – North America – Japan – India – Malaysia – China

Emerald Publishing Limited
Howard House, Wagon Lane, Bingley BD16 1WA, UK

First edition 2019

Reprints and permissions service
Contact: permissions@emeraldinsight.com

British Library Cataloguing in Publication Data
A catalogue record for this book is available from the British Library

ISBN: 978-1-78973-438-6 (Print)
ISBN: 978-1-78973-437-9 (Online)
ISBN: 978-1-78973-439-3 (EPub)
ISBN: 978-1-78973-440-9 (Pbk.)

INVESTOR IN PEOPLE

Acknowledgments

I wouldn't be able to write this book without a support and intellectual stimulation of my family, friends, and colleagues. Thank you all; and especially Rolf, Lutz and Christophe; for sharing your wisdom, encouragement, and patience while I was "suffering through" a creative process. Without you this journey wouldn't have been possible. And of course, special thanks to Aline the first reader and critic of this book whose valuable advice and comments made it much better.

Contents

List of Figures

List of Tables

List of Abbreviations or Acronyms

AIDA	Awareness Interest Desire Action
AMEC	The International Association for Measurement and Evaluation of Communication
B2B	Business to Business
B2C	Business to Consumer
CC	Corporate Communication
CCO	Chief Communications Officer
CEO	Chief Executive Officer
CFO	Chief Financial Officer
CIO	Chief Information Officer
CMO	Chief Marketing Officer
COP	Conference of Parties
CR	Corporate Reputation
CRM	Customer Relationship Management
CSP	Corporate Social Performance
CSR	Corporate Social Responsibility
EACD	European Association of Communications Directors
EC	European Commission
EU	European Union
GRI	Global Reporting Initiative
GSMA	GSM Association
HR	Human Resources
IGO	Inter-governmental Organization
IO	International Organization
ISO	International Standards Organization
KPIs	Key Performance Indicators
MDGs	Millennium Development Goals
NGO	Non-governmental Organization
PA	Public Affairs
PESTEL	Political Economic Social Technological Environmental Legal
PPP	Public Private Partnership
PR	Public Relations

RACI	Responsible Accountable Consulted Informed
ROE	Return on Engagement
ROI	Return on Investment
SDGs	Sustainable Development Goals
SWOT	Strengths Weaknesses Opportunities Threats
UN	United Nations
UNGA	United Nations General Assembly
UNGC	United Nations Global Compact
UNICEF	United Nations Children's Fund
USP	Unique Selling Proposition
WEF	World Economic Forum
WHO	World Health Organization
WOMM	Word of Mouth Marketing
WTO	World Trade Organization

Prologue

This book is a summary of research and reflection about advocacy. I am an advocacy and communication consultant with an interdisciplinary background from social sciences (ethnology and cultural anthropology), media studies, and finally management. My career started in advertisement, passed quickly through market research to land in communication and advocacy consultancy. Ever since I started, I was fascinated to what extent communication and engagement can have a transformative role on the organizations. Not to preach too high, I would claim that communication and advocacy can positively change the lives of many. The issues that once where just short news snap-shots somewhere far away are brought home through digital and traditional media requiring global action. At the same time communication and advocacy change the organizations. The companies need to act in a way that responds to the requirements coming from their stakeholders. This changes the business models and also shifts the role companies have in the society and broader system.

Influence is the most natural thing people do. We want to have "better deal" for us, for our families and for those about whom we care. In order to get what we want, we need to win the argument or convince the others about our points and to do what we want. We do it all the time and in many circumstances. This is why advocacy is accompanying us throughout our lives. We advocate for ourselves, for our families, for organizations that we represent. Paradox being that oftentimes, we do advocate without knowing that we advocate. Similarly, organizations and companies need to permanently advocate for themselves in a busy multi-media and multi-stakeholder environment. Making people care about the issues important for them and making people support their organizational brand and activities becomes a *sine qua non* requirement for an organizational license to operate. Without license to operate businesses and organizations vanish. So, we can claim that organizations can't exist without effective advocacy.

At the same time, the ways of influencing are changing. Social media, virtual reality, big data analytics – all these new tools and technologies change the way organizations and individuals communicate with each other. With a personalization of communication, companies and organizations are more and more often humanized – they are seen almost as human beings. Corporate citizenship requirements make companies build personalities. The companies behave, act, and are perceived as individuals. This changes dramatically the way they see themselves and the way they engage with the external environments. Organizational engagement is driven by these new requirements and redefines the role both advocacy and communication play.

This book is a combination of research, theoretical modeling, and personal experience. It aims to discuss the newest trends in the organizational engagement from a managerial perspective. There are many books that focus on corporate communications, and there are several books focusing on the grassroots engagement and campaigning. However, there are very few that look at advocacy from a holistic perspective. In this book, I claim that advocacy is equally relevant for non-for-profit and corporate sectors. I try to also sum up the key trends impacting advocacy and define "so what" from an organizational perspective.

I was pretty frustrated by the lack of models for strategy development and functional management of advocacy during my time as Co-Director of Executive Certificate in Advocacy – one of the first (if not the first) executive education training in the field. Strategic models lists of considerations as well as recommendations included in this book are response to this frustration. They are developed in a way that favors customization and avoids cookie-cutter approaches in the implementation. This last point is extremely important from an advocacy perspective. In management practice, we often suffer from "best practices" approach. The "best practices" in communication and advocacy are everywhere. They create a safety net for those who design organizational engagement strategies. Companies follow the best practices of the previous campaigns in their marketing and influencing approaches. However, the landscape and stakeholders are changing at a pace that nobody can really keep up with. Therefore, a past success is no guarantee of future good performance. We do forget about it far too often and embark at repetitive campaigns that don't necessarily correspond to the organizational objectives. Moreover, the fact that something worked well for another organization is no guarantee that it will work for ours.

Advocacy professionals can be divided into two main groups. The first one encompasses professionals with business or legal background who see advocacy, public affairs, and lobbying as the key organizational activities linked closely with the core business of the organization or company. The second group presents much more mystical view on advocacy. They want advocacy to be a mysterious activity not scrutinized at a corporate level. For them advocacy is almost like a magic. And magicians are not supposed to report or show how they do their magic. This attitude unfortunately still shared by many advocacy professionals destroys its internal perception. Advocacy brings value to the organization and those managing advocacy need to stand up and measure and report the effectiveness of their activities. This will upgrade perception of advocacy to the level it deserves.

Finally, both communication and advocacy are very often not considered to the core of the business by the companies and organizations. It is true that advocacy professionals in the global international non-for-profit and international organizations benefit from a better statute than their corporate counterparts. But still, in many cases many organizations don't realize that advocacy might be their "raison d'être." Without advocacy they cease to exist. Here we can think about trade associations. Their job is to represent the interests to their members and there is no more obvious way than advocacy.

Yet often companies and organizations don't support these activities with the sufficient budgets. Enough is to compare the EU lobbying budgets of the multinationals (published in the EU Transparency Register) with their regional or even local marketing budgets. Yet the decisions taken in Brussels that are lobbied for or against can define business success or completely destroy a business model.

I would love this book to become for some a simple (simplistic) guide on how to design advocacy strategies. I would love to start a discussion on the organizational positioning of advocacy as a function. At the same time, I would like that advocacy gains the place it deserves among the executives of the organizations. In today's environment many factors impact the business operating environment. Whether we want it or not many people and organizations have a stake in the business of virtually any organization and company. Having a compass to navigate this environment becomes paramount for the future of business. And as I will claim at the end of this book the landscape is set to change and evolve further. This evolution both from a social perspective as well as from the perspective of the advocacy tools and strategies will elevate an importance to engage with even broader ranges of audiences and stakeholders.

Creating engagement means bringing people closer to the organization. While we need to be strategic in both advocacy and communication, we cannot forget about an emotional component. People and stakeholders alike need to believe in the values and purpose of the organization in order to support it. Without this belief the organizations fail to deliver on their promises. As a result, these organizations fail to obtain their license to operate. Being strategic about emotions might sound like a dichotomy but is not, and I hope this book will convince the readers. This dual rational-emotional approach requires though a transformation of the way we think about the role of organizational engagement.

Let's start the journey and make advocacy strategic …

Introduction – Why Advocacy? Why Now?

The role of corporate reputation for business results has been analyzed and described for years (Chun et al., 2005). Many researchers studied the correlation between a good reputation and financial performance of the companies (e.g., Roberts & Dawling, 2002):

> Good corporate reputations are critical because of their potential for value creation, but also because their intangible character makes replication by competing firms considerably more difficult. Existing empirical research confirms that there is a positive relationship between reputation and financial performance. (Roberts & Dawling, 2002)

Focus of certain researchers on reputation studies has helped to elevate the discourse around corporate reputation to the key concern for communications and external relations management (Barnett, Lafferty, & Jermier, 2005). The role of corporate communication and public affairs department within many companies and organizations is summarized by management of organizational reputation. At the same time, management of the corporate reputation is one of the key functions for the marketing department (Balmer & Greyser, 2006). It also led to commercial success for the organizations that help to manage and benchmark corporate reputation. The example of the Reputation Institute that assesses the companies according to their external reputation is the best witness of this tendency.

The world has changed – this statement can sound trivial and stating the obvious. And to a certain degree it is true that saying that the world has changed doesn't bring much to the discussion. There is no new argument, or unknown fact. However, it is surprising to see how few of the organizations and companies are actually embracing the change that the world has undergone and include it in their communications and external engagement strategies. This change happens at all levels:

- the way organizations are perceived (externally and internally);
- the way organizations are expected to behave and act (higher expectations accompanied with a much more humanized view on the organizations); and
- the way organizations communicate and engage (through different tools, channels, and platforms).

These changes are the direct results of the global trends impacting communications and influence agenda. For the purpose of this book we selected five trends that in our view impact the advocacy stakeholder agenda the most.

Trend #1: Low levels of trust – the trust studies show year by year decreasing levels of trust in the society toward the channels (media), organizations (companies and institutions), and information in general (Edelman Trust Barometer 2010–2019). This adds a challenge of influencing opinions and beliefs of those who matter for business as people don't believe the messages they see nor the institutions carrying these messages. It also means that traditional communications model is not effective anymore. Sending messages and hoping for people to interact doesn't work. Organizations need to focus less on information and content they want to promote and more on the engagement with the right stakeholders and influencers. It means creating the new and direct ways of engagement as well as looking for the stakeholders to support the messages.

Trend #2: Segmentation of influence – on the one hand, the number of actors influencing the political and social agenda is increasing. On the other hand, the stakeholders and influencers that are focused on the precise and concrete issues can be more influential than the ones with higher scope or reach. This trend is the most visible in social media. The influencers that are focused on the niche issues/markets have much higher impact on their target audiences than the ones with big audiences (Influencer Marketing Hub, 2019). It creates a real need for the companies to gain an in-depth understanding of their operating environment and develop engagement strategies that are segmented to the needs of all types of influencers. It doesn't mean focusing only on the micro-influencers. It requires deeper understanding of the landscape and better grip on the ripples of influence.

Trend #3: Confirmation bias – people tend to believe more on what reaffirms their preexisting beliefs (Klayman, 1995; Nickerson, 1998). This is hardly a new news. There are several definitions of the confirmation bias which in brief can be described as:

> Confirmation bias, as the term is typically used in the psychological literature, connotes the seeking or interpreting of evidence in ways that are partial to existing beliefs, expectations, or a hypothesis in hand. (Nickerson, 1998)

In fact, it is an old psycho-sociological finding that is further accentuated by the digital media environment (Knobloch-Westerwick, Johnson, & Westerwick, 2015). Indeed, social media users are rarely exposed to the information that challenges their perception of the status quo and of the world (Knobloch-Westerwick et al., 2015). More often than not, they see and consume information that is confronting them in their vision of the world and in the vision of a particular issue (Knobloch-Westerwick et al., 2015). Looking at the algorithms of social media, the information that we see in the social media feeds is based on the pages we follow and interactions that we have (Yin et al., 2016). The advertisement — the best example here is remarketing — meaning targeting of the messages and advertisements based on our previous visits. The same tendency can be observed in the way online audiences are created. One of the most used tools looks at *"alike audiences"* meaning repeating targeting toward the individuals who are similar to the ones previously engaging with the organization. While effective, it can be also limiting in terms of the scope and future opportunities to engage beyond current circle of interest. Equally, results in the search engines are based on our previous searches (Knobloch-Westerwick et al., 2015). Yet interestingly enough search engines top the list of the media that are most trusted by the users (Edelman Trust Barometer, 2019). In fact, it is not in anyone's business interest to challenge our views as then we might shift to the other media that are more comforting and provide the security of affirmation. As a result, we are constantly reaffirmed in what we already believe in (Nickerson, 1998). This is even more visible in the case of the "digital natives" — growing up in the environment in which digital is the primary source of information. The whole generation is growing up in the environment which is not challenging the status quo of personal believes.

Trend #4: Changing expectations from stakeholders and consumers — the consumers and stakeholders expect from organizations to be the active actors in the society (Scheyvens, Banks, & Hughes, 2016). Looking at Trust Barometer study from Edelman, it is apparent that businesses have a growing license to position themselves in the broader social context and lead the discourse beyond their core operations (Edelman Trust Barometer, 2019). At the same time, the decision-makers (including regulators and legislators) expect companies to have a position on the broader societal themes such as sustainable development (Scheyvens et al., 2016). The Sustainable Development Goals (SDGs) framework created by UN in dialogue with private sector and non-for-profit partners created a platform for companies and other actors to work together addressing world's pressing issues. At the same time, the SDG framework created expectations for the stakeholders to address together the societal issues (Scheyvens et al., 2016). It also provided companies with the opportunities to move away from defensive approach toward proactive one (Scheyvens et al., 2016). While there are still questions about operationalization of the SDGs and the ways the success of SDG implementation can be measured; it is clear that they did change the discourse around sustainability even before they were adopted (Sachs, 2012).

Trend #5: VUCA — volatility, uncertainty, complexity, and ambiguity are the words that define today's operating landscape for organizations and companies (Breen, 2017). It is important to note and recognize that the change impacts both companies (commercial entities) and non-for-profit organizations. The context of VUCA requires much more agility in business models; it also requires much more flexibility in communications and engagement (Breen, 2017). It also requires constant challenging of the existing engagement and influence models (Mack, Khare, Krämer, & Burgartz, 2015). This needs to be paired with a constant foresight related to the stakeholder landscape (Mack et al., 2015). This all means that advocacy is even more important for the companies and organizations alike. Interestingly, companies oftentimes do the foresight into the future of their business model and consumers, but rarely use foresight techniques and methodologies to define their advocacy models.

Based on these trends and a complexity of the environment, advocacy moved from being considered as an "emerging" discipline into the core strategy of marketing and corporate communication. It is reflected by a growing number of professionals having job titles related to "advocacy." In some cases, this shift is motivated by a willingness to get away from using the "public affairs" job title which is associated with a classical lobbying activity. However, in more and more cases this change reflects a profound shift of priorities within the organizations. The shift which recognizes that in order to be truly influential, the companies need to gain support from multiple stakeholders (Scheyvens et al., 2016; Wood, 2010). And gaining support from the stakeholders requires a concentrated effort and building relationships going beyond the "business as usual," or current business needs (Scheyvens et al., 2016).

In addition, growing importance attached to sustainability in the corporate context means that companies and non-for-profit organizations work more together (Carbonara, Costantino, & Pellegrino, 2014; Chan et al., 2010; Deaton & Heston, 2010). It goes from punctual cooperation through partnerships to fully fledged public private partnerships (PPPs). The PPPs can be seen as the ultimate vehicles of advocacy for multiple stakeholders (Andonova, 2010). Successful PPPs are built around the common understanding of the interests by stakeholders coming from the various sectors of activity (Andonova, 2010).

I.1.   Changing Communications Landscape

Today, people are confronted with more information that they can process at every stage of media consumption. Whether it is traditional media or social media, the information, data, facts, and visuals are everywhere. Frequently, the information is conflicting. Media make lower distinction between the facts and commentary (Maigret, 2007). Navigating this landscape is increasingly difficult. Every single communication channel is getting saturated with facts, data, and knowledge.

At the same time, due to the multiplication of the channels it is increasingly difficult to distinguish between the "real" and the "fake." Ongoing discussions about the influence of fake news and fake social media on electoral results are a great example of this trend. The scandal of Cambridge Analytica showcased the issue in a pinnacle. The fact of illicit usage of data in order to impact the election results created a buzz all around the world. It can be attributed to a consequence, the trust toward digital information and social media further decreased (Edelman Trust Barometer, 2019). We also observe a simultaneous decrease in trust toward traditional media and institutions. It creates an unprecedented challenge for companies and organizations to influence their audiences.

The multiplication of data, data sources, and influencers make it even more difficult for companies and organizations to "cut through the noise." At the same time, thanks to social and digital media, they can engage with their audiences directly. Also, for the first time in history, they don't have to rely on media broadcasters and can engage with their audiences directly. This created an environment in which organizations need to look holistically at their landscape in order to engage better. The traditional focus and distinction between the key customers and key stakeholders are by far not sufficient in order to influence the agenda and position the company/organization in this changing landscape. In order to position itself in the landscape, organizations need to:

- *Gain in-depth understanding of the communications channels.* Understanding of the technical features of the channels and audience profiles needs to be paired with a good grasp of demographics of the audiences one each of the platforms.
- *Identify the key issues that impact the operating environment of the company or organization.* The key issues usually go beyond the traditional and direct concerns that were on the corporate agenda. It means also understanding of the global issues which can impact a core business of the organization.
- Following from that, there is a *need to identify the ones who influence the opinions and beliefs around these both core organizational issues and global ones impacting them.* This goes beyond an understanding of the legislative and regulatory agenda. In order to do it right, companies need to see who are the ones shaping the discourse around the global topics of a direct or indirect relevance for business.
- *Seek for external partners and organizations* that can be impacted by the same developments in order to build partnerships and coalitions beyond the "usual suspects." Managing advocacy campaigns in coalitions brings multiple benefits: it shares the burden of the campaign, it showcases a broader industry voice and creates unity between various actors impacted by the social, regulatory, and legislative developments.
- *Communicate with a large group of stakeholders and influencers* in order to shape the landscape and create an enabling environment in which organization can position its messages and its interests. These influencers and stakeholders can ultimately become the advocates of the organization and bring an external support when needed.

Navigating this complex landscape represents a challenge and opportunity at the same time. This is why identifying and understanding the agenda of those who matter becomes paramount for organizational and business success. Without this understanding, the organizations continue to broadcast their messages into the vacuum without being able to identify whether they are impactful or not. We claim that this broadcasting model defining the way communications and public affairs work is redundant and can create adverse results to the intended ones. For instance, many campaigns focus solely on raising awareness among target groups. However, raising awareness needs to be accompanied by a clear call to action – people need to know "what should they do" with the issues. For instance, several studies have showcased that pure awareness raising without supporting target audiences with a clear call to action can lead to the behaviors that are opposite to the desired ones (Christiano & Neimand, 2017). The study about famous campaign "Dumb ways to die" launched by Sydney public transport authority showcased that campaign led to an increase in numbers of suicides in the public transport – effect opposed to the intended one (Christiano & Neimand, 2017). It happened because the campaign lacked a good understanding of its target audiences and as an effect created adverse effects to the intended ones (Christiano & Neimand, 2017).

> Too many organizations concentrate on raising awareness about an issue—such as the danger of eating disorders or loss of natural habitat—without knowing how to translate that awareness into action, by getting people to change their behavior or act on their beliefs. It's time for activists and organizations to adopt a more strategic approach to public interest communications. (Christiano & Neimand, 2017)

Too often, companies and organizations focus solely on what they want to convey or achieve. The needs of their audiences are frequently forgotten (as is the need to identify who those audiences are). As a result, multiple companies and organizations fall into the trap of over-communicating or communicating missing the target (Christiano & Neimand, 2017). They multiply the channels and messages without any real focus. And focus is essential to engaging with those who matter the most and ultimately driving lasting change (Christiano & Neimand, 2017).

I.1.1.   Place of Communications in the Corporate Strategic Management

Corporate communications department traditionally focused on managing the channels used by organization to interact with external world (Cornelissen, 2011; White, 1994). These included owned channels such as website and earned channels (e.g., traditional media reached through media relations activities). The role of the communications department has evolved with the rise of social media channels (Bochenek & Blili, 2013). The new channels created an opportunity for communication professionals to become the drivers of engagement with the new audiences. Communication professionals claimed internal ownership of the social media engagement (Bochenek & Blili, 2013). Indeed, social media combine all media functions in one (Bochenek & Blili, 2013). It includes earned, owned, and paid aspects. As a result, the role of communications departments in organizations where this department was responsible to manage social media engagement was elevated and entered the territory traditionally reserved for marketing professionals (Bochenek & Blili, 2013). However, with a rise of paid engagement in the social media platforms, the landscape changed again. It is now more and more frequent that social media and digital engagement are driven from the marketing side of business.

At the same time, the role of external relations and public affairs in companies is further strengthened. The role of consumers in the public policy processes has been studied for over 40 years (Ferrell & Krugman, 1978). Multiplication of the stakeholders and their agendas requires from companies to have a more holistic approach to their public affairs activities. Also, the influence techniques evolve from a traditional lobbying to more sophisticated engagement strategies requiring both political communication and campaigning. Consequently, the role of public affairs professionals is more and more focused on building lasting relationships as opposed to gaining access to the decision-makers (Zetter, 2014). Thought leadership and content strategies are rising to become the key tools used in the public affairs activities.

The evolution of the role of communications department within companies is heavily dependent on an organizational learning of the company (Bochenek & Blili, 2013). In an article published in 2013, we proposed a model that looked at the different level of integration of corporate communication department depending on the learning level of organization. It led to the development of five archetypes for organizational models of corporate communication management (Bochenek & Blili, 2013). These were put in the context of three loops of learning: tactical, strategic, and network. Using organizational learning theory was very useful to describe the changes and challenges faced by corporate communication function (Bochenek & Blili, 2013). One of the main conclusions of this study was that the internal position and influence of the corporate communication department depends on the sensitivity of the industry to crisis and focus put into measurement and evaluation of the communications activities (Bochenek & Blili, 2013).

This trend evolved further with the changes and developments of the stakeholder landscape. The role of communications becomes increasingly focused on managing change for organizations (Mazzei, 2014). This requires new types of skills and competencies from the communications professionals (Cornelissen, 2013). In addition, it also redefines the place that corporate communications department has within the organizational structure (Mazzei, 2014). In several cases, it leads to the change of the name of the department in order to include the variety of the functions it has within the organization. It is more and more often seen that the head of corporate communications department reporting directly to the CEO of the company and/or sitting in a management board. Gravity center of the communications department is depending on the leadership view of communications (Communication Monitor, 2018).

The questions on leadership and organizational culture in the ECM 2018 draw out some interesting findings. For example, although 76.5 per cent of the respondents state that the top leader in their organization understands the value of communication, only 57.8 per cent confirm the same for other leaders like those of most work units. At the same time, about 20 per cent of the communication leaders in the organizations surveyed are said to lack leadership excellence. (Communication Monitor, 2018)

I.2. The Art and Craft of Influence

It is increasingly difficult to identify who influences whom in the international socioeconomic context. The traditional distinctions between stakeholders, decision-makers and consumers are less and less relevant with all groups constantly interchanging. In the recent years, often non-traditional actors have had stronger leverage on decision-making than well-established institutional ones (Hall & Biersteker, 2002). There is a similar tendency when looking at the legal operating context. The so-called soft laws (including standards, rankings, and industry-driven frameworks) have more impact on businesses than traditional laws and regulations (Abbott & Snidal, 2000). Soft laws become also an area for lobbying and advocacy. Self-regulation is often used by the industries to mitigate the risks related to industry regulation (Gunningham & Rees, 1997). Indeed, companies might benefit from self-regulation in order to avoid being subject to a regulation/legislation, which could have higher impact on their business model for instance (Gunningham & Rees, 1997). In consequence, often time proactive advocacy approaches (like self-regulations such as creation of industry code of conducts, industry rankings, etc.) become more effective for the companies than the defensive ones (fighting with the regulation or legislation) (Zetter, 2014).

Traditionally, influencing strategies were executed on behalf of companies and industries by lobbyists and public affairs professionals (Zetter, 2014). Simplistically speaking the most important asset of a good lobbyist was his/her list of people on speed dial in their phone. Lobbying was traditionally about *"who does the lobbying professional know."* Nowadays, the access is less of an issue. Many country and international legislations require decision-makers to consult the constituencies before processing the laws and regulations (Zetter, 2014). Therefore, the challenge is what to do with the access. In the context where meeting regulators and legislators become a right – it means also that more influence groups gain this access. The legislators and regulators are confronted with even more data, positions, and lobbyists. As a result, in order to be effective, the lobbyists and advocates need to come with a clear value proposition for the stakeholders (Zetter, 2018). This value proposition needs to have a cohesive character and showcase consideration toward all the parties impacted by an issue.

Meanwhile, decision-making processes are influenced by a multitude of actors, so it is impossible to know *"everyone that matters"* in any given subject.

In fact, effective influencing strategies now have to start with identification of those who can actually impact decision-making both directly and indirectly (Zetter, 2014). And effective identification requires looking at both prominence and relevance of an individual. While prominence comes from personality and level of activity, relevance is still rooted in a social capital (e.g., position). The second level of analysis requires to look at the influence from a network perspective (Bruni & Teli, 2007). It helps to identify who influences whom in the decision-making process (Bruni & Teli, 2007). As a result, that allows to focus the lobbying activities and develop two-pronged strategies. These strategies focus first on influencing decision-makers. Secondly, they seek to influence those who influence them. Network theory is a very useful tool to identify these individuals and organizations (Lin, 2017).

I.3. Toward a Consolidated Approach

Complexity of an influence landscape calls for an integrated approach to influence and advocacy strategies. Therefore, the advocacy strategies are more and more often based on a "campaign approach." Indeed, in this view advocacy is a permanent campaign which aims at building positive and supportive behaviors of the target audiences toward an organization. Both words – advocacy and campaign – still bring to mind thoughts of examples of grassroots campaigns and social activism, but there is so much more to both.

The campaign approach provides clear benefits: structure, cross-channel focus, creativity, edge and focus on the desired outcome, and campaign goals. This last is so important, as the clear and correct definition of the desired outcome (the "so what" of the campaign) will determine the success of its efforts. It is also time bound – the campaign needs to lead toward an end result and should have an end embedded in the planning. This helps to shape the timeline, define the milestones, and structure an approach toward the activities. Finally, it helps defining measurement and evaluation and links the measurement with the final goals.

This broader and more inclusive approach to influencing strategies recognizes the complexity of the international environment, providing a focus. Organizations that take this approach build direct relationships with those who matter to them in the context of the issues which are the most pressing from an organizational perspective. As a result, the ongoing question faced by advocacy and public affairs professionals about who owns the relationship becomes irrelevant, as it is relationship that owns relationship. Building relationships is an ongoing organizational activity which engages multiples stakeholders. This multiplication poses a challenge of alignment. It provides also a benefit of avoiding on relying on personal relations between individuals.

I.4. Defining Advocacy

Advocacy becomes increasingly important for international companies and organizations. For good and bad the role of advocacy within organizations and companies is evolving. In the past advocacy was synonymous of third-party endorsement for the causes, organizations, and products. Now advocacy term is used in the corporate context as a synonymous of public affairs and lobbying. At the same time, there are more and more professionals that identify themselves as advocates.

In this context comes a question – how to define advocacy? Some authors look at it from a process perspective – advocacy in this sense is a process of influencing public agenda for a cause (e.g., UNICEF Advocacy Toolkit).

> Advocacy is the deliberate process, based on demonstrated evidence, to directly and indirectly influence decision makers, stakeholders and relevant audiences to support and implement actions that contribute to the fulfilment of children's and women's rights. (UNICEF Advocacy Toolkit)

Others still see advocacy as a third-party endorsement (the act of advocating on someone's or an organization's behalf). This showcases the difficulty and complexity of what advocacy is. Combining the two approaches leads to logically challenging situation in which advocacy becomes a process and a result of the same process.

This duality of advocacy makes providing a clear definition challenging. However, as we explore in Chapter 5 of this book these approaches are not mutually exclusive and can indeed build on each other. For the interest of simplicity, we call it a duality of advocacy. Having this holistic view on advocacy allows to clearly define the benefits it can bring to the organization. It also focuses on recognizing the advocacy process, which leads to the third-party endorsement (Figure I.1).

Therefore, advocacy becomes both the strategy and the result of the strategy. This definitional issue is part of the reason why advocacy is still relatively misunderstood.

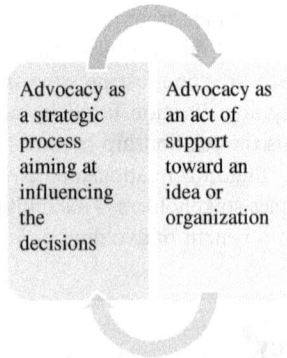

Advocacy as a strategic process aiming at influencing the decisions

Advocacy as an act of support toward an idea or organization

Figure I.1.   Duality of Advocacy.

I.5. Structure and Flow of the Book

This book proposes a blend between theoretical reflection about advocacy and its imperatives together with the analysis of practice. This holistic approach aims to look at advocacy without ideological lenses that often times tainted the analytical approach to the issue. It recognizes that advocacy is a function of organization in shaping and influencing the environment in order to follow its organizational needs and agenda.

We have never communicated as much. Individuals, organizations, companies all want their messages to be "out there." However, to be heard and to have an impact, companies need to cut through the noise. And they can achieve this only by focusing on quality and originality. In this context communicating less often means having more impact.

Many books describe corporate communications (Argenti, 2006a, 2006b; Cornelissen, 2011; White, 1994). Even more books look at marketing and advertisement trends, and several books look at public affairs (Boddewyn, 2012). However, very few authors look at intersections between the disciplines. Advocacy is situated at the nexus of organizational engagement disciplines and provides a great opportunity to look at influencing landscape holistically.

This book aims to fill this gap by providing a comprehensive overview on how to design, set up, and execute effective advocacy strategies for organizations and companies. It looks at both organizational design and the most effective content approaches. Its comprehensive approach focuses both on the management and structural side as well as on the communications side. Its structure starts with definition of the playing field, which is followed by more theoretical reflection on various contextual aspects of advocacy. It moves then to practical implementation of advocacy strategies and campaigns. Finally, it touches on the notion of crisis in advocacy and ends on an outlook toward the future scenarios for advocacy. More precisely the chapters are structured as following.

The first chapter introduces the main concepts of advocacy. It defines the main professional and theoretical concepts surrounding advocacy. By looking at different types of advocacy, it aims at describing the background of advocacy and state the ground for the concepts discussed further in the book. It also provides an overview of the advocacy trends and how do they shape an influencing landscape. There are many tools which are used by advocacy professionals and several ways in which advocacy approaches are structured. The chapter proposes a journey to discover them and see advocacy as a profession. We introduce the similarities (many) and differences (few) between advocacy approaches seen in non-for-profit versus corporate sector. Finally, it seeks to look at advocacy as a business and describes the ways advocacy is set as a business within the organizations and companies.

The second chapter of this book reviews the state of the art related to advocacy in corporate communication, business, and marketing studies. This review allows us to define how advocacy is understood in different contexts. It helps also to understand the challenges that we face while defining advocacy strategies due to its complexity. Finally, in this chapter we propose a conceptual model for organizational advocacy management. This model is a dynamic managerial model that is applicable both for private sector companies and for the non-for-profit organizations.

In addition, we propose an advocacy diagnosis tool that can be used by communications and advocacy professionals to benchmark their advocacy strategies against best practices. This diagnosis tool which consists of a questionnaire allows to:

- benchmark advocacy strategy against best practices and define the advocacy profile of the organization;
- identify gaps in advocacy strategy and showcase the possible corrective actions in order to cover these gaps;
- see how the advocacy profile (archetype) of organization fits into international landscape and which advocacy tactics and actions are the most effective;
- define the template for advocacy strategy development. This template can be used for both organizational and campaign advocacy strategies;
- enhance advocacy efforts and ensure the best return on investment from advocacy activities within the organization; and
- showcase the opportunity for strategic alliances and the path that can be used in order to build these alliances (relevance, value, return).

The third chapter looks at the evolution of the expectations from stakeholders toward the companies and organizations. It looks at an evolution of what used to be called Corporate Social Responsibility (CSR) in the corporate discourse. The concept of the CSR evolved toward sustainability, and companies more often talk about their sustainability strategies and engagements as opposed to the CSR. Indeed, the term CSR became associated with *old* and *outdated* strategies seeking to build public support toward organization through philanthropic activities. These are now replaced by more comprehensive approaches that touch even business models and product definition often branded as sustainability strategies.

Further involvement of companies in the societal issues is based on the stakeholder expectations toward the corporations. Indeed, the studies indicate that both the stakeholders and the consumers require from companies to have a position on the key social issues. This position should be broader than just declarations and defensive reporting on the supply chain performance, which was the center of CSR strategies.

This shift in societal involvement of the companies provides a great advocacy platform of cooperation between the actors from the sectors that not necessarily used to work together. In this context, UN SDGs and underlying targets provide a great framework of cooperation for all the actors. SDGs are an inclusive platform that encourages cross-sector cooperation. In addition, the SDGs favor looking at the issues from a broader perspective that goes beyond a narrow view frequently presented in the past CSR approaches.

At the end of the chapter, we present what we believe are current advocacy opportunities and thought leadership model. Interestingly, the popularity of the thought leadership concept led to a certain dilution of the term. Many companies call whichever executive profiling or leadership communications a "thought leadership strategy," yet when properly defined and consistently executed thought leadership can become a very powerful vehicle for advocacy and public affairs strategies. This requires several conditions:

Condition #1 – clearly defined desired outcome of the thought leadership approach.

Condition #2 – alignment between thought leadership approach and corporate strategy.

Condition #3 – strong communications platform that allows thought leadership to build connections with the stakeholders beyond regular group of corporate contacts.

Condition #4 – strategic and creative narrative that builds emotional connection with organizational involvement and with the corporate brand.

Condition #5 – commitment from the organization at all level from executive engagement to employee advocacy.

This holistic approach helps organizations to become both more effective and more efficient in their defined sustainability strategies.

The fourth chapter seeks to provide a better understanding of influence landscape.

Who influences whom? Why are these decision-makers influenced by these particular influencers and with what results?

These are the vital questions that each organization needs to ask before embarking on an influencer strategy. The influencer strategies used to be based on corporate engagement, with social media influencers selected on the basis of their digital followership. This led to high spending on campaigns that were proven to be relatively ineffective. This came with a realization of the need for more qualitative indicators while looking at the influencer strategies.

The recent rise of popularity of so-called micro-influencer strategies in marketing and public affairs is one of the examples of this shift of focus. Micro-influencer strategies mean focus on the individuals with smaller social media following but more active and resilient communities. This new marketing trend is based on a good assessment that relevance can be more important than reach. However, as each of the big marketing trends it leads to an important amount of supply of services of varying quality levels that seek to identify, engage, and manage corporate relationships with these micro-influencers.

In our approach we propose to look at influence holistically. In fact, the global influencer strategies and micro-influencer ones don't necessarily need to be mutually exclusive. In contrary, they can co-exist and fuel each other in the advocacy funnel. In fact, when well defined they have different aims and contribute to the different levels of engagement between an organization and its public.

We believe that additional questions and mapping digital influence using anthropological and sociological methodologies is the most effective. Humans interact on various channels based on their social needs. The role of social capital in building relationships between stakeholders and companies is often times underestimated, yet it can bring tangible benefits.

At the end of the chapter we propose a questionnaire that can be used by the managers to define and assess their influencer strategies. It combines the questions related to the aim of the campaign and advocacy effort with the questions focusing on the quantification and qualification of the selected influencers. We believe that some of the *"common sense"* considerations that it includes are worth reminding people of, as they are oftentimes overlooked during advocacy strategy development.

We also propose a "health check" list of considerations that we believe are relevant for monitoring and evaluation of the relationships with the external influencers of the organization. This includes both quantitative considerations related to the return on investment (ROI) combined with qualitative considerations focusing on the progress and depth of the relationship. This list is driven by the following considerations:

- What are the costs associated with management of the relationship?
- What are the benefits that the organization has thanks to this relationship?
- How did the engagement start? And how did the relationship evolve?
- What are the measurable benefits from this engagement?
- Is there a room to deepen the engagement?

Following on these considerations and "health check," we establish the maturity level of the relationship and suggest the steps to further benefit from mutual engagement.

The fifth chapter proposes an advocacy campaign model. The model is defined in such a way that can be applied for both public affairs and public campaigning activities. It follows the strategic steps that are needed to plan, implement, and measure an advocacy campaign in an international context.

Many of the advocacy campaigns fail to align what they are seeking to achieve with the communications tactics. Therefore, it is crucial to follow a structured planning process. This process we believe includes 10 key steps.

Step 1: Landscape mapping and definition of a unique point of engagement (UPE). We propose the concept of unique point of engagement as an enhancement of the unique selling point/proposition from marketing. We believe that definition of the main value proposition of an organization should be the first step before identification of any campaigns. This should come from an in-depth landscape mapping including competitive benchmarking and organizational foresight. This would allow for any campaign to address not only the known issues, but also the unknown ones that can impact the business or reputation in the future.

Step 2: Setting up of the impact and ambition level. This step allows us to define an overall impact of the campaign on an organization and/or business.

We believe that clear definition of the desired impact is important in order to link the advocacy campaign with the core of the organizational considerations. It also allows to align the advocacy and public affairs goals with the organizational goals. It is recommended that the desired impact includes both short- and long-term components.

Definition of the advocacy outcomes. It is important to distinguish between the advocacy outcomes and advocacy outputs. The advocacy outcomes are the final results of the campaigns within the target groups (AMEC, 2019). Many of the advocacy campaigns fail to align define their outcomes and as a result the focus is lost, and activities are driving the campaign and not a strategy. Definition of the campaign outtakes focuses on desired reactions of the target audiences toward the messages (AMEC, 2015). It includes recall of the message, emotional connection with the key messages, and imminent interactions.

Definition of the campaign outputs looks at the levels of coverage and reach of the campaign messages (Macnamara, 2012). This also includes the numbers of the meetings, partners aligned with the campaign plan, and members of the coalition (AMEC, 2009, 2015).

Step 3: Context analysis. It includes further landscape mapping and analysis. It is complemented by the SWOT and PESTEL analysis. The idea is to have in-depth basis and understanding of the broader landscape. In this step, we look also at potential backlashes and push back related to the campaign (defining the need for defensive advocacy). The idea of this step is to understand a resilience of the campaign and the organization. Finally, at this moment we develop alternative scenarios.

In the context analysis, we also look at defining the links between the issues of the campaign with the broader social context. This helps to define the common points with the other socioeconomic subjects that are related to the advocacy campaign. These analyses help uncover potential additional partnerships and coalitions for the campaign.

Step 4: Target audience identification and opinion tracking. Based on the context analysis we define the primary and secondary target audiences. The primary target audiences are those who have a decision power over the issue of the campaign (decision-makers or power-brokers) (Subacchi, 2008). The secondary audiences are the ones who have a leverage over those with decision power (influencers) (Subacchi, 2008).

Having identified all the target audiences we need to understand the sentiment among them toward the campaign theme and toward the organization running the campaign. In addition, it is important to understand the sentiment toward the competing campaigns. The most effective methods for initial opinion tracking include a combination between qualitative and quantitative methods. This analytical process uses both big and small data analytics to define the context holistically.

Step 5: Platform identification. It is important to see the main advocacy platforms that are relevant for the issue of the campaign. Oftentimes, the organizations use the same platforms to advocate on a variety of issues without analyzing their particular effectiveness. In this step, we identify the platforms that are on one hand the most useful to address all the target audiences (both decision-makers and influencers). At the same time, we look for the most effective media platforms to leverage campaign messaging (including traditional media and digital platforms).

Step 6: Definition of the main communications tactic. Using the data of opinion tracking and sentiment analysis together with a knowledge of the platforms, we identify the main campaign lever. This lever needs to be in line with an organizational DNA of the organization behind the campaign. At the same time, it has to contribute in creating a change among the target audiences. It should also address the issues identified in the PESTEL and SWOT analysis.

Step 7: Development of strategic narrative. This is the most defining step for an external view of the campaign. Strategic narrative drives all the engagement of the campaign and provides a guiding point for all content development. It is important to base a campaign narrative on an in-depth understanding of the context of the campaign and of the issue. It avoids the campaign being driven by the creative aspects as opposed to strategic considerations. It also puts the target audiences in the center and allows us to focus on the issues and needs identified among them.

Step 8: Creative and user-first content development. Strategic narrative needs to be translated into the content that has a potential to engage target audiences on an ongoing basis. It is crucial to ensure that the content developed for the campaign resonates with the target audiences. This is executed through A/B/C testing and analysis of the performance.

Finally, the content needs to be focused on the needs of the target audiences and not assumptions from the organization developing a campaign. In order to achieve that the content creation process and planning needs to be based on research among target audiences focusing on the channel preferences.

Step 9: Measurement and reporting protocol. Advocacy campaigns need to be measured and evaluated as any other communications and marketing activities. Both measurement and evaluation have to be linked with the desired impacts of the campaign (as defined in the step 2). We believe that measurement of the advocacy campaign is used to improve the performance and allow adjustments of the campaign. As such, the reporting needs to be agile and focus on ongoing improvements.

Step 10: Engagement calendar and campaign plan. The activities of the campaign require proper advanced planning. The calendar of the campaign is the last step of the strategic design. In our view, it should combine the team composition (for instance, based on RACI model) with a detailed planning of the activities.

The sixth chapter analyses the role of the content and content marketing in the advocacy strategies. Storytelling has become one of the most used communications strategies to reach target audiences (Salmon, 2007). Yet the popularity of storytelling leads to many organizations using it without a strategic focus. We believe that in order to harness the power of storytelling the organizations need to use it in a truly focused and strategic manner (Salmon, 2007).

The attention spans of the target audiences are more and more limited. Social media create an unlimited amount of information and content to engage with. The content marketing becomes an essential tool for building the relationships between the brands and their stakeholders and consumers. In order to be effective in this busy environment, companies, and organizations need to stand out. Content marketing goes beyond development of the proprietary stories and collateral. It requires a truly holistic approach.

At the same time, companies benefit from the probably biggest shift in communications power ever. Thanks to the social media and digital channels, the companies don't have to rely on the media anymore in order to reach their audiences. They can build and manage the relationships with their stakeholders and consumers directly.

Several organizations use this opportunity and develop content hubs and magazines as their thought leadership vehicles. Some of the companies and organizations go even further and build their communication departments around a concept of a newsroom. This redefines the role of corporate communication and advocacy. Using these strategies, they shift their role from being provider of information and news to become the creators of information and news.

At the end of the chapter, we analyze the types of content that work best in the current advocacy campaigns. We do challenge a common view that the campaigns which "make the most of noise" are the most successful ones. We do argue that the most successful campaigns are the ones that serve the defined advocacy goals the best and deliver the highest return on engagement (ROE). The notion of ROE has been proposed as an alternative to ROI in the context of campaigns. We believe that it is an interesting proposition as long as we continue focusing on the main campaign outcomes. Rarely, engagement for the sake of engagement is an advocacy goal.

Outcome focus in the content marketing requires rethinking what does successful campaign mean and how do we measure the content formats' success. We propose a checklist framework which can be used by advocacy managers to assess the quality of the content formats in their campaigns.

The seventh chapter looks into the notion of organizational and corporate reputation in the advocacy strategies. The corporate reputation is a multi-factor concept which links the communications elements with an overall organizational value (Barnett et al., 2005). There are several models that look into the valuation of corporate reputation (Barnett et al., 2005; Gotsi & Wilson, 2001). The Reputation Institute is probably the most known company focusing on reputation management. Their purpose is described as:

> We help the world's largest companies build credibility with the people that matter most to them by delivering data-driven insights about how they are truly perceived. (Reputation Institute, 2019)

At the same time, it is impossible to talk about corporate reputation without talking about looking at the issues and crisis management. Social media created an environment in which corporate reputation can be destroyed within a minute. This requires companies and non-for-profit organizations alike to be ready and prepared. Companies don't benefit from any time for reflection or preparation while managing a crisis.

In this chapter we will look at the steps of communications crises. We analyzed a selection of the crises caused by both internal and external factors and looked for the commonalities. We also differentiated the crisis spread on social media and traditional media. Interestingly, there are several patterns that occurred in all of these crises.

We then analyzed the common patterns of the corporate crises and looked at the learnings from an organizational perspective. As a result, we propose a model for issues monitoring and management. We believe that many of the crises could have been avoided through issues monitoring and management work. It would also have been easier to manage the issues before resulting in a crisis.

This chapter discusses also a difference between crisis management and defensive advocacy. It proposes a defensive advocacy management model: DEFEND aiming at structuring an issues management approach.

The eighth chapter looks at the evolution of advocacy and communications as disciplines. We seek to develop a broader organizational model for advocacy management that is "future-proof." We base our proposed model on considerations looking at the foresight of future development of communications and advocacy.

Virtual reality, augmented reality, artificial intelligence, big data all these trends will impact the way advocacy strategies are designed and executed. We claim that advocacy thinking is at the edge of a paradigm shift moving from engagement toward experience. The technologies allow companies and organizations to provide their stakeholders and consumers with the (virtual) experiences during the advocacy campaigns.

This will require further changes in the way advocacy campaigns are planned and executed. However, several of the principles are to remain valid, or become even more important:

- Advocacy needs to be clearly linked and interconnected with the business objectives. Growing expectations from stakeholders and consumers mean that the organizations willing to be successful and impactful need to integrate advocacy in all levels of their activities.
- Advocacy needs to be vertically and horizontally integrated within the organization. It is paramount to align advocacy positions between the organizational leadership, the experts and employees. As the employees of the company are considered to be the most credible source of information about its activities, there is an additional need for a horizontal integration of the advocacy.
- Advocacy has to be considered as a business discipline that delivers value for the organization and is considered as a profit line as opposed to being an expense line. The costs associated with a lack of advocacy action are in

majority of the cases far exceeding the costs of advocacy strategies. However, the considerations of ROI need to be part of advocacy design. Therefore, advocacy has a power to become a profit line for an organization as opposed to being only an expense.

- Advocacy needs to be considered as a profession — growing popularity of the term "advocacy" led to multiple individuals calling themselves advocacy professionals. While we claim that vertical integration of advocacy means that "advocacy is the job of everyone within the organization," at the same time we see a need for advocacy to be managed by a designated organizational unit.

- Advocacy activities have to be monitored, measured, and evaluated in line with the other organizational activities. Advocacy still suffers from perception created by the lobbying professionals that were averse to performance measurements. As a result, there was an impression that lobbying activities are limited to "wining and dining," which in turn limited the recognition of the business value lobbying brought.

These principles underlie a model which combines advocacy trends considerations with an organizational learning theory. It is inspired by the model developed around corporate communications sophistication; however, its application is broader (Bochenek & Blili, 2013). It proposes a clear model for advocacy strategic management from a managerial perspective. It also includes proposed engagement patterns that organizations can undertake depending on their advocacy management profiles.

Overall, this book aims to help scholars and practitioners to develop a better understanding of advocacy and what advocacy can bring to companies and organizations. It can be also used as a manual for advocacy strategy and campaign development. At this moment, there is already a growing recognition of the importance of advocacy for international nonprofits and organizations. Also, more and more trade associations consider advocacy to be at the core of their business. Multiple internationally operating companies involved in the sustainability discourse place advocacy in the center of their public affairs considerations. This all creates a fertile ground for advocacy professionals to step up and drive the agenda of the organizations they work for.

In the context of the VUCA world, the time for advocacy is now. However, it is the time for advocacy to be strategically planned and integrated vertically and horizontally within organizations. The opportunity for both advocacy and organizations embarking on an advocacy journey is huge. However, it comes with several risks if not executed properly. Focused, strategic, and integrated approaches will help to mitigate these risks.

Chapter 1

What Is Advocacy and Why It Is Important?

1.1. Introduction

Advocacy becomes in certain circles of communications and marketing professionals a buzz word used to describe all the types of public affairs and communications-driven engagements. It is also used by some as synonymous to lobbying and public affairs. For the others, advocacy is "lobbying for a good cause." This is the case especially in the context of international companies seeking to differentiate their sustainability and CSR-related activities from their core business and political lobbying. In the case of non-profits an international organization's advocacy term is used to describe all the activities these organizations do in order to achieve their organizational aims. Just looking at the above and the dichotomy between the two approaches, we can see that it can be very confusing for people to understand what advocacy stands for and what is the difference between advocacy and other activities organizations do in order to engage their audiences.

At the same time, there is a recognition that the requirements from consumers, stakeholders, and audiences in general are evolving and seek for organizational engagement in a broader range of themes (Communications Monitor, 2018; Edelman Trust Barometer, 2019). The organizations are expected to play a constructive role in the socioeconomic system. This requirement is not new but aggravated by the context built around Sustainable Development Goals and shift of the discourse within the non-for-profit sector. Indeed, non-profit and international organizations recognize the need for support from private sector in order to achieve their missions. This support goes beyond donations and sponsoring. As a result, there is an increased number of initiatives that are built on the principle of involvement of various actors (Pennec & Raufflet, 2016; Wood, 2010). Public-Private Partnerships are the most obvious example. In order to cooperate and partner with one another, the organizations need to create a common ground and common platform. It means aligning of the respective agendas and defining the space of compromise that the actors not used to working together are willing to go for (Andonova, 2010). This requires a significant advocacy effort on both sides.

There is also demand from consumers and general public to see more in-depth engagement from companies in the societal issues. The times of CSR "feel good" or *greenwashing* tactics are well over. At this moment, the expectation is that the companies are much more deeply involved in the issues and drive a positive change agenda. In order to be credible, they need to work together with the other actors from the system, which includes governments, nonprofit organizations, and social movements (Cui et al., 2016; Pennec & Raufflet, 2016).

People are being influenced by other people in their choices both in terms of ideas and finances. "Others," meaning individuals are much more credible than the institutions and organizations. Third-party endorsement was always very important for marketing and public affairs. However, nowadays Word of Mouth Marketing (WOMM) and influencer strategies become the core of marketing and public affairs respectively. All this creates an environment in which advocacy becomes the key enabling factor.

1.2.   Definition of Advocacy

What does advocacy actually mean? The question is often asked to the advocacy professionals and those using the term. It is true that advocacy means many different things to many different people. However, this constant is not very helpful in driving the understanding of advocacy. As we stated in the introductory chapter of this book, the main issue in understanding and defining advocacy comes from its dual nature. On the one hand, it is the process that organizations and companies undertake in order to influence the agenda and create an enabling external environment for their operations. On the other hand, advocacy is an outcome of organizational engagement with the key stakeholders which results in supportive behaviors of these audiences vis-à-vis an organization, its products, its agenda, or its people. The latter definition brings advocacy to being synonymous of the third-party endorsement.

There are several professional and academic definitions of advocacy. We will have a closer look at different ways of defining advocacy in the next chapter, focusing on the place advocacy has between various external engagement functions of the organization. The definition from a Merriam-Webster dictionary captures both sides of advocacy:

> the act or process of supporting a cause or proposal: the act or process of advocating something. (Merriam-Webster, 2019)

1.2.1.   Duality of Advocacy

This definition of advocacy considers its dual character. From this perspective, the organizations work toward a desired defined outcome, which is time-bound and can be measured against the timeline and final success of the campaign. At the same time, advocacy is a sort of a *perpetum mobile* − an activity in which organizations need to permanently gain and re-gain the trust from the external stakeholders in order to be able to successfully develop their organizational landscape.

1.2.2. *Advocacy vs Lobbying*

At the common-sense level both advocacy and lobbying aim at influencing people's views and decisions. Both use similar strategies and tactics. Why does it make sense then to make a differentiation? Question about the difference between advocacy and lobbying comes a bit from the ambitions of the two disciplines. Lobbying professionals would like to see the term demystified and use alternative names such as advocacy to label their work. On the other hand, they claim that modern lobbying strategies are far more advanced than simple direct stakeholder approach (Zetter, 2014). Therefore, lobbying strategies are increasingly sophisticated. At the same time, advocacy professionals enhance the scope of their activities related to engagement strategies. As a result, advocacy uses more and more often lobbying techniques in order to achieve its goals (Zetter, 2014). Chapter 2 provides more comprehensive discussion on the difference between the two. For the purpose of this book, we consider lobbying as one of the advocacy strategies. Here we talk about lobbying in the context of legislative and regulatory environments.

1.2.3. *Advocacy Funnel*

Advocacy is a process. The process of advocacy requires several stages. One of the most common errors done by the advocacy professionals is to focus purely on the awareness aspect of influence strategies. There are many marketing and communications funnels with awareness interest desire action (AIDA) being probably the most widely used one (Duncan & Caywood, 1996). We looked at multiple funnels and developed an advocacy influence funnel which is based on the same principle and yet aims to capture a dual nature of advocacy. It is based on five steps that are aimed at driving the change among the target audiences. The proposed model is based on the following stages (Figure 1.1):

- Awareness – knowing about an issue.
- Reaction – forming opinion about an issue.
- Engagement – sharing point of view around an issue.
- Endorsement – agreeing with the advocacy call to action related to an issue.
- Action – making decision over an issue.

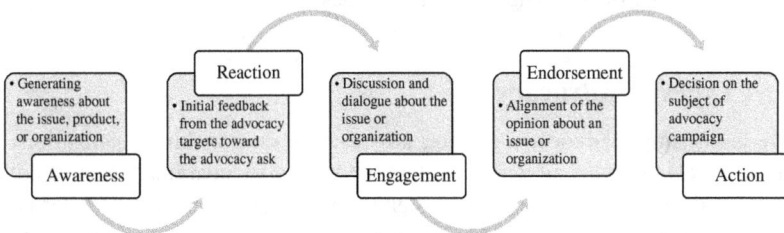

Figure 1.1.   Advocacy Funnel.

Table 1.1. Advocacy Funnel Management.

Stages	Tactics	Measurement
Awareness	Media relations	Media impressions
	Social media	Social media reach
	Influencer engagement	Prompted and unprompted awareness among target audiences
	Stunts/"big" events	
	One pager	
Reaction	White papers	Social media (reactions, shares, and comments)
	Scientific research	
	Coalition building	Number of press articles
Engagement	Meetings	Number of engagements
	Political campaigning	Non-prompted mentions of the issue
	Social media engagement	Queries/Requests
	Conferences	
	Congresses	
Endorsement	Direct engagement	Commitments from the target audiences
	Digital and media amplification	Public endorsement
Action		Legislative changes
		Regulatory changes

These stages are equally relevant for both types of advocacy. From a campaign planning perspective, it is important to take into account these steps and select the right engagement strategies for each of them. Table 1.1 showcases a summary of engagement tactics and measurement methods for each step of the advocacy funnel. This simple funnel seeks to help advocacy professionals in better strategizing of their engagement activities.

1.3. Types of Advocacy

There is no simple advocacy. In fact, advocacy is used within organizations at multiple levels. Regular advocacy professionals tend to have this vision of advocacy limited to an external stakeholder engagement; however, in a broader landscape there is a need to look at various types of advocacy. Below we present the main types of advocacy that can be seen in the professional discourse:

External advocacy – what we could call a "classic advocacy." This term usually means all the activities developed in order to influence an external stakeholder landscape of a company or an organization. It seeks at creating a favorable external environment for the activities of this company or organization. It also means engagement with external audiences in order to stimulate an external support and endorsement for an organization, or its ideas or products. This is the most developed and most structured form of advocacy present in multiple organizations. For many advocacy professionals, external advocacy is synonymous of advocacy in general.

Employee advocacy – engaging employees of an organization in order for them to become the active supporters of the organization's agenda. Employee advocacy is becoming more and more popular as employees are perceived to be the most credible source of information about the company and its operations (Edelman Trust Barometer, 2019). The employee engagement strategies look at leveraging the employees' goodwill and empowering them to take active stance in support of their employer. This trend of employee engagement in advocacy is especially visible on the social media channels. There are multiple tools and platforms (such as Everyone Social software) that seek at creating the communities of advocates based on the employees' social media presence.

Consumer advocacy – strategies seeking to engage brand consumers to endorse the company and its products. Consumer advocacy was for a long time considered to be synonymous with seeking for third-party endorsement. With a growth of digital media and permanent presence of review and ranking features on the websites, this type of advocacy is even stronger embedded in the marketing strategies. Sometimes consumer advocacy is seen as synonymous to WOMM.

Public advocacy – strategies seeking to engage general public in favor of a cause. In general, public advocacy is synonymous with public campaigning. These advocacy activities are often driven by non-for-profit or governmental institutions. Frequently public advocacy campaigns focus on raising awareness of a particular issue. As a result, it has a limiting result on their effectiveness. Conversely, the public advocacy strategies focusing on the whole advocacy funnel tend to be a very effective tool to shape the public opinion.

Influencer advocacy – strategies seeking to engage external influencers to support the company and its products. The term gained a lot of popularity recently with a fashion of using digital influencers in campaigning. Success of influencer advocacy depends a lot on the preparatory work – selection of the right influencer to engage with. Ultimately, this type of advocacy looks at transforming external influencers into ambassadors of the organizations in order to leverage their external reach.

Digital advocacy – advocacy strategies seeking at leveraging digital channels (especially social media) to engage the external audiences. Digital advocacy has become lately a sort of buzz word which in many cases covers all digital engagement activities of the organization. However, done right, digital advocacy can be an excellent lever to support all other advocacy activities. In order to be effective, it needs to be embedded into overall advocacy media mix.

In fact, from a corporate perspective all types of advocacy are extremely important as they lead toward the same goal – building an enabling environment for an organization to achieve its objectives. Therefore, it is very useful to look at the types of advocacy as a sort of a toolkit from which we can choose the best tactics to achieve the set results.

1.3.1. *Advocacy in Non-for-Profit Context*

Non-governmental organizations (NGOs) and international organizations are founded with a mission to address an issue or several issues that impact a socio-economic context. The narrowness or broadness of these issues varies from one organization to another. However, they all have in common a need to influence a stakeholder environment and leverage the support in order to achieve desired outcomes. In addition, nonprofit sector organizations need to constantly seek for funds in order to be able to survive and continue to deliver on their missions. This again requires connecting with the broader external audiences and at the same time clear unique value proposition. Both of them are achieved through effective advocacy strategies. Looking at the nonprofit sector from this perspective brings advocacy to the center of organizational priorities. The question is not whether the organizations should embark on advocacy or not; it is about how to design the entire organization in order for it to be able to deliver on its advocacy needs.

The structures for managing advocacy within non-for-profit organizations differ. Some have a dedicated department called "advocacy department." Several others put advocacy together with communications under one leadership under external relations umbrella. Other organizations link advocacy with public policy and place advocacy professionals within these structures. Finally, there are organizations that decentralize advocacy efforts and put advocacy professionals within their programs or business lines. This approach seeks to generate synergies between the core of organizational activities and external stakeholder engagement. It is similar to corporate approach where marketing/communications professionals are placed directly in the brand teams as opposed to creating a central strong corporate team.

Certainly, for several years, more and more professionals have "advocacy" in their job title and even more professionals have "advocacy skills" in their job descriptions. This is a good sign of the growing importance that advocacy has within the international non-for-profit community. At the same time, this tendency calls for a professionalization of the advocacy-related jobs. It also calls for a structure delivering professional training in the strategies and skills needed for international advocacy management. It is less trivial than it appears to be to state that advocacy is gaining a professional momentum and moves from one of the activities done within organizations toward the core focus and core activity.

1.3.2. Advocacy in Business

There are two main approaches in using the term advocacy among international businesses. The first consists in using advocacy as a synonym of public affairs and lobbying. In this view, all external relations activities seeking at improving operating environment and market position of the company can be labeled as "advocacy." The second way of looking at advocacy is to link it with sustainability and CSR engagements of the company. In this view, advocacy would be dissociated from the "classic" public affairs activities and focus purely on the "doing good" type of activities like with the corporate citizenship. The latter way of seeing corporate advocacy is limiting and doesn't really link back to the holistic contribution of advocacy for an organization. Paradoxically the companies representing second view still place advocacy within their public affairs and/ or external engagement structure.

In both cases, the role of advocacy within the company is to help the organization connect with the relevant stakeholders, which have an impact on its business. This can include regulatory impact (legislators, regulators, law-makers), reputational impact (NGOs, IGOs, activists, thought leaders, scientists), or financial impact (analysts, financial community at large). Connecting with these stakeholders and building meaningful relationships becomes paramount for future success of the corporation. Therefore, an effective advocacy strategy needs to look at direct stakeholder engagement, communications, influencer engagement, public relations, lobbying as well as sustainability and compliance. This inclusive and holistic approach mitigates the risks of too narrow, or too broad, focus of advocacy. It also mitigates the risks of missing out on stakeholder evolving agendas.

1.4. Aims of Advocacy

There are multiple reasons why the organizations advocate. While ultimately, they do it in order to support their organizational objectives, the aims of respective campaigns can vary. Given the complexity of the stakeholder landscape there are many potential calls to action that can be integrated into the campaigns. The list of aims of advocacy is not exhaustive, but already showcases the complexity of the influencing environment:

- block or introduce regulation or legislation;
- protect market position;
- increase sales of the products;
- improve living conditions;
- increase brand recognition;
- support corporate or organizational reputation;
- increase donations;

- increase brand loyalty; and
- attract or retain best talent.

Even this non-exhaustive list reinforces the idea that advocacy is an activity that needs to be embedded in the whole organizational structure. Many of the aims listed above would be managed at the same time through different campaigns. This in turn reinforces a need for an internal alignment.

1.4.1. Key Components of Advocacy

Advocacy is definitely a multi-faced discipline. It includes communications, engagement, research, foresight, socioeconomic analysis, and corporate affairs. This holistic approach strengthens the message that advocacy needs to be grounded in the research and knowledge. In order to influence the landscape and decision-making processes, the advocates need to be armed with the facts and data. However, they also need to be able to convey the messages in a simple manner. For this, strategic narratives are paramount. These narratives need to be expressed in the formats that resonate with the stakeholders (Figure 1.2).

1.4.2. Advocacy Strategies and Tactics

Independently of the aim of advocacy there are several strategies, which are almost universally used across the campaigns. They all seek to shape the discourse and influence decisions in the socioeconomic and political system.

- *Direct stakeholder approach and lobbying* – most classic advocacy strategy. It consists in identifying those who matter in an issue and addressing them directly with the advocacy asks. In some legal contexts, for instance US/EU/UK, this type of activities is regulated and subject to a public disclosure (Zetter, 2014). This strategy is especially pertinent in the advocacy campaigns aiming at changes (or lack of changes) in the legal and regulatory system.

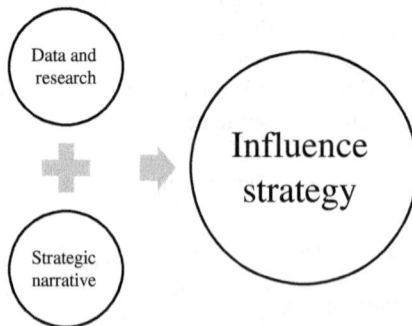

Figure 1.2.   Influence Strategy Components.

- *Public campaigning* – leveraging public opinion in order to put pressure on decision-makers. This strategy was traditionally used much more by non-profit organizations than by the corporates. However, this is changing, and we are seeing more and more public campaigning driven by the corporations. This strategy usually requires creative concept and marketing-like delivery.
- *Coalition building* – enhancing the number of organizations aligned in a campaign. This works best in the punctual campaigns which are time-bound and have a clearly defined objective. As coalitions include organizations that don't usually work together and even compete between themselves, it is important to define an agreement space and agree to disagree on everything else. While very effective and allowing to spread a burden of a campaign among multiple organizations; coalition building can also lead to diluting of the message and final result where "nobody is really happy."
- *Thought leadership* – defining the space which organization can "own" with its contributions to the socioeconomic system. True thought leadership strategies require an in-depth understanding of the external landscape and creation of the proprietary research and knowledge. This strategy is very effective for a long-term positioning and reputation building of the company.
- *Omni-channel engagement* – using all available digital and classic communications channels of the company to convey advocacy messages. After several years of belonging more to marketing activities; this strategy is increasingly used in corporate advocacy. It aims to leverage public opinion and broader audiences in order to influence policy processes and decision-making. This approach can be very effective to amplify other advocacy delivery mechanisms.
- *Grassroots engagement* – creating movements for social change. This strategy is used much more often by nonprofits. It can be very effective in driving change; however, it can be challenged at the level of authenticity. The most effective forms of grassroots movements require participants to believe in their ethos. Therefore, when the engagement is driven top-down it can lose its emotional appeal.

Global advocacy campaigns tend to combine several of these strategies in a meta strategy to influence various stakeholder groups. It is important to remember that there is no "one fits all" advocacy strategy, and effectiveness of one strategy in a particular context doesn't guarantee repeated success in the other subject or target group.

1.4.3. Advocacy Tools

Effective advocacy strategies tend to use multiple tools to address various target audiences. While toolbox and an effective number of the opportunities to engage seams endless, there are several tools, that are worth noting and keeping in mind while executing advocacy strategies.

- *White papers* – short research-based papers explaining an issue and/or position of the organization. It is one of the basic tools of advocacy. Recently, there is much more focus on design and visual elements of the white papers in order to grab attention of the target audiences.

- *One-pagers* – very short document presenting the issue, position of an organization, and call to action for the stakeholders. With the ever-short attention spans of the target audiences, one pager becomes a very effective tool to influence key stakeholders.
- *Infographics* – visual representations of data and call to action. While infographics are primarily used in digital formats, there are more and more instances where their elements are also included in the hard copy material.
- *Videos* – all statistics show a growing impact of video on the target audiences. The videos are frequently used in advocacy both in the context of large public facing campaigns as well as the more targeted stakeholder approaches.
- *Position papers* – presenting opinion about a legislative process from an industry or organization's perspective. Position papers tend to be more explicit in terms of the "ask" than white papers.
- *Company/organization/industry statements* – used to present advocacy demands in the context. They present purely argumentation in favor of the organization's position in a given subject.
- *Exhibitions* – presenting advocacy context in a visual manner. The role of exhibitions evolves with an increased use of virtual and augmented reality applications. The exhibitions become increasingly focused on creating experiences and immersing target audiences in the realities of advocacy organization.
- *Events (and side-events)* – help shaping the agenda and focus attention on an issue. Recently, face-to-face meetings and events gain importance as an effective advocacy tool. It is especially visible around global annual meetings such as World Health Assembly or United Nations General Assembly. Many organizations take benefit of an important presence and concentration of stakeholders and organize side-events. The side-events represent a good opportunity; however, need to be based on strong value proposition as usually there are multiple competing co-occurring events.
- *Conferences/panels and round tables* – allow the combining of academic and professional audiences. They can be used to leverage this presence and launch campaigns. Frequently, conferences are co-organized and co-hosted by multiple organizations.
- *Congresses/Summits* – help putting the organizer on the public agenda. They bring visibility and help in raising the profile of the organization. They are usually periodic events (every year or every two years) often driven by one organization. The congresses tend to be expensive to organize and attend; however, for trade associations, they are one of the prime sources of income.
- *News releases* – reaching media with the message related to a development. It is important to think about press releases as news releases. It helps to focus and qualify what kind of information is appropriate for this mean of communications.
- *Press conferences* – ultimate media relations tool. It is important to remember that journalists are extremely busy and under tight deadlines and pressure.

Therefore, they tend to be selective in terms of their time and focus. Press conferences are only effective in the context of important news and announcements.

The list above is, of course, not complete. However, these are the main and most commonly used advocacy tools. The most effective approaches require using a combination of the tools according to the target audiences and the campaign phases.

1.5. Key Advocacy Shifts

The way advocacy strategies are executed varies according to:

- types of organizations which advocate;
- range of stakeholders they are seeking to engage; and
- the ways they address their target audiences.

It all leads to a change in the way advocacy strategies and approaches are designed within the organizations and companies. The trends listed below ultimately are a witness of a growing role and importance that advocacy plays in the organizational and business strategies.

Holistic advocacy approaches – engaging multiple departments and job functions within an organization in order to achieve advocacy goals. These approaches require an internal alignment and coordination of the professionals from across the organization. They can be very effective in addressing complex and multi-dimensional organizational challenges. However, the broad focus means also that they might miss on very precise individual goals.

Omni-channel advocacy – using all the communications and marketing channels to engage with the target audiences. These include all suite of digital and social media channels in addition to traditional direct stakeholder approaches and media relations. Omni-channel approach is a reply to a need of engaging broader audiences in the organizational engagement.

Advocacy as a profit center – advocacy used to be considered as a (necessary) expenditure which allowed business to operate. However, at this moment more and more organizations see advocacy as a business line and a separate P&L. This means advocacy has a chance to evolve and become a profit center, which sells services to internal stakeholders.

The above trends showcase a changing face and role of advocacy within the companies and organizations. It definitely becomes more strategic and closer to the core business. Further alignment will require even closer link between advocacy and strategic management.

1.6.   The Business of Advocacy

Because advocacy is seen as more and more critical to the business success of an organization, it also means that there are certain budget levels allocated to these activities. There are several actors who make money out of advocacy activities based on several business models. Contrary to lobbying which was associated with the external agencies managing direct stakeholder engagement on behalf of their clients (Zetter, 2014), advocacy was more often considered to be an in-house activity. This is still true; however, there is an increased number of consultancies offering advocacy services. Below we list several models in which advocacy activities are structured:

- *Advocacy consultancy (retained services)* – client paying fixed amount of money on a monthly basis for a defined scope of services and consultancy being on stand-by.
- *Punctual advocacy consultancy* – advocacy services linked to a particular case or issue. Usually doesn't involve a long-term commitment on a client side. Often multiple services are sourced from the same vendor under "umbrella" type of agreement.
- *Services linked to advocacy sourced externally* – specialized services and consultancy purchased from external vendors in support of organizational advocacy activities.
- *Services linked to advocacy sourced internally* – advocacy support provided by different internal business units. This can include the international organizations research department; fundraising department; or communication department.
- *Internal service line focused on advocacy* – advocacy department of an organization coordinating and managing external engagement of an organization.

With regard to the consultancy services, the fee models are evolving. While in public relations and lobbying retained contracts have been the standard agreement models for years, the field moves increasingly toward project fees and project agreements. The latter offer the client more flexibility and allow the sourcing of different types of services from different suppliers. Also, putting smaller budgets toward competitive bids is supposed to increase financial returns and reduce costs. The retained agreements in contrary benefit from the scale and knowledge of the consultancy team of the client's business. They provide stability of relationship and alignment between the activities. It is true that with multiplication of small project contracts and suppliers there is a risk of loss in consistency and internal alignment. As stated above, the need to attract attention of the target audiences requires a focused messaging.

Independently of business model and relationship model, the business of advocacy is changing. There is a growing requirement for the professional services as opposed to the payments for access to the decision-makers. The unique selling proposition (USP) of advocacy consultant or advocacy professional is not the size of their speed dial list in their phone. It is the types of services they bring to the table that can contribute to achieving the overall desired outcomes of organizational engagement. Professionalization of services will also bring increased competitiveness between the service providers.

1.6.1.   Advocacy Professionals

The organization of advocacy activities within a company or organization was discussed earlier in this chapter. It showcased that there are more and more people who "do" advocacy. These are professionals coming from various backgrounds not necessarily working in the core of external relations of an organization. At the same time, advocacy as a function needs to be managed at a corporate level. This creates a challenge to maintain right proportions between matrix organization and leveraging all types of advocacy while maintaining consistency and alignment between these various activities. For several organizational functions, advocacy is the key component of the required skillset: external relations, public affairs, member relations, stakeholder engagement, sustainability, and communications. Advocacy is also a key for marketing professionals as well as those who manage the projects on behalf of international organizations and non-for-profits.

There is no real professional structure which would group advocacy professionals as is the case for other external engagement functions. Therefore, those working on advocacy belong to the professional associations from the other disciplines. In consequence, there is also a lack of a common ethics code or professional standard under an umbrella of "advocacy." Setting the professional standards for advocacy becomes more and more urgent as there is an important number of professionals working on the advocacy initiatives. The closest existing structures and codes of conducts come from lobbying and public affairs professions.

Growing professionalization of the field of advocacy will also require existence of the professional training and certification. There are very few professional level trainings (executive education) that would deliver diplomas in advocacy. However; we can definitely observe, in recent years, an increase in the offer. However, it is difficult to judge whether the training offer in advocacy increased, or as the term is very fashionable there are more and more trainings that are called "advocacy" in order to attract additional audiences without real innovation in the curriculum. In any case, this should be seen as a positive trend as it grounds advocacy as one of the key organizational functions driving engagement with external audiences.

1.7.   Key Challenges for Advocacy

Current stakeholder environment poses multiple challenges for advocacy professionals. There is a general level of distrust toward the institutions. Social media and digital engagement changed the notions of influence. People take decisions before knowing the facts. Stakeholders are confronted with an unprecedented number of interest groups and influence campaigns. These are the main external

Table 1.2. Challenges of Advocacy.

External Advocacy Challenges	Internal Advocacy Challenges
• Busy influencing environment • Multiplication of interest groups and individuals working in advocacy • Lack of ethical and professional advocacy standards • Limited attention spans of external stakeholders • Low levels of trust toward advocacy messages and advocacy professionals	• Many people "doing advocacy" within the same organization sitting in different organizational departments • Frequent lack of internal alignment around the priorities • Multiple messages and confusing narratives of organizations • Coordination between marketing, advocacy, and public relations activities • Financial and human resources dedicated to advocacy vs expected results

challenges of advocacy. At the same time, there are challenges coming from within the advocacy profession. There are more and more people who are involved in the organizational engagement. They represent different agendas and their professional levels vary. More and more campaigns are launched with a low level of internal alignment. Within the same organization there are multiple people involved in the influence-oriented activities. This might create confusion and requires an additional coordination between various sets of actions.

The combination of both external and internal challenges showcases the need for a strategic approach to advocacy. It also requires looking holistically at organizational engagement and influence strategies. Without this there is a risk of managing counterproductive activities that don't deliver on the organizational aims (Table 1.2).

1.8.   Ways to Measure Advocacy

For a long time, advocacy professionals were relatively averse to measurement and evaluation of their activities. This led to a certain misconception around advocacy itself. Numerous executives saw external engagement as a mysterious function within organization which might deliver tangible results; however, advocacy professionals have a difficulty to prove its importance and effectiveness for the organizational activities overall. Some of the organizations measured top level outcomes − the example here could be whether a legislation that was promoted or blocked passed or not. Other organizations measured the activities − numbers of meetings held, numbers of people reached. Colloquially, one can say they measured "how busy they were." Obviously, both of these

Inputs
- Number of content items produced
- Budget of the campaign
- Data collected
- Research performed

Outputs
- Number of meetings held.
- Number of stakeholders reached
- Number of coalition partners
- Number of social media messages
- Number of press releases
- Reach of messages.
- Impressions of the paid (social) media activities

Outtakes
- Number of social media engagements
- Number of stakeholders recalling the message
- Initial reactions of the target audiences on the message
- Sentiment around organization or issue

Outcomes
- Number of commitments from the target audiences
- Changes in the legislative processes
- Political decisions
- Regulatory changes
- Behavioral changes
- External third-party endorsement

Impacts
- Socio economic benefits or losses coming from the regulatory changes
- Business environment changes
- Societal change

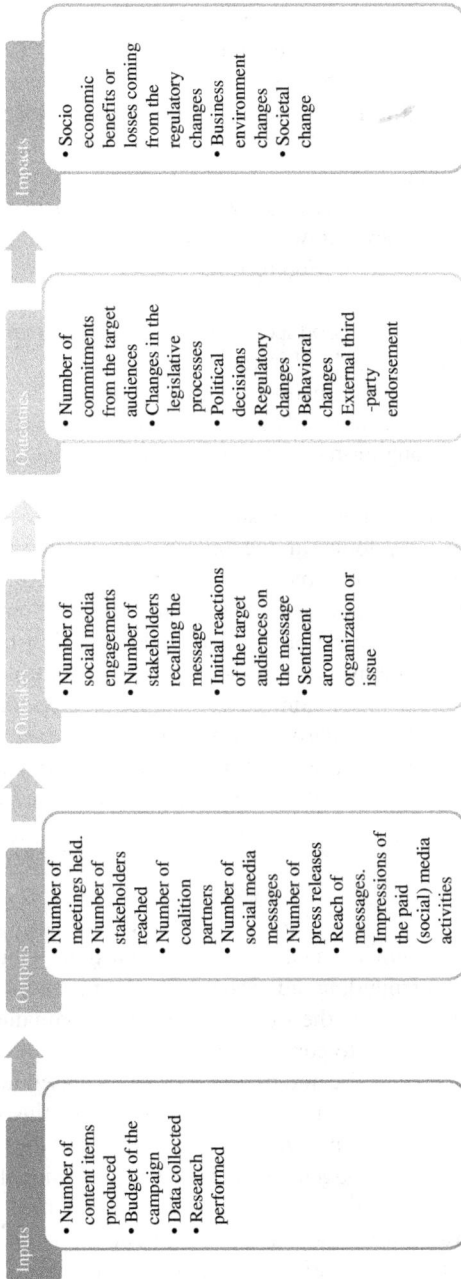

Figure 1.3.   Advocacy Measurement Framework.

approaches have apparent limits and don't allow us to showcase to the full extent the value delivered by advocacy to the organization.

As there is no professional structure for advocacy, there is also no common framework from measurement and evaluation of the activities. The closest measurement framework that can be applicable comes from communications profession. It was developed by the International Association for Measurement and Evaluation of Communications (AMEC). This framework puts the communications activities in the funnel (similar to the one proposed above) and looks at indicators according to the phases of organizational involvement. We adapt similar principles to the advocacy below and look at the campaign and activity development from this perspective (Figure 1.3).

- *Inputs:* What did organization produce in the context of the campaign?
- *Outputs:* What was the activity level in the campaign?
- *Outtakes:* How did the target audiences react to the message?
- *Outcomes:* What was the result of advocacy activities on target audiences?
- *Impacts:* What are the long-term consequences of the campaign?

This way of measurement allows us to showcase the value advocacy brings to an organization. It not only looks at the final results of the campaign (outcomes), but also at the chain of activities. This approach helps to answer the question: "how did your activities lead to the final result?". Sometimes, advocacy professionals struggle to single out their own contribution to the outcome of a campaign. There are many good reasons for that: multiple stakeholders involved in the same subject, many campaigns focusing on the same issue, omnichannel mix making influencing environment very busy. However, a comprehensive approach to measurement and evaluation of advocacy campaigns mitigates some of these risks and provides evidence of the effectiveness and efficacy of the selected approaches.

1.9.   Conclusions

Complexity of influencing environment creates a context in which there is an increasing momentum surrounding advocacy. More and more professionals work on external engagement of the organizations and companies. More and more organizations see the need to connect with a broader group of external stakeholders. This leads to more noise and presence of an increased number of messages in both regulatory and legislative landscapes. In turn, this means that in order to be effective, organizations need to focus their activities and be more strategic about their external engagement. It favors a professionalization of the advocacy activities. However, this is not necessarily accompanied by the professional structures and frameworks such as codes of conduct. It makes it difficult to distinguish between the quality of professional services offered. Since advocacy is a business of trust, any misbehaviors of the others lead to an overall decrease of trust toward the profession.

There are many types of advocacy starting from employee advocacy and ending with public advocacy. This creates a rich influencing environment, where organizations have to be very precise about their end goals and select the right strategies that deliver to the expected results. Many of the available tools are used by other businesses and organizational lines. In addition, other professionals within the organizations frequently address the same target audiences as advocacy. Therefore, an internal alignment and coordination become "mission critical" for a success of organizational engagement. This alignment happens at two levels: structural (shaping the departmental structures in a way that favors internal collaboration) and content (aligning the messaging across various externally focused activities).

For the future of the profession it will be crucial to move forward with formalization of the advocacy structures and behaviors. This will also create a clear differentiation between the professionals and allow the best ones to be more successful. In addition, it is important that companies and organizations align their external engagement structures in order to take benefits from synergies between the activities. It will lead to creation of a consistent external engagement model. Finally, advocacy activities need to be measured and evaluated as any other business. Therefore, while measurement should be outcome driven, it should also include on going monitoring and reporting of the activities. This ensures a possibility to single out the contribution of advocacy toward the final landscape shifts and changes. Definitely, there was no time when organizational engagement was more crucial.

Key Takeaways

- *Advocacy is a multi-dimensional concept and discipline. It encompasses both strategic process toward achieving of the legislative and regulatory goals and activating external stakeholders to endorses these goals and organization in general. Holistic approaches are required in order to bring organizational and business benefits of advocacy.*
- *There are more and more professionals involved in strategic advocacy. Therefore, the competition for attention among the key external stakeholder audiences is growing. It means that the organizations need to look for creative ways to convey their messages.*
- *Engaging political stakeholders and decision-makers needs to be based on both evidence and strong messages. This dual rational-emotional approach structures strategic engagement. This means that advocacy and lobbying need to be more and more creative both in concept and delivery.*
- *Advocacy is a process that aims at converting target audiences to supporters of the ideas or organizations. An influence funnel model helps to track the evolution of the audiences and structures the phases that are required to observe the evolution of the target audiences.*

- *Advocacy and engagement efforts need to be measured and evaluated in order prove their strategic value to the organization. The framework for advocacy measurement should be focused on the outcomes and impacts of the activities. However, it should also track the activities in order to draw a correlation between the organizational efforts and campaign results.*

Building a resilient advocacy function requires commitment from both organizational management and advocacy professionals. Setting the goals and ambition levels together and linking advocacy with organizational priorities builds the strength of the function and allows better integration across all external engagement activities of an organization.

Chapter 2

Strategic Advocacy Management – Looking for a Managerial Model

2.1. Introduction

Corporate reputation is important for companies and organizations alike (Gotsi & Wilson, 2001; Reputation Institute, 2019). Good corporate reputation not only influences the choices of consumers and helps to attract and retain the best talent, but also creates an enabling environment among the stakeholders and those who create an operating environment for a company (Reputation Institute, 2019). In order to benefit from a positive reputation there is a need for trust toward both organization and its brands (Reputation Institute, 2019). Trust in turn becomes increasingly difficult to gain and needs to be maintained and regained every day (Reputation Institute, 2019). Increased demands from stakeholders and shareholders (e.g., impact investment, or even simpler sustainability-driven investment choices) require companies to rethink the way they communicate and engage. This also creates an opportunity for a fundamental shift of the role of corporate communications and external engagement within the organizations. The calls for alignment of the external engagement functions of the organizations are not new (Balmer & Greyser, 2006). However, a current context with increased scrutiny from stakeholders and the general public amplifies this tendency further.

Traditionally, corporate communication was serving the business and managing the external image of the organization (White, 1994). It was managing the channels of engagement with the public (Cornelissen, 2011; White, 1994). Therefore, corporate communication professionals played a role which could be summarized as "channel management." Since before the emergence of social media organizations had limited chance to engage with their stakeholders directly, communications professionals relied heavily on media amplification and third-party channels (Cornelissen, 2013). The main role of communications professionals was to build and manage the relations with the external stakeholders and amplifiers with a special focus on media (Cornelissen, 2013).

Until the 1980s, professionals responsible for communication within their organizations had used the term "public relations" to describe communication with stakeholders (a term still used in academic circles across the world). This public relations (PR) function, which was tactical in most companies, largely consisted of communication to the press. When other stakeholders, internal and external to the company, started to demand more information from the company, communication professionals within organizations subsequently started to look at communication as being more than just PR. The roots of the new corporate communication function started to take hold. This new function came to incorporate a whole range of specialized disciplines including corporate design, corporate advertising, employee or internal communication, issues and crisis management, media relations, investor relations, change communication, and public affairs. An important characteristic of the new function was that it consolidated a range of communication disciplines and expertise into a single corporate communication or corporate affairs department. This department has a single mandate that is focused on the organization as a whole and on the important task of how an organization is presented to all its key stakeholders, both internal and external. (Cornelissen, 2013)

A shift of the channels and opportunity to engage target audiences directly means that the role of corporate communication is changing (Communication Monitor, 2018). Organizations need to engage broader ranges of stakeholders in their communities (Balmer & Greyser, 2006). Thanks to digital communications and social media, they effectively can engage these publics directly by building their own channels. Building communities, third-party endorsement, and advocacy become the key functions of the communication department (Communication Monitor, 2017, 2018). This way communication becomes a central piece of business and driver of the strategic decisions (Du et al., 2010).

It comes without surprise that the place of corporate communication within organizational structure can define its efficiency and effectiveness (Bochenek & Blili, 2013). We looked at integration of the corporate communication and its positioning within the organizational structure. As in the case of the model developed in 2013, we develop the model with help of the organizational learning theory (Bochenek & Blili, 2013). It looks at three levels of organizational learning: operational, tactical, and strategic.

Multiple authors describe the ways and models in which corporate communication is managed as a function (Cornelissen, 2011, 2013; White, 1994). This chapter looks at these models and contrasts them with the current stakeholder landscape. Finally, it proposes a new model for communication management that considers a profound paradigm shift based on these four principles:

- The boundaries between the roles of communications, marketing and public affairs are blurred (Balmer & Greyser, 2006). Many functions address the same target audiences. Therefore, an internal and external alignment is key.

- Effective engagement strategies are based on content and not distribution channels. This requires a holistic redesign of an organizational structure and outcome-focused performance evaluation.
- Social media and digital channels empowered companies to become broadcasters in their own right and don't need to rely on traditional media to connect with their audiences.
- Advocacy and lobbying rely stronger and stronger on the communications channels and political campaigns to engage stakeholders. Direct stakeholder engagement needs to be increasingly supported by multi-media campaigning.

As a result, an alignment between the corporate functions looking at external engagement with the stakeholders is paramount for organizational effectiveness (Balmer & Greyser, 2006). Ultimately, in the current setting corporate communication, marketing and public affairs professionals all try to target the same (or very similar) audiences. Historically, each of these functions has been managed by a different set of professionals. However, in the current digitally driven landscape this differentiation loses its relevance. On the contrary, an internal alignment between the functions brings synergies and mitigated the risks related to a "siloed" approach (Balmer & Greyser, 2006).

2.2. Socioeconomic Context and Need for Multi-stakeholder Cooperation

Organizational communication doesn't happen in the vacuum. Every subject in the public domain attracts communication from multiple actors and stakeholders. As stated before, social media create a platform through which organizations can address their audiences directly. The ease of communication through social media poses the biggest challenge of digital communications: social media are used by multiple actors coming from multiple sectors each trying to influence their constituencies and stakeholders. As a result, the amount of information produced exceeds the capacity of individuals to absorb. The notion of information overload in consumer research is not new and has been a subject of research since the 1970s (Jacoby, 1984).

> The two questions posed at the outset may be answered as follows. Can consumers be overloaded? Yes, they can. Will consumers be overloaded? Generally speaking, no, they will not. This is because they are highly selective in how much and just which information they access and tend to stop well short of overloading themselves. (Jacoby, 1984)

It also means that the attention spans are lowered – therefore organizations participate in a constant uphill battle to grasp attention and ensure their messages reach and impact desired target audiences – reaching the audiences effectively becomes one of the key challenges for external communications management (Communication Monitor, 2018).

The digital audiences expect information to be short and presented in an easy to understand and digest way and visually attractive way (HubSpot, 2018). It is interesting to see that the global statistics related to performance of the digital content indicate every year "best practice" content to be shorter and shorter. The individual preferences for the content formats change as well. For instance, video has become the prime vehicle of information on the social media channels.

> This trend toward video has been in the making for some time now. What's different is that millennials, an age group which roughly spans 18 to 34, aren't just buying sneakers and gadgets anymore. Increasingly, millennials comprise a cohort of people purchasing homes, baby clothing, and B2B software. And their strong preference for video, social, and mobile-first content has implications for marketers working across an expanding array of industries. (HubSpot, 2018)[1]

Global issues such as global warming, plastification of the oceans, management of opportunities, and risks related to technology require cooperation and understanding between multiple types of stakeholders (Andonova, 2010; Sachs, 2012; United Nations, 2015). These issues that are at the forefront of the global public's minds will not be addressed without a concentrated effort of actors coming from various sectors (Sachs, 2012). There is a growing awareness of global businesses that the global issues impact their bottom line and therefore they are in a need of addressing them (Communication Monitor, 2018; Edelman Trust Barometer, 2019).

Good illustration of this shift could be the changed status of World Economic Forum which became an international organization (IO) in 2015 (World Economic Forum). It evolved from a business networking platform into a multi-stakeholder platform for dialogue and engagement. This was confirmed by granting of an IO status by the Swiss government. The 2019 Annual Meeting in Davos was chaired by six Global Shapers (individuals active in their communities being below 30 years old, who work on social impact initiatives). The recent images of discussions and participants in Davos are far from the CEO-led event of the past.

> The World Economic Forum is the International Organization for Public-Private Cooperation. The Forum engages the foremost political, business and other leaders of society to shape global, regional and industry agendas. (World Economic Forum, Mission)[2]

---

[1]https://blog.hubspot.com/news-trends/content-trends-preferences
[2]https://www.weforum.org/about/world-economic-forum

A growing number of initiatives combines the public, private, and non-for-profit sectors. The Public-Private Partnerships (PPPs) grow both in numbers and in scope of issues the focus is on (Andonova, 2010). Their scope is also increasingly complex starting from infrastructure and ending on a global sustainability agenda (Andonova, 2010). According to the World Bank, the characteristics of PPPs include:

- Risk-sharing between public and private sectors.
- Long-term relationship between parties.
- Public service and ultimate regulatory responsibility remain in public sector. (World Bank).

These characteristics show a need for cooperation by different types of actors and push from multilateral organizations toward multi-sectorial cooperation.

2.2.1. Sustainable Development Goals as a Platform for Engagement

The United Nations have seen the need for a global cooperation in order to achieve lasting change across the globe. Its first big initiative was the Millennium Development Goals (MDGs) framework introduced at the turn of the century. MDGs were criticized for being top-down structure by the developed countries and imposing the agenda on the developing world (Sachs, 2012). Also, their ambitious goals were not translated to a working framework which would allow us to engage a broader group of stakeholders; however, they did shape global policy priorities (Sachs, 2012, 2015). Therefore, they have had a limited potential to engage the stakeholders coming from the different sectors and actors beyond political ones.

> The eight Millennium Development Goals (MDGs) − which range from halving extreme poverty rates to halting the spread of HIV/AIDS and providing universal primary education, all by the target date of 2015 − form a blueprint agreed to by all the world's countries and all the world's leading development institutions. They have galvanized unprecedented efforts to meet the needs of the world's poorest. The UN is also working with governments, civil society and other partners to build on the momentum generated by the MDGs and carry on with an ambitious post-2015 development agenda. (United Nations)[3]

It is generally accepted that MDGs were successful in putting the issues on the agenda, but not creating a framework through which these issues could have been addressed (Sachs, 2012). Some would claim that it was a missed

---

[3]https://www.un.org/millenniumgoals/

opportunity for a global community, while others would argue that the fact of entering some of the issues into the global discourse was a success per se (Sachs, 2012). However, they didn't enter to the common language and the interest in MDGs didn't go beyond informed circles of decision-makers (Attaran, 2006). The MDGs were also rarely quoted as a corporate priority by the businesses or as an organizational priority by the NGOs.

In 1999 the United Nations established a Global Compact (UNGC) with a mission of: *Business as a force of good.* Its purpose is described as:

> By committing to sustainability, business can take shared responsibility for achieving a better world. (United Nations Global Compact)[4]

The Global Compact allows business membership and measures the impact of the business activities on the external environments. The premise of the UNGC was to engage the businesses in the global agenda subject in the platform that is driven by a multilateral engagement (UN Global Compact website).

With the introduction of the Sustainable Development Goals (SDGs), the UNGC activities have been aligned into the framework (UN Global Compact website). The scientific research around UNGC is not conclusive. Some researchers see it as a successful platform that linked business objectives with the societal goals (Rasche, Waddock, & McIntosh, 2013). Others suggest that it had a limited value and was more directed into building of the reputational assets of its members (Rasche et al., 2013). However, UNGC was definitely successful in creating a platform for dialogue and engagement linking the actors who did not work together in the past. It also supported the evolution of the business approach toward the Corporate Social Responsibility and taking more evidence-based stance toward stakeholder engagement.

> Corporate sustainability starts with a company's value system and a principles-based approach to doing business. This means operating in ways that, at a minimum, meet fundamental responsibilities in the areas of human rights, labor, environment and anti-corruption. Responsible businesses enact the same values and principles wherever they have a presence and know that good practices in one area do not offset harm in another. By incorporating the Ten Principles of the UN Global Compact into strategies, policies and procedures, and establishing a culture of integrity, companies are not only upholding their basic responsibilities to people and planet, but also setting the stage for long-term success. (Global Compact, 2019)[5]

---

[4]https://www.unglobalcompact.org/what-is-gc/mission
[5]https://www.unglobalcompact.org/what-is-gc/mission/principles

The SDGs were introduced in 2015 at United Nations General Assembly. The SDG framework including both goals and targets have been developed in a dialogue with civil society and business (United Nations, 2015). The idea behind was to avoid the criticism of alleged top-down approach from MDGs framework that led to a low level of their operationalization and create an inclusive structure for cooperation (Sachs, 2012). Some critics of the SDGs highlighted that the goals were created in possibly too large collaboration between various actors (Scheyvens et al., 2016). As a result, the goals and targets have been enlarged to a great extent in order to get "something for everyone involved in the process" (Scheyvens et al., 2016). The consequence of this approach is that they lost some level of boldness that could drive stronger action and change. The others would argue that this is the force of the SDGs as by creating an inclusive platform the UN provided a neutral engagement ground for actors coming from various sectors and backgrounds (Sachs, 2015).

> The Sustainable Development Goals are the blueprint to achieve a better and more sustainable future for all. They address the global challenges we face, including those related to poverty, inequality, climate, environmental degradation, prosperity, and peace and justice. The Goals interconnect and in order to leave no one behind, it is important that we achieve each Goal and target by 2030. (UN)[6]

It is difficult to assess the effectiveness of the SDGs in addressing the issues they were designed for since they are looking at the 2030 horizon. However, it is interesting to see how businesses embraced (or not) the SDGs in their activities. An early research conducted in consulting environment suggests that the companies embraced SDGs in a declarative way (Leidar, 2016)[7].

> Only nine per cent of the companies we analyzed have a dedicated SDG section on their corporate website, although 40 per cent have issued at least one SDG-related statement. The degree of commitment varies from a simple acknowledgement of the importance of the SGDs to a concrete declaration committing support to achieve the goals. Interestingly, companies headquartered in Europe are more likely to have a dedicated SGD website section and/or statement. (Leidar, 2016)

The SDG involvement was happening more in declarative sphere with a low level of binding declarations and measurement (Leidar, 2016; Oxfam, 2018; PwC, 2018). These findings were confirmed in the recent studies from both PwC and Oxfam (Oxfam, 2018; PwC, 2018).

---

[6]https://www.un.org/sustainabledevelopment/sustainable-development-goals/
[7]https://www.leidar.com/wp-content/uploads/2016/11/Leidar-Insight-nov-2016-SDGs.pdf

We assessed 76 companies, of which 47 stated they support the SDGs. Of the subset of 47 companies in our sample that have stated they support the SDGs, we found that more than 40% (21 of 47) only loosely link their sustainability strategy with the SDGs. Companies in this group made the link by merely mentioning the SDGs in the introduction to their sustainability reports or in relation to sustainability areas (e.g. by placing an SDG icon next to sustainability priorities) but without articulating how their strategies are aligned to help meet the goals. These companies risk paying lip service to the SDGs without meaningfully grappling with the goals' implications for their business and sustainability strategies.

A second significant group of companies within the subset referencing the SDGs (51% or 24 of 47) has gone a step further by more clearly linking their sustainability strategies with the SDGs. The most common approach is for companies to map and align their sustainability priorities across the SDGs and list concrete activities and initiatives. Only two companies in our sample are using the SDGs as the guiding framework for their sustainability strategy and showing efforts to realign their practices to meet the ambition of the goals. (Oxfam, 2018)

Notwithstanding the reservations around an actual business involvement in tacking the SDGs; it is important to note that they constitute a great advocacy and cooperation platform for stakeholders coming from various sectors. SDGs are also considered to be the reference for all discourse and work related to the sustainable development.

2.3.   Shifts in Corporate Communications Management and Convergence of the Functions

Corporate communications have been studied in different forms (and under different names) for a long time – the span of the studies includes almost 60 years of studies. It is even longer if we consider all studies around organizational communications and its impact on the target audiences (Katz & Lazersfeld, 1955). The studies traditionally focused on the various operational aspects of corporate communications management as well as on the applications of the corporate communications channels in organizational campaigning. This focus meant that corporate communications was not really studied from the multi-dimensional strategic perspective. For a long time, the researchers discussed whether the studies on corporate communications should belong to management studies or journalism (Argenti, 1996). There were very few studies looking at the corporate communications function from a corporate perspective (Bochenek & Blili, 2013). In a way corporate communication was considered as a support business function and analyzed accordingly (Bochenek & Blili, 2013). This led to a very low focus on studying the organization of the communications departments and internal positioning within the companies and organizations (Bochenek & Blili, 2013). As a result, it is not easy to provide an evidence-based evolution of the corporate communications concept and function (Bochenek & Blili, 2013).

Beyond that the scholars from social science and especially from sociology studied communications as an act of social exchange (Maigret, 2007). It was an act of social interaction. However, there were very few studies looking at communications from a corporate or organizational perspective. In fact, the acts of communication were studied much more from a media perspective (Maigret, 2007). The interpretation of the message was the subject of numerous studies in the media and communication science (Maigret, 2007). There were several models that analyzed in depth the act of communication. These models included Stuart Hall's encoding-decoding, which claimed that it is important to take into consideration the cognitive filters which influence perception of the messages (Hall, 1980). While this theory was slightly "forgotten," it becomes very pertinent in analyzing digital interaction that oftentimes suffers from cognitive bias (such as confirmation bias to name the most quoted one) (Nickerson, 1998). The intercultural aspect of communication is important from the organizational perspective (Hofstede, 2001). An important study by Hofstede provides insights into organizational communication (2001). While generalization of the conclusions to the overall intercultural communication is controversial, companies' communication systems are described interestingly. There were multiple new studies that focused on describing the intercultural aspect of corporate communications including further operationalization of the Hofstede's model in the context of international reputation management (Swoboda & Hirschmann, 2017). These focused on the organization of communication, messaging of the organization and its public perception through cognitive lenses of cultural perception (Swoboda & Hirschmann, 2017).

Corporate communications were also considered as a tool/technique to build and sustain corporate image and/or reputation − these studies were often situated in the nexus of management studies and business ethics (Du, Bhattacharya, & Sen, 2010; Wood, 2010). Several studies analyzed the impact of corporate image on corporate performance in terms of competitive advantage (Orlitzky, 2008). The multi-level analysis focused more on organizational techniques than on dialogue with stakeholders (Wood, 2010). However, again these studies focused limited attention on organization of corporate communications within the organizations (Bochenek & Blili, 2013).

From the 1990s on, there is an agreement that the role of communications within companies is more important and that it is evaluated positively by senior executives (Argenti, 2006a, 2006b). However, corporate communication has been often analyzed from the perspective of corporate identity and reporting (Wood, 2010). Corporate reporting in the context of corporate image brings the question of CSR reporting and CSR information management (Du et al., 2010). Disclosure and communication with stakeholders can bring a competitive advantage (Melo & Garrido-Morgado, 2011). There is also a clear correlation between executive perception of corporate communications and executive "buy in" and position of the corporate communications within the organization (Communication Monitor, 2018). The role of communication professionals as providers of information for the senior executives is critical to the perceived importance of the function and its place in the organizational structure (Communication Monitor, 2018).

Corporate communications, public relations, and marketing communications – all these functions manage corporate reputation (Balmer & Greyser, 2006). Moreover, the department managing corporate communications can be called by all these names. The fact that various terms describe this job function shows certain confusion about the role that the function should have within the organization (Argenti, 1996; Cornelissen, 2013). As the definition presented at the beginning of this chapter suggests, the naming issues are also due to the evolution of the concept and place of corporate communication in the organizational structure. Also, the hierarchical level of the supervisor of corporate communications varies (Communication Monitor, 2012–2018; Malaval & Decaudin, 2005). In some organizations, actually very few, it is a board level function, while in the others corporate communications, it is situated in the marketing department (Argenti, 1996) or even HR department (Communication Monitor, 2017). The structure and reporting line between the head of communications and senior leadership of an organization plays an important role in an overall perception and position of the department (Forman & Argenti, 2005). As stated before, it is highly driven by perceived usefulness of the function to provide insight and information (Communication Monitor, 2018).

The place of corporate communications in the structure depends also on the corporate profile (industry vs. services). It depends also on the customer type (b2b vs. b2c). It is also driven by the corporate culture in general and senior executives' agenda in particular (Argenti, 1996; Communication Monitor, 2018). The fact that similar challenges are listed in the studies throughout more than 20 years showcases a dilemma of the role that communication plays and should play within the organizations.

From the 1990s, corporate communication is a subject of studies as well as a title for a function in many organizations (Argenti, 1996; Cornelissen, 2011). Both the term and the research on corporate communication are relatively new (Argenti, 2006a). There is an ongoing discussion between scholars whether the domain of corporate communications belongs to the communication and mass media departments, or management studies (Argenti, 1996, 2006a). This changes with involvement of multiple external engagement functions under the corporate communication umbrella.

The ownership issue also defines the problems of research (Argenti, 1996; Wright, 1999). These divergences lead to a situation in which the subject is relatively under-studied, especially in the context of a growing role for corporate reputation in competitiveness (Argenti, 1996; Berens & Van Riel, 2004). Cornelissen provided the following definition of corporate communication:

> Corporate communication, in other words, can be characterized as a management function that is responsible for overseeing and coordinating the work done by communication practitioners in different specialist disciplines, such as media relations, public affairs and internal communication. (Cornelissen, 2010)

This definition is interesting as it focuses and positions corporate communication as a service provider for an organization and other departments. At the same time, the changing context requires corporate communications professionals to step up and manage a broader range of functions. The companies have to communicate to build relationships with stakeholders in order to communicate with them and build trust (Edelman Trust Barometer, 2017, 2018). The models of trust are also differing (Edelman Trust Barometer, 2018). We are observing constant decrease in trust levels toward traditional institutions and organizations (Edelman Trust Barometer, 2019). Interestingly, the trust in traditional and local media after years of decrease started to pick up again in the last year (Edelman Trust Barometer, 2019).

Therefore, corporate communication governance needs to become more professional and strategic (Argenti, 1996, 2006a; Communication Monitor, 2018; Zerfass, Verčič, Verhoeven, Moreno, & Tench, 2012). It also raises a question about a qualification of those who manage the function. More and more often the corporate communication structures are managed by professionals who are more educated in the domain (Communication Monitor, 2018). A growing number of academic and professional trainings in communication is a good example of this tendency. This brings the structure to the communications management and creates common frameworks for an organizational design of the function. It also changes the supply of educated and trained professionals that enter into the corporate communications field, making it more competitive and result-driven. Therefore, the sophistication of corporate communications governance is accompanied by the professionalization of its managers (Bochenek & Blili, 2013).

2.3.1. Changing View on Communications Management

Multiple stakeholders pose a growing challenge to organizations to impose their issues on stakeholders' agendas. Communication cannot be perceived through a static model like the one developed by Lasswell (1948). Indeed, because of social media, communication passes through multiple channels, so that recipients and senders are interchangeable (Communication Monitor, 2018; Winkin, 2001). Many authors analyze the impacts of this change on the public sphere and communications model. Yves Winkin introduced the model of orchestral communications, where different voices are expressed individually to form overall message and opinion (Winkin, 2001). However, this change was not perceived exclusively in the context of social media. Before, the rise of the nonprofit sector and the multiplication of communications channels changed the model of public sphere. Multiplication of the number of stakeholders embraced the division of the public sphere (Mouchon, 2005). According to Mouchon it became mutated.

Bastien and Neveu (1999) proposed the model of the mosaic to describe the current public sphere. The multiple elements composed an overall picture all together. They were not dependent on each other; however, they were elements of the phenomenon. Traditional actors in these models lost their importance while unofficial ones gained power (Miller, Fabian, & Lin, 2009). The empowerment of groups of interest and NGOs is one of the faces of this phenomenon. It had been amplified by the rise of social media (Mills, 2012). This requires new models of corporate communication for organizations, which need to deal with non-market stakeholders (Lawrence, 2010). New means of communications have empowered the structures which already existed and were established in the social system (Tapscott, 2008).

Maxwell McCombs and Donald Shaw introduced the theory of agenda setting in 1972 following the research on the presidential campaign in 1968. The study discussed the findings of the school of limited media effects (i.e., Katz and Lazersfeld). The media were supposed to shape the opinions of stakeholders by increasing the prominence of certain themes. As Bernard Cohen (1963) stated, the media were not saying what to think but about what to think. The majority of the studies in communications tried to assess the impact of the media on the public (Maigret, 2007). However, there was far less attention on the techniques on how the media are actually influenced by the organizations. In that view, the journalists would be the public that is exposed to the communications efforts of the organizations. Therefore, the success of any organization is based on its ability to place its core subjects on the media agenda. CC executes this principle by creating public relations programs (Egri & Herman, 2000). In this context media are the intermediary audience and recipient in the process. The organization influences the media in order to place its messages in the channel and afterwards, influence the public and stakeholders. It can be seen as a double agenda setting (McCombs & Shaw, 1972). The latter process involves also framing and priming (Bateson, 1972a, 1972b; Iyengar, Peters, & Kinder, 1982). These processes were considered as the elements of the media effect on the public (Dayan & Katz, 1992). However, again, few analyzed the effects of corporate communications and media relations on the media.

The social media change these processes. The importance of media relations and media coverage in the corporate/organizational communication decreases, as there are other channels of communication available for the organizations. It is possible for organizations to address the public directly through social media channels and maintain direct dialogue. This dialogue can be managed on the global scale (Barbier, 2011; Veil, Buehner, & Pakenchar, 2011). However, these media are neither owned nor controlled (Tapscott, 2008). They remain in the sphere of influence while creating an opportunity for a direct dialogue. Jean Missika says that the digitalization means the end of television (2006). It seems to be valid for television understood as a linear medium. However, there is an increasing exposure to the content that can be consumed on-demand through technologies. Therefore, the customization of the content offering becomes crucial. David Meek studied the opportunities provided by YouTube to NGOs and humanitarian organizations to amplify their issues on stakeholders' agenda and further action (2011). He analyzed an example of the NGO Invisible Children and the impact of its videos. The link between the field, cyberspace, awareness, and action of stakeholders is analyzed. He contributes to the discussion by considering offline actions, that is, events as an important element which helps to "galvanize" the community online (Meek, 2011). In that overall context, the social media have a dual role for corporations; on the one hand they are a tool for corporate communications and social media marketing, on the other hand they provide a research toolkit to assess brand sentiment and overall reputational health of the company (Beuker et al., 2010). This connection management becomes a strategic concern of corporations (Hancock, 2010).

2.3.2. *Public Affairs − State of the Art and Definitions*

Public affairs is the field that has been studied for the last 30−40 years. It even has its own dedicated scientific journal, *Journal of Public Affairs*. There are several definitions of public affairs, but for the interest of this book we selected the one coming from PR Council:

> We can define public affairs as "issues arising from the relationship of the public to an organization such as a government body or a financial institution." Substitute the word "client" for "public," and you arrive at the essence of a public affairs practice. (PR Council)[8]

In this context public affairs are a tool that companies and organizations use in order to shape their regulatory environment (Zetter, 2014). This includes both lobbying and broader political communications. It is important to note this duality as it is what makes public affairs being close to advocacy. Historically, public affairs tools and techniques were associated with the corporate engagement in the policy issues while advocacy was a domain of the non-for-profit sector (Zetter, 2014). However, these distinctions are blurring. The non-for-profit organizations use more lobbying and public affairs tools to shape the decisions in their key issues. This is recognized by Transparency Register of European Union where NGOs and companies need to follow same requirements of disclosure (Transparency Register, 2019). At the same time, the companies engage with a broader thematic framework and range of stakeholders (PwC, 2018). Finally, both cooperate more and more frequently to address the international issues coming from a sustainability framework (Scheyvens et al., 2016).

In the public discourse we can observe multiple misconceptions around public affairs and lobbying. This leads to the naming issues and search for other names to describe the same activities:

---

[8]https://prcouncil.net/inside-pr/public-affairs/

Some organizations are uncomfortable with labelling their activities as "lobbying", as an American survey of US non-profit organizations revealed. Organizations were asked what activities they undertook to influence policy: 29% said they never lobbied, 15% never advocated and 12% never educated. Simultaneously, 86% answered that they did participate in the public policy process.

The negative connotations associated with the word "lobbying" have prompted most lobbyists to use other terms to describe their profession: in Europe the most used term is "public affairs." Even the European Commission has dropped the term "lobbying" used in its 2006 Green Paper, to become "interest representation" in its Communication establishing a voluntary Register in 2008 and in the current Transparency Register set up in 2011, it is being referred to as European institutions interaction with citizen's associations, NGO's, business, trade and professional organizations, trade unions, think tanks, etc. (EPACA, 2018)[9]

In some countries, lobbying has become almost a synonym of corruption – to the extent that "lobbying activities" are forbidden (Zetter, 2014). These misconceptions are very harmful for the public affairs professionals as they are facing a strong negative bias from the general public and in many cases from the political decision-makers (EPACA, 2018). This bias is being addressed through an increased openness with regards to the decision-making processes and transparency (Zetter, 2014). The initiatives in the United States and European Union (including Transparency Register) are a good example of the work done to de-mystify lobbying activities (Zetter, 2014). The below quote introducing the Transparency Register of EU provides a clear view on the change of the way lobbying should be perceived:

Citizens can, and indeed should, expect the EU decision-making process to be as transparent and open as possible. The more open the process is, the easier it is to ensure balanced representation and avoid undue pressure and illegitimate or privileged access to information or to decision-makers. Transparency is also a key part of encouraging European citizens to participate more actively in the democratic life of the EU.

The transparency register has been set up to answer core questions such as what interests are being pursued, by whom and with what budgets. The system is operated jointly by the European Parliament and the European Commission.

Source: Transparency Register, 2019[10]

---

[9] https://epaca.org/about-lobbying/
[10] http://ec.europa.eu/transparencyregister/public/homePage.do

At the end of the day, the lobbying questions often boil down into the access question (Zetter, 2014). For a long time, the public affairs professionals have been focusing on gaining the access to decision-makers and politicians (Zetter, 2014). As a result, access to decision-makers was considered to be a commodity that was sold by public affairs professionals and lobbyists. From our perspective we find the SEAP's definition of lobbying as both simple and well structured:

> In a nutshell, it simply means seeking to influence policymaking, policy implementation and/or the EU institutions' decision-making process.
>
> The European Parliament, European Commission and Council of Ministers are the three main EU bodies involved in adopting policy and legislation.
>
> As the EU has grown in size and areas of competence, its decisions affect more and more areas of business, civil society and individual citizens.
>
> As such, more and more people seek to influence the shape of legislation so that it reflects their concerns or needs. (SEAP)

However, the access (direct or mediated) becomes much easier for the interested parties (SEAP).

> Why lobby? Lobbying is a legitimate part of the decision-making process and an integral part of the democratic process. When done well, it should inform decision-makers' thinking, thus allowing them to take well-informed decisions. Lobbyists can provide information and expertise of a particular field, which decision-makers or politicians will not necessarily possess. As such it should aid better law-making. (SEAP)[11]

The main issue and challenge nowadays is "what to do with this access?" (Zetter, 2014). That requires the whole rethinking of the public affairs profession and re-focus on the content and quality of interaction as opposed to a simple access toward decision-makers (Zetter, 2014). Therefore, public affairs research needs to also focus on a more holistic view of public affairs as a profession (Zetter, 2014). It would also benefit from a higher level of neutrality of researchers who are still oftentimes presenting a certain level of bias toward this profession.

---

[11]https://seap.be/lobbying/

2.3.3.   Advocacy – State of the Art and Definitions

The research on advocacy is still somewhat limited in its scope. Frequently, advocacy is defined from a non-for-profit perspective. A definition from UNICEF is a good example. It includes both definition of advocacy itself and what advocacy means for an organization together with the overarching advocacy goals:

> Advocacy is the deliberate process, based on demonstrated evidence, to directly and indirectly influence decision makers, stakeholders and relevant audiences to support and implement actions that contribute to the fulfilment of children's and women's rights.

> Elaborating on this: advocacy involves delivering evidence-based recommendations to decision makers, stakeholders and/or those who influence them. Advocacy is a means of seeking change in governance, attitudes, power, social relations and institutional functions. It supports actions which are taken at scale, and which address deeper, underlying barriers to the fulfilment of children's rights.

> The goal of advocacy can be to address imbalances, inequity and disparities promote human rights, social justice, a healthy environment, or to further the opportunities for democracy by promoting children's and women's participation. Advocacy requires organizing and organization. It represents a set of strategic actions and, at its most vibrant, will influence the decisions, practices and policies of others.
>
> *Source*: UNICEF Advocacy Toolkit

A lot of researchers focused on analysis of the grassroots movements and campaigns. For a long time, the advocacy was associated directly with the non-for-profit sector and international organizations. The act of advocating was almost antonymous to the act of lobbying (associated with the international companies and businesses) (Zetter, 2014). This complexity makes difficult to clearly define the role advocacy plays and can play within the organizations.

At the same time, the term was used as a synonym of supportive behaviors of the target audiences vis-à-vis products, services or organizations. As such advocacy was understood as third-party endorsement. The act of advocating on behalf of a company or organization was described in the marketing studies under "consumer advocacy." With a growing role of consumer activism, consumer advocacy became one of the most important tools used by the companies to ensure their market position. We can observe three main streams in the research related to advocacy in international affairs:

- The first focuses on the advocacy strategies and driving of social change (Jordan & Van Tuijl, 2000; Nelson, 2000).
- The second looks at advocacy campaigns and campaign tactics/tools from an engagement perspective. Many of the researchers from this stream analyze the efficiency of the advocacy campaigns from the target audience engagement perspective (Fox & Brown, 1998; Stroup & Murdie, 2012).
- The third focuses on consumer advocacy and is closely linked with the marketing studies (Urban, 2005). In this stream advocacy is considered to be one of the marketing tactics focusing on engaging the consumers in brand support.

There are several research focus areas in advocacy including: NGO advocacy and campaigning, business advocacy, advocacy campaigns, grassroots movements, employee advocacy, and advocacy networks. Even this short list illustrates well the challenge faced in the advocacy field – advocacy means many things for many people. Therefore, even the term advocacy strategy can be misunderstood depending how the person perceives it.

Following these considerations, we suggest a definition of advocacy that caters to the duality described above. Advocacy becomes in fact a strategic process aimed at creating behaviors of defined target audiences vis-à-vis an organization, its products, brands, or services. A proposed definition of advocacy is pretty broad. We believe that this broad approach is the most effective one.

> Advocacy is a strategic approach to influence stakeholders and gain third-party endorsement in order to shape an organization's/ company's operating environment.

The most important element of our definition is that we believe advocacy requires being strategically driven. Without the link toward the organizational strategy it becomes a vacuum of activities which bring a limited value to the organizational performance. We also believe that advocacy is directed toward those who shape an operational environment of an organization. This is very important as it requires an in-depth understanding of the business and socioeconomic context. Finally, advocacy is about shaping the environment and decisions with a clearly defined outcome. Therefore, the campaigns and activities need to be grounded in a defined outcome-focused approach.

2.4. Toward a Conceptual Model of Strategic Advocacy Management

The proposed model for advocacy management is inspired by both academic literature about public affairs and advocacy management as well as management theory of organizational learning (Argyris & Schon, 1978; Huber, 1991). We propose a dynamic model that considers the changing landscape around influence and communications tools. At the same time, the model is flexible enough to be applicable for both companies and not-for-profit organizations. We define the organizational profiles and build dynamic maturity levels inspired by the model developed for corporate communications management (Bochenek & Blili, 2013).

The categories included in the conceptual maturity model are based on the basic managerial functions namely: planning, organizing, staffing, leading, and controlling (Koontz & O'Donnell, 1972). In this dynamic model we look at the conceptual idea learning profiles according to the main managerial functions. We believe that this approach is pertinent as it allows to see advocacy from a processual perspective and gets away from typical content-centered analytical models. Dynamic character of this model means that it can be used as a diagnosis tool for those managing advocacy in the organizations as well as assessment tool for those who review the advocacy organization.

2.4.1.   Organizational Advocacy Profiles

The organization's learning patterns can be seen as the typical learning paths. The researchers suggest four or five learning profiles that apply to a majority of the companies (Crossan & Guatto, 1996; Huber, 1991). In this research we follow a previous corporate communications maturity model developed by Bochenek and Blili and adapt it to the advocacy context (Bochenek & Blili, 2013). The five learning patterns described below are the archetypes of an "ideal learning path" (Bateson, 1972a, 1972b). Proposed archetypes are ordered in ascending maturity levels (Crossan & Guatto, 1996; Huber, 1991).

2.4.1.1. Sleeping

The companies that don't see advocacy as core to their communications and engagement. These organizations tend to ignore the external developments in their operating environments. Their usage of communications tools is limited, and if they use them, it is driven by marketing and sales activities. They don't see the need for advocacy in order to create their competitive advantage. Their channel listening and socioeconomic scanning are limited in scope and developed on an "ad hoc" basis. These organizations don't use employee advocacy and in general communications and public affairs are not the executive level concerns. Finally, the measurement and evaluation protocols are non-existent.

2.4.1.2. Delegative

The organizations representing this learning pattern relay heavily on external parties to deliver their advocacy. They delegate the initiative for industry/sector wide initiatives to the competitors and/or trade associations. Their individual positioning on the issues is non-existent or replicating an overall industry positioning. Their internal processes related to advocacy focus heavily on monitoring of the developments as well as risk mitigation. They don't proactively engage with the discussions nor shape the discourse. These organizations tend to engage external suppliers to drive the engagement on their behalf. They do participate in the industry coalitions, but rarely to never take the leading position within them. The tone of voice and positioning of these organizations is conservative and not daring.

2.4.1.3. Following

These organizations participate in the advocacy efforts beyond their own area of business. They follow the industry trends and participate in multi-company and multi-stakeholder initiatives. These organizations shape their own influencing agenda based on the industry trends and best practices. They invest in the advocacy both in terms of the staff and the content; however, they don't come out with the industry-wide initiatives. These organizations observe external developments and adjust their own narrative accordingly. Within these companies advocacy is considered as a function – it is usually placed within the public affairs or government relations remit. These companies tend to be quite reactive and build their competitive advantage based on marketing differentiation and consider advocacy as a market access tool.

2.4.1.4. Shaping

Representing this pattern are the organizations that take a leading position in the industry associations. Their executives consider advocacy as a key enabler for business and build their positions around it. The investment in advocacy goes beyond communications and public affairs. These organizations participate actively in the PPPs as a part of their sustainability strategies. They also see public affairs and advocacy as the functions beyond market access. Their external profile is much more visible and tone of voice bolder. They integrate advocacy and sustainability messaging in their corporate communications and marketing. From the measurement and evaluation perspective these organizations monitor and report their advocacy activities in an ongoing basis. Advocacy is considered to be a business line that can generate the profits for business as a whole.

2.4.1.5. Leading

Organizations representing this learning pattern consider advocacy as the core of their activities. It is perceived as an enabler for business and has a very high level of executive buy-in. They tend to participate actively in the industry-wide initiatives that go beyond their core business. These companies act and represent the business as a whole and not only their area of focus. The advocacy structures are complex and integrated across the business lines. As a consequence, sustainability, corporate positioning, business strategy, and leadership agenda are all fully integrated. These organization go beyond existing industry representations and platforms and create their own initiatives. They tend to have very daring tone of voice and center all their external engagement around advocacy and sustainability. Finally, they build industry-wide measurement and evaluation protocols (Table 2.1).

Table 2.1. Advocacy Learning Profiles.

	Sleeping	Delegative	Following	Shaping	Leading
Planning	Lack of formalized advocacy plans Objectives not defined Advocacy not integrated in the business strategy Lack of alignment between external engagement activities	Defined public affairs/advocacy plans Objectives developed in line with the market access strategy Advocacy activities planned in a reactive manner	Formal advocacy plans developed Objectives aligned with industry objectives Clearly defined advocacy outcomes	Advocacy strategy as part of the business strategy Formalized planning and approval processes Multiple stakeholders consulted within and beyond organization in the advocacy planning processes Clearly defined advocacy plans	Business strategy shaped by advocacy strategy Formal planning processes and procedures throughout the organization Long-term and short-term advocacy planning Clear timelines and long-term impact-driven objectives
Organizing	No separate job function for advocacy Activities (if any) organized on ad hoc basis Lack of formal structure for advocacy or public affairs	Public affairs/government relations department function within the organization Advocacy integrated in the public affairs and communications function High level of externalization of the advocacy activities	Advocacy function driving external engagement of the organization – formal structure of external engagement Advocacy function/sub-function present across the organization	Formal advocacy structure throughout the organization Internal structure of advocacy reflected in the external participation and leadership from the company in the industry associations	Advocacy function driving external engagement of the company Alignment of marketing and corporate communications activities with advocacy goals

Staffing	Possible externalized monitoring function	Dedicated public affairs/government relations professionals Advocacy staff with communications/political background Lack of career progression possibilities within the function Majority of the advocacy function delegated to trade associations/external consultancies	Dedicated advocacy resources within the organization Advocacy integrated in the HQ office and main centers of influence Partial delegation of the advocacy function and activities toward external consultancies and trade associations	Advocacy function integrated both in HQ business lines and regional/country offices Direct reporting line between the head of advocacy and CEO Access to internal and external resources for advocacy professionals External expertise supplementing internal function	Advocacy professionals integrated in the strategic planning department Advocacy as an executive level function
Leading	Lack of executive oversight on the advocacy function Advocacy and external engagement not-focused on	Advocacy activities seen as supporting the business Possible advocacy reporting toward senior management on ad hoc interest basis	Advocacy as an executive concern integrated in internal and external leadership communications Alignment between external sustainability positioning and advocacy activities	Advocacy as an Executive Board level function Alignment between internal and external leadership of advocacy function Company representatives taking roles in external industry associations	Advocacy and sustainability agenda aligned with the executive agenda CEO as the key spokesperson on industry related advocacy issues Alignment of advocacy with internal communications

Table 2.1. (*Continued*)

	Sleeping	Delegative	Following	Shaping	Leading
			Employee engagement programs	Driving initiatives beyond closed stakeholder group	Staff ambassadorship and employee internal and external advocacy
Controlling	No formal measurement and evaluation protocol Lack of internal and external reporting KPIs not defined	Guidelines for external engagement with the political stakeholders Code of conduct/ ethical guidelines in line with the industry association best practices Ad hoc auditing of external perception of company	Defined measurement and evaluation framework in line with the objectives Regular benchmarking against the key competitors Formulated codes of conducts and rules of external engagement Formal external evaluation procedure	Comprehensive measurement and evaluation framework Regular external auditing of the advocacy strategy and activities Regular perception audits among key stakeholder groups	Outcome-based comprehensive evaluation framework Multi-layered reporting on the advocacy progress Clearly defined KPIs for the advocacy teams External auditing of the advocacy plans and performance

2.4.2. *Diagnosis Tool for Advocacy*

A majority of management theories boil down to the main functions that management has in the companies. For the purpose of this model we chose the view on basic function of management consisting of the five functions: planning, organizing, staffing, leading, and controlling (Koontz & O'donnell, 1972). As in the dynamic model for advocacy management we used these functions and developed the questionnaire that is broken down accordingly. The questions aim at helping define the organizational profiles of advocacy management and in consequence develop action plan to improve the strategic advocacy management.

This diagnosis tool which consists of a simple questionnaire allows us to:

- benchmark advocacy strategy against best practices and define the advocacy profile of the organization;
- identify gaps in advocacy strategy and showcase the possible corrective actions in order to cover these gaps;
- see how the advocacy profile (archetype) of organization fits into international landscape and which advocacy tactics and actions are the most effective;
- define the template for advocacy strategy development. This template can be used for both organizational and campaign advocacy strategies;
- enhance advocacy efforts and ensure the best return on investment from advocacy activities within the organization; and
- showcase the opportunity for strategic alliances and the path that can be used in order to build these alliances (relevance, value, return).

The diagnosis tool and maturity model are interconnected. The questions from the diagnosis tool help to position the organizational profile within the conceptual model. They also help to identify the gaps and therefore design corrective actions to ensure consistency of the advocacy strategies and activities.

2.4.3. *Questionnaire for Strategic Advocacy*
Management – A Diagnosis Tool

This questionnaire allows to identify the organizational profile of advocacy in the strategic management of an organization. This questionnaire can also be used to define the role and function of advocacy within the organization. Applying these questions can structure the development of the organizational strategy around advocacy and define the function and role advocacy plays within the organization.

Planning
    (1) How are the advocacy activities planned within the organization?
    (2) Who is responsible and who is accountable for the planning processes?
    (3) Are the advocacy plans clearly defined?
    (4) Who is signing off the advocacy plans?

(5) Is advocacy aligned with the sustainability and external engagement of the organization?

(6) How often are the plans reviewed/updated?

(7) How is the success of advocacy defined?

(8) What is the timeline of advocacy activities?

Organizing

(9) Where does the advocacy function sit within the organization?

(10) Who has the ultimate responsibility for advocacy activities?

(11) How is the external engagement of the organization organized?

(12) What is the proportion of advocacy activities that is externalized versus internally managed?

(13) Is the organization a member of the industry bodies and associations?

(14) What is the level of involvement in the industry initiatives and trade associations?

(15) How is the head of the advocacy function positioned within the structure of the organization?

(16) What is an internal organization of the advocacy function within the organization?

Staffing

(17) How many people work in the advocacy department/structure within the organization?

(18) What is the profile of those who manage external relations and external engagement of the organization?

(19) What are the reporting lines between the executive leaders, business leaders, and those who manage advocacy function within the organization?

(20) What kind of advocacy training and upskilling opportunities does the organization offer to its staff?

(21) What is the hierarchical level of the most senior advocacy professional?

(22) How does the organization recruit its advocacy practitioners?

(23) What is the level of rotation of advocacy staff within the organization (vertically and horizontally)?

(24) Who is responsible for recruitment of the advocacy and external relations staff?

Leading

(25) Who is defining the advocacy agenda of the organization?

(26) Who is the leader of advocacy function within the organization?

(27) What is the process of defining the advocacy priorities within the organization?

(28) What is the degree of alignment between the organizational advocacy goals and overall industry advocacy positions?

(29) What is the involvement of the organization's executives in the industry/trade association initiatives?

(30) Who are the key leaders deciding the advocacy agenda and strategy of the organization?

(31) To what extent is advocacy and sustainability-related messaging integrated in an overall executive positioning and executive communications?

(32) What is the degree of involvement of the company's executives in the business-led initiatives focusing on the issues beyond its main industry?

Controlling

(33) How is advocacy measured and evaluated?

(34) How are the advocacy goals and objectives defined?

(35) What is a degree of alignment between the advocacy goals and business strategy?

(36) Are there internal codes of conduct related to external and political engagement within the organization?

(37) What is the frequency of advocacy reporting within the organization?

(38) What is the overall framework for measurement of external relations of the organization?

(39) How does the organization analyze its external image among key stakeholders?

(40) Is there an external validation of the advocacy and sustainability-related reporting?

These questions aim to support sophistication and strategic design of an advocacy function. They aim to provide a set of considerations toward those who define the advocacy organizational structure.

2.5. Discussion and Further Research

In this chapter, we proposed to apply the basic principles of strategic management to the model of organizational management of advocacy. Even till today and despite all the changes in the business landscape, advocacy is still perceived as non-core function (especially in the private sector companies) or only associated with lobbying activities (Zetter, 2014). While advocacy might be synonymous with lobbying in some cases, in general it requires much broader strategic approaches including communications, marketing and core business functions. Applying a dynamic model can help mitigate some of the risks related to misperception around advocacy. It can also help to understand the contribution that advocacy can bring to the organizations by focusing on the links between advocacy and business objectives and results.

At the same time, the model aims to help and structure the advocacy efforts and define the framework for organizational advocacy strategies. Bringing controlling element through robust measurement and evaluation framework supports perception change around advocacy as a profession. It is visible that the advocacy professionals face similar challenges to the communications professionals in terms of recognition of their function within the organizations. The professionalization of the job function and subsequent growth in numbers of employees with the titles related to advocacy will help to overcome these issues.

A future scientific research around advocacy will definitely benefit from a strategic management approach and seeing advocacy as one of the core functions. Our proposed model invites discussion on the ways to increase efficiency and effectiveness of the corporate advocacy efforts. This field is relatively understudied, and we believe that a cross-discipline research would bring additional insights and perspective valuable for both scientific community and practitioners. For instance, studying "in organization" models of advocacy management would be important for the future research in the field. This would include analyzing and benchmarking various models and structures used in the organizations to manage advocacy function.

Finally, studying concrete advocacy initiatives through qualitative methodology (for instance business ethnographic research) would bring a better understanding around the issues faced by the multi-stakeholder initiatives. These studies could include for instance benchmarking of the perceptions between corporate and not-for-profit advocacy agents within the same campaigns. We talk a lot about the need of different actors to work together in order to achieve advocacy goals. However, the experience of this work and organizational culture elements are rarely part of the discussion. Oftentimes advocacy campaigning is studied exclusively from the perspective of the "end recipients" of advocacy messaging. The view from "within" would for sure provide additional insights and allow a much deeper understanding of the constraints and benefits of multi-stakeholder initiatives from a management science perspective. In all cases, advocacy as a field of study is set to expand as advocacy is growing both as a profession and consideration of the organizations.

Key Takeaways

- Landscape is changing; advocacy becomes more and more critical for organizational results for both companies, not-for-profits and international organizations. Therefore, the definition of organizational advocacy requires an inclusive approach looking at whole range of activities.
- Corporate reputation management needs to be structured and strategic. Given its importance for an overall performance of the company it needs to have appropriate structures and processes. These need to be linked with an engagement strategy and stakeholder approach.
- There is a need to manage advocacy activities strategically and to see it as an integrated part of organizational design. It means applying the same management principles to advocacy as to any other business line in the organization.
- In the growing field of advocacy, organizational learning is critical. A sophistication of advocacy models and practices can elevate the way organizations manage their influencing strategies. It is important for

organizations to document and analyze their advocacy activities in order to drive an improvement agenda.

- Advocacy requires an integrated approach combining all engagement functions of the organization: communications, marketing, public affairs, market research as well as core business functions. An internal alignment is critical factor for a success of advocacy initiatives.
- There is a growing need to measure and report the results of the advocacy initiatives. Measurement and evaluation practices constitute the best advocacy for advocacy in the organizations – helping to gain executive attention and recognition.

Chapter 3

From Philanthropy to Sustainability through CSR – What's Next? Societal Context and Changing Role of the Companies

3.1. Introduction

A lot was said about the changing role of the companies in the socioeconomic ecosystem. The companies are supposed to play a new role in the society where their focus is to be shifted from the profits toward the values and contributions. Some research suggested that this shift of discourse and focus on a "triple bottom line" helped companies to hide their unethical practices and constituted a substation of real action (Norman & MacDonald, 2004). While the studies present different views about the direct positive impact of corporate social responsibility (CSR) activities on the financial performance of the companies, it is easily visible that the companies that are socially active benefit from a better reputation among their stakeholders and consumers (Wood, 2010). The reputation in turn is one of the most important intangible corporate assets (Bernett, 2006).

Interestingly, it was noted by some researchers that CSR involvement alone doesn't necessarily have a positive impact on the financial performance of the companies. At the same time, other researchers suggest the contrary. However, this is also due to the definitions of what CSR is. There is also a discrepancy between how the companies see CSR and how researchers define it. Oftentimes, CSR is measured and considered as a philanthropic expense of the company aimed at influencing its direct stakeholder environment (Moon et al., 2010; Orlitzky, 2008). That raises also a question on how to actually measure the CSR performance of a company (Wood, 2010). The views on the best and most appropriate metrics differ. Several researchers suggest that CSR measurement suffers from a multiplication of the vanity measures (Wood, 2010). It leads to contrasting conclusions in the research about the impact of CSR on the performance of the companies (Du et al., 2010; Minor & Morgan, 2011). There is a certain level of agreement that communication and stakeholder engagement bring the benefits of reputation to the organization (Du et al., 2010)

Given these discussions and a general lack of consensus around CSR, we propose to focus in this book on the notion of sustainability. As the definition of corporate sustainability is larger than typical and most repeated definitions of the CSR, it is also more relevant for the discourse around advocacy.

> Corporate sustainability is imperative for business today – essential to long-term corporate success and for ensuring that markets deliver value across society. To be sustainable, companies must do five things: Foremost, they must operate responsibly in alignment with universal principles and take actions that support the society around them. Then, to push sustainability deep into the corporate DNA, companies must commit at the highest level, report annually on their efforts, and engage locally where they have a presence. (United Nations Global Compact Guide to Sustainability)[1]

In addition, the stakeholders of the companies (especially coming from the non-for-profit sector) tend to have a critical view of the term CSR as a synonym of "green-washing" of the international corporations in the 1980s and 1990s (Norman & MacDonald, 2004). Initially, the companies were reporting their CSR achievements almost exclusively in terms of the environmental performance. Then the companies moved toward more comprehensive frameworks of compliance reporting (Crane, 2008). The communications aspect started to be supported by the reporting. It is generally accepted that the Cadbury Report was the first comprehensive CSR report issued (Crane, 2008). It was also a milestone in thinking about CSR. The reporting created the basis for multi-stakeholder dialogue around the social performance of the companies. After that the reporting moved from compliance to voluntary commitments and then toward a stakeholder engagement (Porter & Kramer, 2011). This evolution of the CSR concept was strengthened by the change in view about the role companies should play in the society and social issues. After 2008 financial crisis there is a move to push companies toward more comprehensive engagement in the causes beyond their business operations. At the same time, the companies need to strengthen their profile and respond to the expectations from the multiple stakeholders.

The expectations from customers coming from the Millennial generation change the way companies look at social performance and sustainability. Indeed, the good practices and sustainable business models become an asset in marketing and communications (Romani, Grappi, & Bagozzi, 2016). This also goes beyond that. Millennials expect their employers and providers to act in an ethical manner and play a positive role in the socioeconomic system (Lippincott, 2012; Taylor & Keeter, 2010). At the same time Millennial consumers are more likely to buy the products coming from companies benefiting from good

---

[1]https://www.globalcompact.de/wAssets/docs/Nachhaltigkeits-CSR-Management/un_global_compact_guide_to_corporate_sustainability.pdf

reputation and known for sustainable practices (Johnstone & Lindh, 2018; Hanks, Odom, Roedl, & Blevis, 2008). All this creates a strengthened demand for multi-layer sustainability. However, this expectation is not unique to the Millennials – the reputation of the companies becomes one of the strongest intangible assets that build the value of the companies (Roberts & Dawling, 2002). Therefore, managing corporate reputation becomes the key function of the external affairs, communications, and marketing departments (Agnihotri, 2014).

The research on corporate reputation indicates that having a "good reputation" brings multiple benefits to a company or an organization (Roberts & Dawling, 2002). Of course, the definitions of what the good reputation means differ (Bernett et al., 2006) and again there is no consensus on what constitutes a good reputation for a company (Bernett et al., 2006).

> To achieve "one vision, one voice" on corporate reputation, and to have a more thorough impact on practice, we believe it to be particularly important that future studies move away from the omnibus-type definitions—those encompassing statements that include content that configures reputation as awareness and assessment and even asset. Omnibus definitions have helped bring corporate reputation researchers together under one common tent in recent years, but in order to make our union academically and practically fruitful, we need to work from a common and more concise definition. (Bernett et al., 2006)

Several researchers prefer the normative definitions, while the others look for more comprehensive ways of defining what corporate reputation is (Bernett et al., 2006). For the interest of this book we follow the definition of corporate reputation coming from Gotsi and Wilson:

> A corporate reputation is a stakeholder's overall evaluation of a company over time. This evaluation is based on the stakeholder's direct experiences with the company, any other form of communication and symbolism that provides information about the firm's actions and/or a comparison with the actions of other leading rivals. (Gotsi & Wilson, 2001)

In general, all the researchers agree that positive reputation is important and beneficial for the companies at multiple layers. There are several benefits that are associated with the companies that enjoy a good reputation, notably:

- It supports attracting and retaining talent. In the current job market space, the companies need to fight for the most skilled employees (Calk & Patrick, 2017). These sought for employees in turn expect companies to act in an ethical manner and positively contribute to the socioeconomic landscape. The compensation and other financial benefits are less important drivers of the choice of the employer (Chau, 2012). Therefore, the image of the company can become the driver of choice.

- It allows them to connect with those who shape a regulatory landscape in which company operates. The regulators and legislators alike are highly influenced by the broader context in their actions and decisions (Zetter, 2018). An effective lobbying requires an in-depth understanding of their organizational and personal agenda of the stakeholders (Zetter, 2018). At the same time, the perceptions of the external stakeholders are strongly driven by the corporate reputation of the organization (Zetter, 2018).

- It mitigates the risks related to crises (Coombs, 2007) (see Chapter 7). The companies that benefit from a good reputation are more likely to suffer less image damage during the crises (Benoit, 1997; Coombs, 2014). During the first phase of the crisis, which is often decisive for a long-term impact of the crisis, they also benefit from a doubt among the stakeholders and regulators (Coombs, 2014). The same applies to general public. As a result, they "win" the time to address the crisis and take care of their constituencies. On the contrary, the companies with a "bad reputation" are being immediately judged and suffer from longer term image damages (Coombs, 2014).

- It makes it easier to build business partnerships. The pressures from the stakeholders concern the whole value chain of the company (Coombs, 2014). The partners (especially from not-for-profit sector) are much more likely to cooperate with the companies, who benefit from a good reputation. This leads to creation of the partnerships and cooperation bringing benefits to the advocacy campaigning.

- It supports the sales of the products and services (Moon, Lee, & Oh, 2015). The ethical considerations become increasingly important for the choices of consumers to select one product over the other (Moon et al., 2015). The sustainability is also increasingly a consideration to pay the premium on the products and services. As a result, good reputation is also directly good for the business.

In a nutshell, the change of landscape and expectations requires the companies to adjust their strategies and approaches to the social subjects. This in turn impacts positively their image and reputation. In this chapter we will explore more in detail the nature of this change, how it impacts the communications and advocacy, and finally how the companies can benefit from this change to build more resilient advocacy strategies in the context driven by the social considerations and growing stakeholder expectations.

3.2. Notion of Trust

There are several studies that analyze the changes in the trust toward companies, institutions, and individuals. Probably, the most comprehensive and covering the highest number of markets is "Trust Barometer" from Edelman. The study is commissioned by a private company, and there might be some methodological questions related to its sample – notably in terms of the per market/par category significance. However, it is the most regularly commissioned and published study looking at notion of trust in multiple countries. It provides a good overview of the global trends around trust and perceptions of the general public toward the different socioeconomic actors.

Since 2009 the trust in institutions and traditional system is decreasing (this includes media, government, and expert community). At the same time "new actors" both in political and social contexts benefit from variable levels of trust. For instance, the trust toward social media started to decrease in the recent years (Edelman Trust Barometer, 2019). We can also observe that in multiple countries and markets the society is increasingly polarized. The old traditional system of power is rejected as it doesn't answer to the growing expectations coming from the society. Brexit, results of 2016 elections in the United States and France followed by several other countries constitute a good example of this polarization and search for new solutions that don't belong to the traditional power system.

This is a real challenge for corporate advocacy strategies. In the past, there were general references of trust on which it was possible to build the campaigns and work toward the influence goals. Social capital was relatively static and based on an individual's background. At present, the challenge is the lack of reference point. It means that advocacy professionals need to constantly seek for the trust references in each case they are influencing. They also need to constantly monitor shifts in trust and look at their impacts on the strategies. This makes the whole advocacy and influence journey even more challenging and requires additional agility in the process and delivery.

In addition, the companies (institutional communications) are not the most trusted sources of information about themselves. Their managers and executives are also not the most trusted spokespeople. The most trusted source of information about the companies are their employees (Edelman Trust Barometer, 2018, 2019). It is interesting to see as at the beginning of the 2010s the "person like yourself" was the most trusted source of information (Edelman Trust Barometer, 2012). The changes in the trust levels and main trust sources are parallel to the changes of the views of the social media channels. The trust in social media is decreasing and goes toward the levels of other media channels. For instance, local press gains recently in trust levels among key audiences in multiple countries (Edelman Trust Barometer, 2019).

Described trust challenge is universal as it doesn't touch exclusively private companies. The non-governmental and international organizations are equally concerned (Edelman Trust Barometer, 2019). Paradoxically, this landscape creates and environment in which the new forms of cooperation can be beneficial for all the involved actors. Public-private partnerships, multilateral organizations – the new forms of cooperation bring together the actors that had limited experiences of working together in the past (Andonova, 2015). Therefore, they build the platforms that can benefit from being a novelty without a past legacy of the institutional system.

3.3.   Managing Expectations toward the Companies

Sustainable Development Goals (SDGs), Global Compact, FTSE for Good – from international frameworks to financial benchmarks the companies are requested to include their social contributions in their strategies and operations. At the same time the consumers are increasingly demanding that products and services be delivered in ethical manner. The push toward measurement and reporting of the social performance accompanied by the global standards such as ISO 14001 showcases the shift toward substantiated influencing strategies.

The sustainability as understood today is focusing on holistic approaches to sourcing, supply chain, production and sales strategies (see, Global Compact, 2019). The companies that decide to communicate their sustainability commitments need to take these considerations on board as any doubts create an environment in which trust toward the corporation might be lost (Global Compact, 2019).

Responding to the expectations coming from the stakeholders and general public builds consumer advocacy. This also means that the companies need to substantiate their declarations and design their organizational strategies accordingly. Sometimes, it means taking decisions with a short-term negative financial impact. For example, sport and outdoor producer Patagonia decided to support climate change fighting initiatives from the money it saved on the tax relief based on the law passed by the Trump administration (Patagonia, 2018). Patagonia has been already known for its environmental and social commitments and this action just strengthens its image.

3.3.1.   How to Define Stakeholders?

Who are the stakeholders? Who has a stake in the issue? Who can impact the organizational operating landscape? What matters to them and how do we reach them with our messaging?

This is just a simple set of questions that organizations need to ask themselves before embarking on any stakeholder engagement program. Even by looking at these questions, one realizes that the definition of stakeholders for the companies is increasingly challenging. One can see the parts of the challenge in a way that stakeholder theory is being debated (Freeman, 1994: Jemsen, 2002; Phillips, 1997, 2003). The "controversies" that are caused by the stakeholder theory reflect well the challenge that the companies are facing. The stakeholder definitions vary from narrow to very comprehensive ones.

The definitions of the stakeholders used in the corporate and not-for-profit sector are becoming more complex. They need to cater for the complexity of the VUCA-driven external environment. In fact, the organizations need to constantly question their stakeholder environment and look for new players that can impact their business and operations. However, we believe that the simplicity in definition is the key as it allows us to cater for multiple types of influencing factors faced by the organizations. There are also different types of stakeholders with different involvement in the current operations of an organization. The legitimacy question needs to be addressed (Phillips, 2003). Narrow definitions of stakeholders are dangerous for the advocacy strategies as they pose the risks related to "missing" some important individuals and organizations. They also tend to focus advocacy strategy development only on the known factors. Therefore, they don't support building agile strategies in which stakeholder landscape is constantly evolving and has to be constantly renegotiated.

In this book, we propose a dynamic view on stakeholder definitions and stakeholder management. It requires a constant monitoring of the developments in the advocacy landscape of an organization. It also calls for an advanced foresight looking at possible future developments of the landscape of an organization.

For the purpose of this book following closely from Freeman's definition (Freeman, 1994), we define stakeholder as:

> An individual or organization that can impact or be impacted by the actions of an organization.

3.3.2. Corporate Social Responsibility – Concept Older than We Think

The evolution of the discourse about corporate responsibility goes hand in hand with societal changes requiring companies to become actors in subjects beyond their business operations (Arora & Dharwadkar, 2011; Black & Hartel, 2004; Wood, 2010). The perceptions and definitions of CSR shifted from philanthropy to partnerships (Seitanidi & Ryan, 2007). The approach of companies toward CSR is more inclusive than it used to be in the 1990s. One-way philanthropy actually excluded the possibility of dialogue and partnership – conversely it created a "top-down" approach (Du et al., 2010; Seitanidi & Ryan, 2007). In fact, it was the donor (the company) who decided when and who to support and fully controlled the process (Seitanidi & Ryan, 2007). However, the return from these investments was limited as it didn't really connect with the business objectives/ issue of an organization (Seitanidi & Ryan, 2007). Often the impact was limited to mutual mentions of the partners in their communications materials (Seitanidi & Ryan, 2007). Now, the trend has moved toward partnerships and common value creation (Porter & Kramer, 2011; Seitanidi & Ryan, 2007; Ziek, 2009). The concepts of sustainability, Creating Shared Value, and others whiten this tendency (Porter & Kramer, 2011). A similar process can be observed in the overall corporate communications management.

Previously, the aim was to manage corporate image as the latter directly influences business operations of the company as well as the stock performance (Brinkmann & Ims, 2003). The example of the study on Philip Morris International shows that the company, in the early 1990s, considered leaving the tobacco business to preserve its image for other operations (notably in the food and beverage industry) (Smith & Malone, 2003). It is interesting to see this study from a perspective of the advocacy campaign around Reduced Risk Products ran by PMI since 2016 under the slogan of "Smoke Free Future." The image of companies is also reflected in stock recommendations (Fieseler, 2011).

Nevertheless, the approach was rather limited to the external perception of the company.

Corporate reputation as a term and process is gaining momentum both in the academic research and in the business community. Corporate reputation studies focus more and more on external partnerships developed and driven by the organizations. Companies build new models of interaction with the nonprofit sector (Shumate & O'Connor, 2010). The process of corporate reputation-building is based on the principle of partnerships with multiple stakeholders. Corporate reputation is directly linked to Corporate Social Performance (CSP) (Wood, 2010). Therefore, the corporate communication of these efforts plays a crucial role in transferring CSR efforts into business benefits (Du et al., 2010). In that sense corporate reputation is an intangible asset of companies, which is a subject of external and internal evaluation (Wood, 2010).

Growing role of corporate reputation increases a focus of companies on the CSR programs and activities. Management of information and of the stakeholders both contribute to the institutionalization of the corporate communications practice in the companies (Tench et al., 2007). The 37 country European Monitor surveys have, for over 10 years, provided insights into this process. The role of CSR is incremental for strategic positioning of corporate communications within the enterprise's structure (Tench, Verhoeven, & Zerfass, 2009).

From the 1990s CSR started to be defined more in terms of corporate citizenship where organizations were supposed to play an active role in society and social discourse in order to meet the expectations of stakeholders (Crane & Matten, 2005). The Cadbury report is frequently quoted as a turning point in CSR reporting and the moment when companies started to voluntarily disclose information about their social and environmental performance (Boyd, 1996). Reporting and compliance were the first steps in organizational learning of CSR (Baumgartner & Ebner, 2010; Wood, 2010). As Carroll (1999) notes, the scientific discourse about CSR in the 1990s was driven by three main theories: CSP, business ethics, and stakeholder theory.

CSR strategies can bring tangible benefits to the organization (Cochran & Wood, 1984; Maltz, Thompson, & Jones Ringold, 2011; Orlitzky, 2008). The studies also indicate that some companies are engaged in CSR programs while conducting "bad business practices" (Strike, Gao, & Bansal, 2006). This phenomenon can explain some reservations about CSR and sustainability present on the nonprofit sector side. Therefore, the focus on stakeholder dialogue becomes a part of reputational risk mitigation (Alniacik, Alniacik, & Genc, 2011; Husted & Allen, 2006; Lawrence, 2010; Ziek, 2009). Actually, the perception of the importance of stakeholders for the company's performance is one of the main drivers of CSR activities (Henriques & Sadorsky, 1999). In addition, it provides a platform for multi-stakeholder initiatives in a *symbiotic sustainability model* as observed by Shumate and O'Connor (2010). The alliance between corporations and the nonprofit sector (in this case NGOs) is based on communicational alliances (Du et al., 2010). The choice of network partners is multi-dimensional and depends on corporate strategy, sector activity, and the type of NGO communications (Shumate & O'Connor, 2010). CSR is a global concept which applies not only to Western-based companies (Amaladoss & Manohar, 2011; Maon, Lindgreen, & Swaen, 2010). However, the way in which CSR is applied differs according to the business and cultural context (Maon et al., 2010). In the case of the Indian context, as tentatively shown by Amaladoss and Manohar (2011), CSR policies might be strongly driven by the personal views of the owner of the company. Also, the research of Kusku on Turkish-based companies proves the increased interest in CSR even in emerging economies (Maon et al., 2010).

CSR depends on the organizational culture and forms a part of the organizational process (Maon et al., 2010). Managerial preferences play an important role in CSR management (Maon et al., 2010). It is also dependent on internal factors such as organizational culture, internal learning and valuation (Maon et al., 2010). The stages of organizational culture define CSR strategies and processes (Maon et al., 2010; Wood, 2010). The profiles define the learning patterns of the CSR strategic management in the companies (Baumgartner & Ebner, 2010). Nevertheless, the role of business is more political and demands more advanced policies and involvement (Scherer & Palazzo, 2011).

3.3.3. Defining Corporate Social Responsibility

CSR influences corporate communications management. It is also a crucial platform for multi-stakeholder communications and management. The concept of CSR has been studied at least since the 1940s (Dahlsrud, 2008). Historically, CSR was related more to corporate philanthropy. The foundations that reflected the interests of the owner or owners of the company were the most popular in the nineteenth century. They were the industrial reincarnation of the principles of the patronage as understood in previous centuries (Carroll, 1999). The Industrial Revolution created an important number of workers who were required to have more specialist skills in order to work efficiently in the new factories. That and the first union movements shifted the attention of managers to employees (Carroll, 1999). The logic of Henry Ford that every worker is supposed to be able to buy the product, which he is manufacturing, was another view on achieving profitability and an interesting platform for internal communications.

In 1946, managers were asked by *Fortune* magazine about the role of responsibility for their corporations (Bowen, 1953). In the results, 93.5% of them agreed that their actions should be driven by factors beyond profit-loss statements (Carroll, 1999). This shows that the term, as well as the existence of CSR in business strategic thinking, is older than it is perceived to be (Carroll, 1999). During that period there was also an important rise of public relations activities (Malaval & Decaudin, 2005). The public relations (PR) industry developed thanks to public pressure which was driven by the domestication of media and especially TV (Argenti, 1996). The growing importance of business regulation and therefore a need for a third-party endorsement also contributed to the development of corporate communication (Argenti, 1996). The best showcase is the tobacco industry which stems from the 1950s and allowed the development of

PR as a profession. The industry generated the kind of PR activities that are frequently called "spin" and negatively perceived (White, 1994). Nevertheless, third-party endorsement, which was the case of the Tobacco Institute and others, became the most used public relations and advocacy technique.

At the same time, public affairs were also related to sustainability efforts. As Carroll observes, in the 1960s there was a scientific tendency to formalize research on CSR and give some framework to these activities (Carroll, 1999). In the definition proposed by Davis and Blomstrom (1966) CSR was defined as:

> Social responsibility, therefore, refers to a person's obligation to consider the effects of his decisions and actions on the whole system. Businessmen apply social reasonability when they consider the needs and the interest of others who may be affected by business actions. In so doing they look beyond the firm's narrow economic and technical interests. (Carroll, 1999, after Davis & Blomstrom, 1966)

Indeed, as Carroll observes, the 1960s focused attention on the ethical side of business activities to evolve in the 1970s to activities related to the socio-cultural contexts of business operations. Researchers in the 1970s defined also different levels (circles) of CSR that were related to the different groups of stakeholders. Therefore, the issue was studied under a more complex perspective which led to discussions on the need of business to engage in these activities (Carroll, 1999). It was also in the 1970s when companies started to have dedicated sections about CSR in their annual reports. In 1979, Carroll concluded the following definition of CSR:

> The social responsibility of business encompasses the economic, legal, ethical and discretionary expectations that society has of organizations at a given point in time. (Carroll, 1979)

This definition embraces the tendency of explaining CSR in terms of stakeholders' expectations. The following definitions in the 1980s gave an additional insight into the voluntary character of the actions which go beyond legal obligations (Carroll, 1999). As Carroll (1999) notes, the scientific discourse on CSR in the 1990s was driven by three main theories: CSP, business ethics, and stakeholder theory. The new and alternative terms, which appear in the discourse, follow the bases developed in the 1960s and 1970s. The newest definitions and applications of CSR focus on the collaborative and environmental aspects. Alexander Dahlsrud compared 37 most common definitions of CSR that function in the scientific discourse. According to him the most popular one is the definition from the Commission of the European Communities, which states:

> A concept whereby companies integrate social and environmental concerns in their business operations and their interactions with

the stakeholders on a voluntary basis. (Commission of European Communities, 2001)

This definition has five dimensions (voluntariness, stakeholder, social, environmental, and economic) (Dahlsrud, 2008). However, this definition does not include the issue of business benefits from CSR programs. These initiatives can bring tangible benefits to the organization (Cochran & Wood, 1984; Maltz et al., 2011; Ziek, 2009) as well. The studies also show that the companies, which develop advanced CSR programs also have frequently unethical behaviors (Strike et al., 2006). The focus on stakeholder dialogue becomes a part of reputational risk mitigation (Alniacik et al., 2011; Husted & Allen, 2006; Lawrence, 2010; Ziek, 2009). In addition, it provides a platform for multi-stakeholder initiatives in a symbiotic sustainability model as observed by Shumate and O'Connor (2010). The alliance between the corporations and the nonprofit sector (in that case NGOs) is based on communicational alliances. The choice of partners for the network is multi-dimensional and depends on corporate strategy, sector activity, and type of NGO communication (Shumate & O'Connor, 2010). CSR is a global concept that does not only apply to the Western-based companies (Amaladoss & Manohar, 2011; Maon et al., 2010). However, the applications of CSR differ according to the business and cultural contexts (Maon et al., 2010). As shown in preliminary form in the Indian context by Amaladoss and Manohar (2011), CSR policies might be strongly driven by the personal views of the owner of the company. However, some of the newer definitions of CSR including the one from the European Commission can be even more relevant in the context of a current stakeholder landscape:

> The Commission has defined CSR as the responsibility of enterprises for their impact on society and, therefore, it should be company led. Companies can become socially responsible by:
>
> - integrating social, environmental, ethical, consumer, and human rights concerns into their business strategy and operations
> - following the law
>
> Public authorities play a supporting role through voluntary policy measures and, where necessary, complementary regulation. (European Commission)[2]

CSR depends on the organizational culture and is a part of organizational processes. Managerial preference plays an important role in CSR management (Maon et al., 2010). It is also dependent on internal factors such as

---

[2]https://ec.europa.eu/growth/industry/corporate-social-responsibility_en

organizational culture (Maon et al., 2010). The stages of organizational culture define CSR strategies and processes (Maon et al., 2010). Nevertheless, the role of business is more political and demands advanced policies and involvement (Scherer & Palazzo, 2011).

Scholars have studied CSR with different levels of intensity for over 50 years. There are several trends in studies on CSR which seem to be relevant in the analysis of corporate communication. There are several main research focus areas, namely:

- reputational assets;
- bottom line focus;
- definitions and re-definitions of CSR in the context of society at large;
- gravity center and ownership of CSR;
- communication and multi-stakeholder dialogue;
- evolution and history of the CSR concept; and
- organizational process and part of organizational culture.

3.3.4.   *Ways of Measuring CSR/CSP*

The measurement of the CSR and CSP has been a subject for research since the early 1990s (Wood, 2010). There was always certain reservation toward corporate declarations related to the CSR management and CSR reporting (Wood, 2010). It was accentuated further by the self-regulatory character of CSR reporting (GRI). From our perspective, the shift has happened when the CSR measurement moved toward CSP measurement.

> Corporate social performance is a set of descriptive categorizations of business activity, focusing on the impacts and outcomes for society, stakeholders and the firm itself. (Wood, 2010)

Interestingly, looking at the definition from Wood (2010) and the models used in the GRI measurement we can see certain similarity. Obviously, there are several critics of sustainability reporting by GRI who claim that this reporting "hides corporate unsustainably practices" (Dingwerth & Eichinger, 2010).

GRI itself builds the case for an integrated approach in sustainability reporting:

> A sustainability report is a report published by a company or organization about the economic, environmental and social impacts caused by its everyday activities. A sustainability report also presents the organization's values and governance model and demonstrates the link between its strategy and its commitment to a sustainable global economy.

Sustainability reporting can help organizations to measure, understand and communicate their economic, environmental, social and governance performance, and then set goals, and manage change more effectively. A sustainability report is the key platform for communicating sustainability performance and impacts – whether positive or negative.

Sustainability reporting can be considered as synonymous with other terms for non-financial reporting; triple bottom line reporting, corporate social responsibility (CSR) reporting, and more. It is also an intrinsic element of integrated reporting; a more recent development that combines the analysis of financial and non-financial performance.

Source: GRI[3]

The rise of the concept of integrated reporting where the elements related to financial and non-financial performance are combined in one reporting framework is particularly interesting from the perspective of the evolution of CSR.

3.3.5. *Evolution of the Role of CSR and Rise of Sustainability as a Concept*

CSR did evolve in the corporate discourse toward sustainability (Porter & Kramer, 2011). There are more and more companies talking about their sustainability efforts versus their CSR. The level of reservations that external stakeholders of the companies especially coming from the NGO sector definitely impacted this move (Lacey, Kennett-Hensel, & Manolis, 2015). However, the efforts to move from reactive CSR and compliance toward integrated sustainability solutions have been noticed since the mid-late 2000s.

The new models of cooperation between the companies and other actors were introduced. Two of the most referred-to approaches were Nestlé's Creating Shared Value and Unilever's Sustainable Brands. They were both redefining the role of the companies in the value chain. The year 2015 and agreement on the SDGs can be considered as a turning point from which the companies became equal actors in the social discourse. The SDGs are the first multilateral framework that was effectively negotiated by the various sectors. The work toward developing the Goals and their subsequent targets involved actors from government, private, and nonprofit sectors.

Nestlé and Creating Shared Value concept is the most obvious example. The term coined by Michael Porter and used by Nestlé was set to redefine the way

---

[3]https://www.globalreporting.org/information/sustainability-reporting/Pages/default.aspx

companies and people think about sustainability (Kramer & Porter, 2011). The term itself was taken on board by Nestlé and set to describe all the activities that company had in the fields of stakeholder engagement and CSR. The way the company describes its approach links the social performance with the business strategy and business returns:

> Our approach to business – Creating Shared Value – has always taken the long-term view. CSV brings business and society together, creating sustainable economic value that also produces wider benefits for society.

> Our efforts for individuals and families, for our communities and for the planet are supported through 41 public commitments, most of which feature specific objectives to 2020. In turn, these commitments will enable us to meet our ambitions for 2030 in line with the timescale of the Sustainable Development Goals (SDGs). Essential to achieving our goals is a robust approach to sustainability, human rights and compliance.

> Our CSV priorities are those areas where our business intersects most closely with society, and where we can create the most value and make the most difference. (Nestlé)[4]

Nestlé explicitly states that the role of CSV is to bring the value to the company while delivering the value to the society:

> CSV generates economic value in a way that also produces value for society. Foods and beverages with a nutrition, health and wellness dimension perform better. Rural development programs for farmers offer commercial differentiation to the consumer, while responsible stewardship of water reduces costs and secures supplies for our businesses. (Nestlé)

In consequence, this dual character of the CSV engagements allows the building of a platform for stakeholder engagement. Both approaches of Nestlé and Unilever that we have seen above have in common the fact of engaging the external stakeholders in two-way cooperation. The traditional CSR models focused much more on the one-way corporate sponsorships.

Similarly, the Sustainable Living concept of Unilever focuses on the impacts the organization has on its key stakeholders. It is also in the center of the organizational essence. The vision of the company includes the sustainability focus:

---

[4]https://www.nestle.com/csv/what-is-csv

> Our vision is a new way of doing business – one that delivers
> growth by serving society and the planet.
>
> *Source*: Unilever

The way of defining the value by Unilever also includes considerations of the multilateral landscape:

> We believe that sustainable and equitable growth is the only way
> to create long-term value for all our stakeholders. That's why we
> have placed the Unilever Sustainable Living Plan at the heart of
> our business model. (Unilever)[5]

The strategy and focus of the Unilever's CEO Paul Polman on the sustainability has been at the same time admired and criticized. Some claimed that he lost sight of the business performance and focused maybe too much on building partnerships with not-for-profit organizations. The others admired the courage and focus beyond the quarterly results of the company. Paul Polman was perceived by those as a new type of CEO, a CEO who is conscious of the external factors influencing company performance and focuses on the long-term strategy of the company. It will be interesting to see whether Unilever will continue on this path after his departure at the beginning of 2019.

3.4. Sustainability and Advocacy – Brining Real Benefits of Corporate Engagement to Business

New approach to CSR described as sustainability, or like some would claim new approach to the corporate citizenship brings great opportunities for building the advocacy strategies. In fact, sustainability and advocacy are interconnected – sustainability requires advocacy to connect multiple stakeholders; advocacy needs to be substantiated by sustainability in order to achieve organizational objectives. Businesses see more and more benefits of sustainability for their operations and engagement with their stakeholders (Wettstein, 2012). At the same time, sustainability strategies open organizations for new forms of cooperation with until recently unlikely partners (Carbonara et al., 2014).

With a growing coverage of sustainability concepts both in business press and literature, one can lose sight of what the businesses are designed for. Independent of a growing importance of sustainability in corporate practices, the companies still need to focus on their actual business and products/services they are selling. Advocacy provides this link. It helps to connect the interests of

---

[5]https://www.unilever.com/sustainable-living/our-strategy/about-our-strategy/

the company with the interests of its stakeholders. As a result, it provides an umbrella for enhanced cooperation.

In the NGO community there are several voices criticizing the companies for using sustainability purely as a vehicle to improve their image. Corporate advocacy is then seen as a cynical tool used to manipulate stakeholders and improve image of the company without real change in business practices. While some of this skepticism could be well-founded, it is also true that without advocacy the meaning of CSR/sustainability action is limited. In fact, the companies need to see tangible benefits from their actions in order to get engaged. Advocacy brings together business objectives, key benefits that come from the engagement and delivers a framework for engagement, which supports sustainability. This creates even more opportunities for companies and organizations to engage in the fields that they wouldn't previously consider as external interaction frameworks (Carbonara et al., 2014).

3.4.1.   Sustainable Development Goals – New Framework of Cooperation

SDGs, adopted at the end of 2015, were designed to change the way society, organizations and businesses interact, engage and behave. Seventeen goals, with 169 targets, were set to define world's agenda till 2030. The framework was integrated first by the international organizations but expanded further to define the activities and focus priorities within multiple companies and industry representation bodies. As a result, it becomes a reference point not only for international organizations, governments, and NGOs but also for the internationally operating businesses (Scheyvens et al., 2016).

Many people, from both the private and public sectors, took part in the debate shaping the SDGs. Given the number of targets, almost everyone claimed they had put their issues on the agenda (see the statements of the international NGOs after adoption of the SDGs in late 2015). But there is a price to pay for this perception of utmost universal success. Multiplication of the goals and targets meant that some of them were somewhat blurred. The study from International Science Council indicates that only 29% of the targets are well defined.[6] In addition, there is a growing gap between the discursive adoption of the goals and real action by companies and organizations in order to support a real progress around the SDG targets: "Three years after the adoption of the Sustainable Development Goals (SDGs), reliable information on how companies are working to contribute to the SDGs remains sparse" (Oxfam, 2018). At the declarative and communication level the SDGs have been introduced in the corporate agenda of multiple organizations. Yet, the actual adoption of the practices and changes in the business models and strategies are by far less widely spread.

As stated by the United Nations and subsequent research, private sector was meant to play an important – indeed pivotal – role in the adoption and

---

[6]https://council.science/publications/review-of-targets-for-the-sustainable-development-goals-the-science-perspective-2015

successful implementation of the SDGs. It is by linking the corporate agenda and business objectives with a sustainable development imperative that change will happen.

> It is clear that the SDGs not only identify where we have to be in 2030 to create a sustainable world, they also outline new markets and opportunities for companies all over the world. To succeed, we must turn the global goals into local business. The UN Global Compact is committed to be a leading catalyst of that transformation. We will devote our capacities and global network to make it happen – based on the sound values and principles that the UN Global Compact is built upon. (UN Global Compact, 2019)[7]

The SDGs become a universal reference point for companies to describe their social engagements. They were also taken on board by the business associations as the reference point in describing corporate engagements.

> As global business faces new and complex challenges and opportunities, our science-based approach and targeted business solutions aim to scale up business impact. We target the realization of the Sustainable Development Goals (SDGs) through six work programs to achieve systems transformation. (World Business Council of Sustainable Development, 2019)[8]

At the same time, there is a gap between the Goals and the respective Targets that are followed by companies (Oxfam, 2018). While multiple companies take use of the Goals to showcase their engagements, a concrete contribution toward listed Targets is missing. That leads to a question on the future of corporate engagement. Will it be based on the measurable quantitative indicators? This leads to questioning of the intentions around engagement for the SDGs. The companies are accused of using "SDG-washing" and just using the framework for their marketing communications efforts without real substantiation of the action. In addition, many companies fail to communicate clearly about the ways of measuring their SDG engagements. As a result, it is impossible to verify positively or negatively the claims around their commitments. Interestingly, we observe similar patterns of corporate learning in the subject of SDGs as with the case of advocacy in general. In fact, the maturity models related to SDG positioning would be very similar to the ones described in the context of dynamic model for advocacy management.

---

[7]https://www.unglobalcompact.org/what-is-gc/our-work/sustainable-development
[8]https://www.wbcsd.org/

3.5.   SDG Integration Model

Table 3.1. SDG Integration Model.

Stage	Actions	Desired Outcomes
Landscape review and foresight for business activities	Foresight in the future of the industry and issue Development of the organizational scenarios for issues future development Identification of the key trends influencing future operating environment	Understanding of the likely and unlikely future business development scenarios
Sustainability goal setting	Definition of the sustainability ambition levels Development of organizational ambition level and organizational purpose	Alignment of the sustainability goals and business strategy
SDG mapping	Mapping of the organizational issues against the SDGs goals and targets Selection of the targets relevant for the organizational sustainability strategy Identification of the actors and issues influencing the discourse around the selected targets	Definition of the SDGs targets and goals relevant for an organizational sustainability strategy
SDG integration	Development of the organizational commitments toward the SDG goals and targets Definition of the KPIs and milestones for SDG integration Alignment of the sustainability strategy with the SDGs	Commitment toward the SDG goals and targets

Table 3.1. (*Continued*)

Stage	Actions	Desired Outcomes
Business alignment	Identification of the operational changes needed to achieve the set sustainability outcomes	Alignment of the business process to support sustainability and SDG efforts
	Definition of the business and organizational processes needed to implement SDG strategy	
	Internal process definition and set up of the monitoring and evaluation protocol	
Engagement strategy	Identification of the influencers and platforms present around the SDG targets	Strategic communications approach for sustainability and SDG engagement
	Identification of the potential partnerships and external partners for the engagement program	
	Definition of the SDG strategic narrative and key organizational messages	
Monitoring, measurement, and evaluation	Periodic information about the progress toward set sustainability targets	Comprehensive framework looking at all aspects of the SDG integration
	Measurement of the progress in the defined framework	
	Ongoing evaluation of the progress and refinement of the processes	
Reporting	Regular progress reporting internally and externally	Strengthened accountability of the organizational SDG initiatives
	Alignment of the sustainability reporting with an overall reporting framework of the organization	
	Distribution of the reporting to the key internal and external stakeholders	

3.6.   Key Conclusions and Conditions for Effective Corporate Engagement

SDGs, Global Compact and other globally led initiatives – all these international frameworks recognize a growing role of private sectors in shaping the socioeconomic agenda. For business advocacy it creates an unprecedented opportunity for engagement with various stakeholders. In addition, it supports corporate efforts to shape the operating environments of the companies. The companies move from being at a receiving end of international initiatives and reactive approaches toward becoming the ones that shape the agenda. However, it also requires companies to substantiate the claims and deepen their engagement beyond regular groups of stakeholders. If not, the increased expectations from stakeholders paired with an increased visibility of corporate actions would risk putting the corporate reputation in danger.

Below we present the conditions that we believe are paramount for success of the corporate sustainability strategies in the context of SDGs. These conditions are based on the thinking around the development of the SDG strategic integration model (Table 3.1). They are designed to inform a strategic thinking around the SDG approaches.

Condition #1 – clearly defined desired outcome of the thought leadership approach

In order to be effective, the organizations need to know what they want to achieve in their sustainability engagements. Interestingly, very few companies and organizations clearly articulate their goals when it comes to advocacy engagement. This clarity ensures that the activities are driven by the strategic outcomes and not tactical opportunities. In addition, it helps to focus the activities on what matters the most for both business and organization. Integration of the SDG component in the thought leadership approach is critical. It provides a substantiation for the corporate declaration as well as a platform to engage external stakeholders.

Condition #2 – alignment between thought leadership approach and corporate strategy

Many organizations use thought leadership concept in their marketing strategies. However, for thought leadership to be effective it needs to be based on the alignment between the declarations and corporate strategies. In fact, thought leadership strategies bring benefits to an organization only when they reflect actual business operations and activities. "Owning an issue" in a discursive sphere comes with a scrutiny and responsibility as it increases stakeholders' expectations. The biggest issue around thought leadership is that it became a fashionable concept in marketing and communications. As a result, many organizations used it to describe any content marketing activities. This led to a misperception of this powerful concept and almost "killed it" for the international companies.

Condition #3 – strong communications platform that allows thought leadership to build connections with the stakeholders beyond a regular group of corporate contacts

It is important to ensure that the right stakeholders are reached and engaged with beyond the regular audiences of a company or organization. Sustainability provides a neutral platform to talk and build relationships with organizations and individuals having various interests in the organization and its work. Engaging these audiences requires a strong communications plan beyond regular means of interaction. It includes delivery of the 360° engagement strategy looking at the social media, media, and direct engagement channels. It also means creation of the channels that are owned by the organization. Moreover, this communications platform should be based on the content and not on the channels. This way we consider the thought leadership holistically.

Condition #4 – strategic and creative narrative that builds emotional connection with organizational involvement and with the corporate brand

In order to connect with the target audiences, the organizations need to create emotional link with their brand. The best way to stir emotions is to create the narrative which spans across all the communications and engagement activities. This way the thought leadership can be conveyed in a way that creates empathy with the target audiences.

Condition #5 – commitment from the organization at all level from executive engagement to employee advocacy

It is crucial that the sustainability efforts have an executive buy in from the senior management. Indeed, it is very effective for the top leadership to "own sustainability agenda." At the same time, it is crucial to ensure that sustainability is a part of organizational strategy as a whole and not simply a "personal crusade of the CEO." Ensuring participation from the employees becomes essential even more so given that they are the most credible source of information about the company's activities.

3.7. Further Research

The field of CSR studies evolved and requires more holistic approaches looking at the full value chain of sustainability. Therefore, we recommend further researchers to study the levels of sophistication in the SDG and sustainability engagements of the companies and organizations. It would be also very pertinent to study the correlation between the holistic changes to the business models driven by sustainability and long-term financial performance of the organization.

It would be also very interesting to see qualitative case-study-based research analyzing sustainability approaches of the start-up and SME companies. The global frameworks are usually first adopted by the global companies. However, it the case of sustainability there is a growing number of start-ups and fast-growing companies building their business models around delivery of sustainable solutions.

In addition, a study differentiating the adoption of the SDGs in the corporate agenda depending on cultural and geographical differences would be interesting. This would help to understand the differences in the local contexts and bring forward any gaps in alignment around the SDG framework around the world.

Finally, we would encourage a further conceptual research on the evolution of the CSR as a concept and executive understanding of the CSR/CSP and sustainability. We believe that a multi-country, multi-industry study would bring insights to a real perception of the sustainability by the executives. It would allow in turn to better understand corporate decision-making processes and the role of executive involvement in shaping sustainability agenda.

With the CEOs of the companies gaining an almost celebrity status, it is crucial to see how their personal agenda impacts the agenda of the companies they lead. To complete this research, we would recommend benchmarking the CEO and executive perceptions with the ones of the middle and line managers and then employees of the companies at large. This would bring an answer to whether the CSR/sustainability efforts are top-down in the organizations or whether they reflect a deeper internal alignment.

Key Takeaways

- *CSR evolved both as a concept and as a requirement for the international businesses. The traditional view on CSR is not sufficient in order to deliver on the organizational goals. Conversely, integrated sustainability approaches are required from the companies willing to influence their operating landscape.*
- *SDGs framework became the reference for all sustainability engagements for both international organizations and companies. The framework favors cooperation between the actors who did not work together in the past. It means that organizational engagement strategies need to embrace the SDGs.*
- *Many companies use SDGs as part of their communications effort providing little action behind their declarations. Effective advocacy requires that the declarations of the organizations are substantiated by the actions and verified in the independent reporting and evaluation.*
- *Expectations from the stakeholders and customers are becoming very similar and merge together. It means that companies need to align all their external engagement strategies and functions. Without this alignment they risk on creating confusion between the target audiences.*
- *Thought leadership remains a very powerful vehicle for the companies and organizations. The concept suffered from being overused and misused to describe all corporate content material. However, when designed*

---

properly and integrated through the organization it can deliver tremendous reputational benefits.

- *Trust is a key driver for cooperation in the international sustainability discourse. In order to be trusted organizations, and companies, in particular, need to be accountable. Bringing robust measurement and evaluation frameworks together with externally audited reporting helps to connecting the narrative with corporate action.*

Chapter 4

Connecting with the Right Audiences for a Better Impact – Imperatives of the Influencer Marketing

4.1. Introduction

Who are the key stakeholders for the organization? How do the opinions of others impact a corporate reputation and view of the company? These are the questions faced by all the communications professionals. As stated in the previous chapter, the organizations are required to act as corporate citizens and engage in the social causes beyond their core business activities (Moon et al., 2015). Even though some criticize the metaphor of corporate citizenship, it is a widely adopted approach to describe the way organizations are required to act (Moon, Crane, & Matten, 2005). At the same time the companies and organizations build relationships with their target audiences in a personalized manner. The model of communications is changing and moves away from one-to-many toward more direct personal relationship building (Zetter, 2014). Companies and organizations seek to build individual relationships with their target audiences and stakeholders (ibid.). This change can be seen at two levels. There is a social change of the expectations and views about the nature of relationships between the individuals and organizations (Mavis et al., 2018; Moon et al., 2015). At the same time, there is also a technological change driven mostly by a rise of social media and digital which favors direct engagement between the companies, organizations, and individuals (Fenton & Barassi, 2011). More and more relationships and interactions happen through digital channels. Therefore, looking at advocacy without focusing on digital engagement would be very reductive and incomplete. While advocacy and engagement cannot be reduced to the digital aspects only, these are a pinnacle of relationships an organization has with its external stakeholders.

It is no surprise that with development of digital marketing, social media engagement strategies of brands and companies become more and more sophisticated. We are far away from the early days of social media when a digital engagement strategy was resumed by "having a profile on a given (or all) social media channels" and the measurement and evaluation focused on the "number of likes we got." Today, social media strategies in some instances can be even more complex than overall communications strategies of the organizations. Current omni-channel engagement approaches include multi-channel strategies with a combination of organic and paid engagement (Romero, Galuba, Asur, & Huberman, 2011). A constant raise of paid marketing solutions on the social media channels presents a pinnacle of the very nature of the strategic change and shift in the ways social media are perceived by marketers and communicators (Bochenek & Blili, 2013; Perrin, 2015). Social media are not seen any more as "pure and innocent" channels in which all the participants have an unlimited access to a global audience and participate in unmediated conversations. They become the marketing and advertising channels on their own right requiring strategic approaches and budgets to fulfill their role.

In fact, the social media channels need to be considered as an integral part of the communications and marketing mix and evaluated in the same way as other media channels of the organization (AMEC, 2015). They also need to be managed in a strategic manner – together with other communications and engagement tools (Bochenek & Blili, 2013). The need for sophistication of the social media strategies is reflected in the numbers. Being "out there" as an organization doesn't necessarily generate engagement (Romero et al., 2014). Looking at constant decreases of the reach and interactions of organic (free) posts on the channels reaffirms this tendency (Brandwatch, 2019). This means that the focus on quality wins over the strategies that were looking purely at quantitative aspects of digital content distribution. It also means that the social media and digital strategies need to integrate full range of paid solutions in order to benefit from the opportunities coming from the marketing targeting tools.

It goes without saying that the social media platforms evolve themselves as well. They become more and more multi-media content platforms with an increased number of opportunities to buy the products. At the same time, a need to keep the users "in platform" means that the social media evolve to create "all in" experiences with no need of switching the channels. Fewer clicks and fewer redirects of traffic are also supposed to improve an overall user experience. And experience inside the platforms is superior. As a result, the companies focus on creating holistic experiences within the social media platforms. Therefore, the effective communications and marketing strategies require taking these changes into account and building comprehensive digital strategies involving multiple stakeholders from within the organization. In fact, an effective digital engagement strategy would include communications, marketing, CRM, sales, human resource, and after-purchase services (Berthon, Pitt, Plangger, & Shapiro, 2012).

Initially, many organizations considered social media management from a very tactical perspective as support channels to distribute corporate messages. Then, the paradigm shifted toward the notion of communities and community management (Bochenek & Blili, 2013). This was reflected in the job titles and the ways social media were represented in communications and marketing departments. It was also frequent to hire young and relatively junior professionals as "community managers" with a sole responsibility to look after social media channels and fans. Today we are observing a move away from a previous notion of "community management." More and more organizations instead take an integrated approach which includes multiple organizational functions: marketing, communications, sales as well as human resources and IT teams.

This comprehensive approach changes the structures of social media management. Indeed, we are moving away from channel management and the approach is much more comprehensive focusing on the value they deliver to organization.

The move toward "all-in" consideration of the social media channels accompanies with a rise in influence marketing. From a social perspective, we have always seen high rankings of "person like myself" in the international trust studies (see, Chapter 3). The bloggers, Instagrammers, and YouTubers are incarnations of this "person like myself" – maybe a more polished or a better-looking version of myself, yet a person with whom I can identify. Indeed, the so-called influencers frequently just tend to be better-looking and outspoken versions of their fan base. The influencers build large communities of fans and followers by appealing to the sentiment of authenticity and proximity, even if this proximity is blurred by the photo filters and photo presets. At the same time, influencer engagement is one of the big trends in social media marketing. The brands seek to engage influencers in order to benefit from their recommendations to increase visibility of their message and in commercial setting to boost sales (CMS Wire, 2019).

Several authors already analyzed the phenomenon of social media influencers and the ways they gain social capital (Booth & Matic, 2011; Freberg, Graham, McGaughey, & Freberg, 2011; Kilgour, Sasser, & Larke, 2015). In the context of social media, social capital is still often reduced to the quantitative expression of the size of the fan base. In the public discourse and media, the term "social media influencer" has been used to describe the individuals with a large digital followership. The criterion in success for an influencer was how many fans and followers this individual had across its social media channels. This led to relatively simple ways of engagement that brands introduced in their influencer engagement programs – they were simply seeking endorsements and product placements. There are numerous examples of successful influencer campaigns that led to increased sales of the promoted products. However, there is also an important amount of "unsaid" and "unreported" campaigns that failed or achieved results below expectation. As there was no initial benchmark, the influencer engagement campaigns have been only compared between themselves and not within an overall marketing mix. Yet the influencer marketing principles have been clear and defined for over a decade (Brown & Hayes, 2008). This leads to the question – "was this influencer campaign more effective than the other one?" as opposed to "is influencer marketing the best means to achieve the results set in this campaign?"

As stated above, the focus on influencers was well justified as the statistics show that consumers tend to trust individuals more than the brands (Edelman Trust Barometer, 2018). The effectiveness of messaging and engagement levels are also higher on the accounts managed by the individuals (Kilgour et al., 2015). One can find many statistics reaffirming the effectiveness of the influencer marketing in terms of the reach and engagement (Brandwatch, 2019; HubSpot, 2018). However, there were several cases of abuses of trust among the community of influencers: followers/fans that were bought, pictures that featured the individuals in places to which they never traveled, etc. These cases were widely reported in the media and lowered somewhat trust between the brands (marketers) and the influencers. A negative trade media discourse around the influencers also led to more critical reception of the influencer content by the target audiences. This decrease of trust was accompanied by an increase of costs associated with the influencer campaigns. The most profiled influencers are charging thousands of dollars per single post or mention. This made influencer marketing a relatively costly way to reach target audiences.

As a result, the companies searched for solutions that would allow a combination of the "best of two worlds" – individual authenticity and trust in messaging. The new "holy grail" of marketing was found in the individuals with smaller followership and much more targeted interests – it was a beginning of the era of micro-influencers (CMS Wire, 2019). The micro-influencers are the individuals with a smaller digital followership (the cap of who the micro-influencers are situated between 10k and 100k followers) who have the activities and content focused around a particular issue/interest (CMS Wire, 2019). In brief, micro-influencers are the individuals known for their interest in a particular subject. They are not the individuals known for being known as was the case with many classic influencers. The statistics coming from the social media platforms indicate that the micro-influencers generate more engagement with their posts and benefit from more active and more resilient communities (HubSpot, 2018).

A move toward influencer-based engagement strategies opens great opportunities for a digital and traditional advocacy. Identifying those with high influencing potential whose interest and communities are focused provides the opportunities for precisely targeted campaigns. At the same time, a good majority of the "traps" related to the reach-focused influencer strategies is mitigated by more precise targeting and lower individual costs. This chapter will look more in detail at the imperatives of current digital engagement and propose a model for influencer engagement strategies.

4.2.   Advocacy on the Rise – Influencing Real Influencers

"Who has an influence over whom and what matters to them?" is the most basic question that any advocacy strategy needs to answer. This question is even more pertinent and relevant in the context of digital influence. Digital engagement strategies have long suffered from an important focus on purely quantitative measures of so-called success (Fan & Gordon, 2014). The size of the community and then the number of likes/engagements were synonymous with success in fan engagement. And surprisingly in many organizations, these are persisting as the metrics of success for digital activities. However, the indicators like size of community or number of likes are the output vanity measures which don't really provide insights into what extent an organization's digital activities support the overall business and marketing goals. Similarly, digital advocacy was limited to engaging the individuals with high digital audiences and working on their support toward a cause or an issue.

Consequently, this led to a focus of digital strategies on awareness building. Awareness was supposed to be a concept which is easy to measure and reported without much of the doubt about the measurement correctness. However, as indicated earlier in this book; awareness has a limited influence on changing the behaviors of target audiences (Christiano & Neimand, 2017). The fact that we are aware of something, doesn't necessarily mean that we will change our behaviors accordingly (Christiano & Neimand, 2017). Social marketing has proved for decades that awareness alone doesn't have a power to change human behaviors (Lee & Kotler, 2015). And even less so, if the required change is for some reason unpleasant, or requires big shifts in habits (Lee & Kotler, 2015). The struggle of campaigners fighting to reduce the consumption of tobacco is a good example. There has been a long time between the moment people were made aware of the health risks related to smoking and an actual decrease in tobacco consumption.

As digital campaigns were focusing mainly on awareness raising, the social media were not used to their full extent in the advocacy strategies. Focus on awareness meant also focus on the reach of social media messages. In this case, a natural consequence was to build the influencer strategies around the notion of the social media followership. The relevance was of a lesser importance. Figure 4.1 explains an evolution of approaches to social media and digital strategies. It showcases that the shift of focus makes digital and social media much more relevant for advocacy and target audience engagement. This is accompanied with a greater focus on real-life benefits and return on engagement as well as return on investment.

This evolution and shift in strategic thinking illustrate well the changes in perception and management of the value of digital for the organizations. It also shows progressive integration of the digital tools and channels into the marketing and business value. Measurement and evaluation protocols followed the same path becoming outcome driven and fully aligned with the organizational business objectives. Typical names used to describe the strategic approaches are also symptomatic with the social media (channel) approach being the least sophisticated and moving toward integrated/omni-channel route.

Social media strategies
- Focus on the channels
- Limited business connection
- Output-driven evaluation and measurement

Digital engagement strategies
- Focus on the engagement
- Integrated horizontally across communications disciplines
- Outtake-driven evaluation

Integrated influence / Omni-channel strategies
- Focus on the whole influence chain
- Integrated vertically across the whole organizaton
- Outcome-driven evaluation and measurement

Figure 4.1.   Evolution of Organizational Digital Strategies.

4.2.1.   *Social Media − Quantitative vs Qualitative Influence*

Influencing the influencers is the key for digital advocacy. While talking about digital influence it is important to define what we mean by influence. There are many definitions of influence in the context of social media. Some of them focus on the ability to reach as many people as possible. These definitions were more frequently used in the early stages of development and sophistication of social and digital engagement channels. The one from CMS Wire is a good example:

> Mega-influencers are the highest-ranking category of social media influencer, they typically have more than a million followers. Gil Eyal, CEO and founder of HYPR Brands, said mega-influencers "are often more famous than influential. They often have a very diverse audience with different topics of interest. Their relation-ships with the individual members of their followership tend to be more distant. They aren't necessarily subject matter experts but they definitely provide a lot of reach in one hit." Eyal said.
>
> [...]
>
> Macro-influencers are a notch down from mega-influencers. One way to identify a macro-influencer is by their follower count, which should fall somewhere between 100,000 and one million fol-lowers. "Your average macro-influencer lies somewhere between micro and mega. There's no exact science differentiating these cat-egories," Deepak Shukla, founder of PearlLemon explained.
>
> "Unlike most mega-influencers, macro-influencers usually gained fame through the internet itself, whether that was through vlog-ging, or by producing funny or inspiring content," he continued. (CMS Wire, 2018)[1]

However, recently there is a general trend to look at social media influence more from a qualitative than purely quantitative perspective. This means looking more at the social capital and linking social media/digital with a whole influence and engagement chain of an individual or organization.

This way of looking at influence is context dependent. As a result, an understanding of influence requires also understanding of the overall organi-zational and marketing goals (Brown & Hayes, 2008). Therefore, the defini-tion of influence becomes dynamic and changes according to the set objectives.

---

[1]https://www.cmswire.com/digital-marketing/social-media-influencers-mega-macro-micro-or-nano/

This dynamism of the concept means that from a marketing perspective an individual can be very influential in one issue and have no influence in the other. This might sound like a common-sense statement; however, in the social media engagement reality, it often wasn't that obvious for many companies and organizations.

While qualitative aspect of social media engagement is critical, it is also important to consider a quantitative aspect of influence in social media engagement. Indeed, with a growth of consideration toward the qualitative aspects and raise of micro-influence the notion of reach is getting neglected or forgotten. This is an error as both quantitative and qualitative aspects are important in order to truly uncover the influence processes (Booth & Matic, 2011; Freberg et al., 2011).

4.2.2. Measuring Influence

Duality of social media influence requires to look for more sophisticated ways of looking at the digital connections between people and organizations (AMEC, 2015). Using network theory and analyzing the relationships between key actors becomes one of the most effective ways to identify those who matter the most (Borgatti & Halgin, 2011; Liu et al., 2017; Merchant, 2012). Applying network theory allows us to see not only how the individuals and organizations are connected, but also the quality of these connections (Liu et al., 2017). It is not only about which individuals are connected between themselves, but also what is the quality of these connections (following/engaging/sharing). In practical terms, it means looking at the issue from a global perspective and identifying the individuals who have the highest impact on the issue. In the second turn it means focusing on the ways these individuals are connected between themselves (Liu et al., 2017). Finally, it means identifying the ones who have the highest influencing potential overall (Borgatti & Halgin, 2011; Liu et al., 2017; Merchant, 2012). Applying this methodology helps with focusing on the individuals and organizations with the highest influencing potential over the network overall (Figure 4.2).

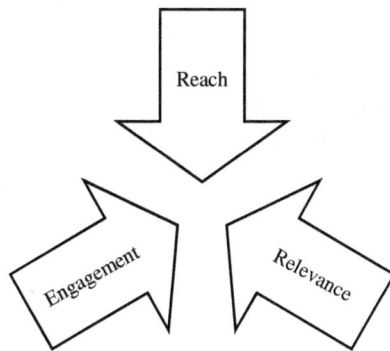

Figure 4.2.   Three-Dimensional Model for Digital Influence.

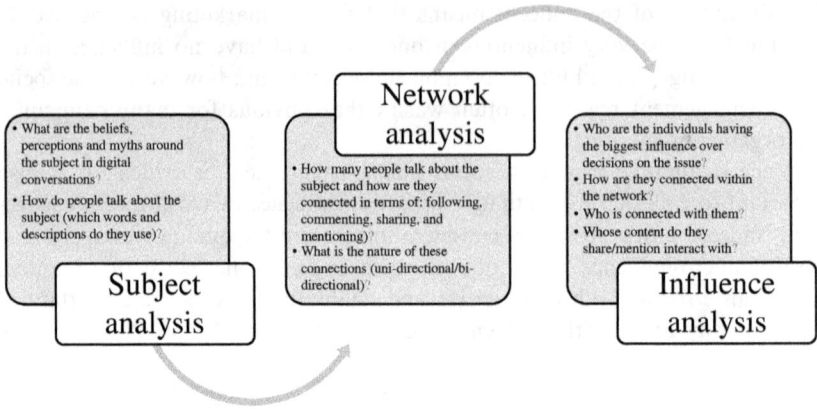

Figure 4.3.   Digital Influence Analysis Funnel.

Applying network theory to social media network analysis requires using big data analytics. Big data analytics provide an effective way to uncover the relationships and how they are shaping the discourse. Again, an effective approach to big data analytics requires application of the human analysis and intelligence in order to benefit from the insights provided by the data (Figure 4.3).

Therefore, looking from a broader engagement perspective, we can see three levels of influence that are relevant for the advocacy strategies:

- *Direct influence on the decision-making processes or resource allocation, etc.* Analyzing this type of influence requires to look at the landscape also from outside of digital perspective. In fact, the socioeconomic and political analysis should be performed before applying it into digital context.
- *Indirect influence through ability to impact those who take the decisions.* This again requires looking at the landscape with a holistic lens that goes beyond digital influence and digital engagement. We can though use a proxy of digital influence to uncover the trends and connections between the individuals and organizations.
- *Shaping influence by ability to define the narratives and discourses around the issue.* This is where big data analytics provide the best insights – it allows us to showcase how the discourse is shaped by the individuals and how the trends evolve over time.

As a result, measurement of digital influence becomes a very complex task requiring an analytical approach far beyond digital itself. At the same time, the complexity of global landscape forces to look for the intersections between the various subjects (Borgatti & Halgin, 2011). It is indeed rare that an issue can be analyzed in isolation. A majority of the issues are interconnected into broader discourses and cross-impact each other (Borgatti & Halgin, 2011). In this case, we need to note the role of the SDGs in shaping the discourse (Sachs, 2016). In fact, SDGs force to see the global landscape from a holistic perspective. The way goals and targets are formulated means that they often reside at intersection of the multiple issues. For example, health issues are often interconnected with the development agenda, gender issues, questions related to the urbanization, climate change, etc. As a result, mapping influencers in one subject also requires mapping the "neighboring ones." This holistic approach is not what the organizations were used to doing in terms of public affairs and lobbying. It requires re-drafting the definition of stakeholders and taking a much broader stance on the aspects influencing the global landscape (Sachs, 2016). It also means that the landscape analysis needs to be more in depth to capture all the changes and potential reputational and/or organizational risks related with the landscape changes and evolution.

4.2.3. *Influencer Engagement – New Mantra, or New Mirage*

While there are reasons to be critical toward influencer marketing, it is also important to see and recognize its value for the companies and organizations. Identifying those who can shape public opinion and public perception becomes an imperative for companies from all the sectors (Kilgour et al., 2015). We argued before in this chapter that a purely quantitative approach to influence doesn't provide a full insight to the effectiveness of the advocacy efforts. We also identified three levels of influence on which we can assess the potential impacts of the influencers. It was also proven that engaging the influencers can be a very effective way to engage target audiences beyond the current community of interest of an organization (Kilgour et al., 2015).

The "how" of influencer strategies is quite complex. In our view it requires a qualitative verification of relevance and influence on the decision-making processes (this can be performed looking at three levels of influence identified above). It also requires looking at potential future influence potential of an

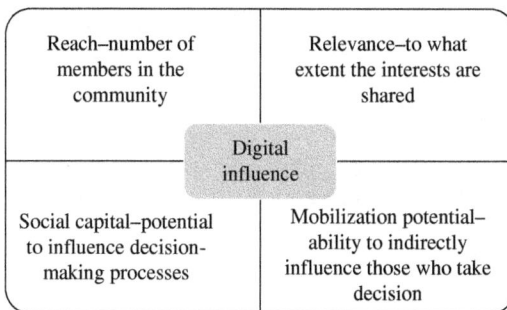

Figure 4.4.   Digital Influence Four-Dimensional Model.

individual or an organization. We propose the following model to describe the imperatives of the social media influence (Figure 4.4):

Reach – we don't underestimate the power of the community. We believe that this is one of the factors that need to be considered when designing digital influencer strategies. In the age of micro-influence (and some even looking at nano-influencers) it is also important to assess a potential reach of an individual. This is especially relevant for the influencer marketing campaigns. However, this shouldn't be the only factor, or even the main factor taken into the account.

Relevance – it is important to select the influence partners that share the similar content interests to the campaign/organizations represented. Many companies and organizations turn toward "generic influencers." While they might have an attractive reach and engaged communities, they don't necessarily fit the purpose for the organizations working with them. In addition, selecting partners that have interests being "too far out" will lead to cognitive issues among the target audiences of the campaign.

Social capital – the ability to influence directly decision-making processes is a basis of advocacy strategies. This should not be different in the context of digital advocacy. We have seen that there are different layers of influence that need to be considered.

Mobilization potential – the decisions are also influenced by the external factors that don't necessarily belong to the official processes. The ability to motivate and mobilize the communities in favor of or against the cause is paramount in strategic design of the campaigns. It is worth noting that this level of influence is potentially the most relevant from a digital perspective. In fact, digital advocacy can deliver the organizational objectives by enhancing the number of people mobilized by the cause and in turn pressuring the ones who take the decisions.

Table 4.1 summarizes in simple terms a way to look at the four-dimensional aspect of the social media and digital influence.

Following these three steps of influence allows us to focus on the influencers that matter the most and that have the highest potential of bringing superior return on investment to the organization. At the same time, it allows us to avoid a too narrow focus looking exclusively at one aspect of engagement.

4.2.4. Rise of Micro-influence

There is a limited research on influencer engagement in advocacy so far. Research body on influencer marketing is far more broad and multi-faceted. Therefore, there are many more references come from the professional studies as opposed to the scientific research. It is interesting to observe a turning point in the way influencer marketing and engagement are both portrayed. After an initial very positive feedback that could have been associated with a certain "hype," we see more and more critical voices around it.

Table 4.1. Management of the Influence Process: Key Components.

	Why	**How**	**What**
Reach	To raise broader awareness about organization's position on the issue	Looking at the numbers of connections and impressions of the messages	Number of connections and connections that connections have – defining potential reach of an individual/ organization
Relevance	To ensure that the advocacy strategy is well-targeted and corresponds to the organizational objectives	Analyzing the socioeconomic landscape and positioning an individual within the issue	The extent to which an individual has a direct or indirect influence over an issue
Social capital	Social capital and trust in an individual or organization will define to what extent it can impact its landscape	Analyzing the trust and positive external mentions on digital channels (in general and within a given issue)	Numbers of positive external unprompted mentions on digital channels
Mobilization potential	To evaluate a possibility for an influencer to generate social media conversation and impact a discourse	Analyzing average engagement rates on the digital posts coming from this digital influencer	Average number of interactions and engagements per post. An overall engagement rate in relationship to an audience size (reach)

Also, the question of the effectiveness of this type of marketing shouldn't be neglected and is increasingly present in influencer campaign evaluation. Having said that we present a more mitigated approach in which the value of influencer engagement is recognized, while we point out some of the considerations that need to be taken into account in order to fully benefit from what it offers.

The concept of micro-influence is not new to advocacy. It was already analyzed and described in the context of social movements, lobbying activities, and consumer advocacy. However, the digital landscape and context made it much more prominent in the professional discourse. The idea that individuals with more focused communities in a particular issue are more effective in setting up the agenda seems to belong at the "stating the obvious" level. However, thanks to big data analytics we are able to identify those who actually are the sources of discourse and in turn can play a transformative role for organizational evolution.

There are several definitions of micro-influence and micro-influencers. The ones coming from marketing field tend to focus more on the quantitative aspect – a number of social media followers that an individual has with a certain cut-off level at which an individual is considered to be a micro-influencer as opposed to just an influencer.

> A micro-influencer is someone who has between 1,000 to 100,000 followers. Micro-influencers focus on a specific niche or area and are generally regarded as an industry expert or topic specialist. "[Micro-influencers] have stronger relationships than a typical influencer. This is often driven by their perception as an opinion leader of [a] subject matter. A micro-influencer, as opposed to a celebrity or regular influencer, often has a very uniform audience," Gyal said. (CMS Wire)[2]

The issue in focusing exclusively on social media influence, on top of the fact that it limits the insights, is very technical. A majority of social media platforms restrict access to their back-end data (API access). This tendency is more and more visible with increase of the focus on value creation and return on investment by the social media companies. Also, raising privacy concerns and prominence of privacy discourse (including all the debate on the GDPR implementation) pushes these companies to protect better the users of their platforms. Therefore, the tools used for big data analytics have only very limited access to the digital conversations. This access is shrinking further with almost each update to privacy policies and API codes. For instance, the big data tools do not cover discussions in the closed or private groups, etc. Yet, the private conversations are real and most valuable exchanges.

At the moment, the channel which grants the most generous access to its back-end data is Twitter. As a result, a majority of the analytics tools rely heavily on Twitter data as the basis of their dashboards. At the same time, Twitter is the smallest of the big social media channels and has a specific demographic of the users – mainly coming from Western countries that are wealthy. This is combined with the open conversations from the other channels. As a result, the data that are used for analysis is limited. Recent study from Pew

---

[2]https://www.cmswire.com/digital-marketing/social-media-influencers-mega-macro-micro-or-nano/

Research Center about Twitter users in the United States gives some indication of this trend:

> The analysis indicates that the 22% of American adults who use Twitter are representative of the broader population in certain ways, but not others. Twitter users are younger, more likely to identify as Democrats, more highly educated and have higher incomes than U.S. adults overall. Twitter users also differ from the broader population on some key social issues. For instance, Twitter users are somewhat more likely to say that immigrants strengthen rather than weaken the country and to see evidence of racial and gender-based inequalities in society. But on other subjects, the views of Twitter users are not dramatically different from those expressed by all U.S. adults. (Pew Research Center)[3]

Basing the conclusions around the discourse only on one of the channels comes with a risk of missing other discussions and trends, or even misinterpreting the trends. It also favors creating of the closed influence circle based on Twitter discussion. It also provides squeezed and biased insight to the effectiveness of the advocacy efforts and subsequent changes in the discourse. In the worst case, an organization looking exclusively at these data points may miss the latest trends, or even apply an ineffective engagement strategy. This strengthens our point for the need of connecting digital and non-digital influence in order to gain real in-depth insights to the influencer landscape (Figure 4.5).

4.2.5. Model for Digital Influencer Engagement

Managing relationships with external stakeholders requires a strategic approach, which permanently links back the engagement strategies to the objectives of advocacy. It also requires considering both digital and offline

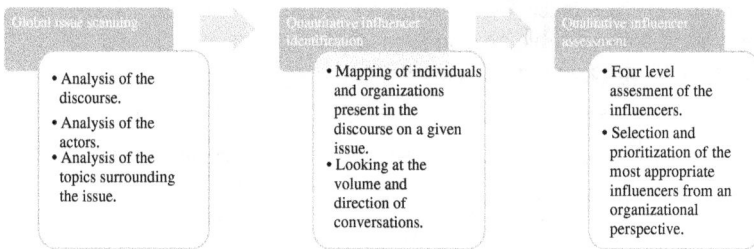

Global issue scanning	Quantitative influencer identification	Qualitative influencer assessment
• Analysis of the discourse. • Analysis of the actors. • Analysis of the topics surrounding the issue.	• Mapping of individuals and organizations present in the discourse on a given issue. • Looking at the volume and direction of conversations.	• Four level assesment of the influencers. • Selection and prioritization of the most appropriate influencers from an organizational perspective.

Figure 4.5.   Digital Influencer Assessment Process.

---

[3]https://www.pewinternet.org/2019/04/24/sizing-up-twitter-users/

landscapes. With this optic, we propose a model looking the influencer management in three phases:

- discovery – mapping the issue, discourse, and landscape;
- analysis – identifying the ones who have the highest potential in shaping the discourse and dialogue; and
- engagement – building relationships with identified advocates and influencers.

For each of the phases we suggest three steps which guide the phases of the concept development (Figure 4.6).

In Table 4.2, we propose accompanying each of the steps from the model with the actions and verification/consideration points. This conceptual model aims to provide a practical application of the influencing model and guide development of the influencer advocacy campaigns. Its practical aspect provides relevance for both marketing and public affairs campaigning models.

4.2.6. Health Check List for Relationship Assessment

Conceptual model presented above guides development of the strategic influencer campaigns. However, there is a constant need to assess the existing relationships that company, or organization has with its influencers. Since influence is a dynamic concept, some of the influencers might lose their ability to impact the company's operating landscape and at the same time there are new emerging ones which need to be attended to. To that end, we also propose a "health check" list of considerations that we believe are relevant for monitoring and evaluation of the relationships with the external influencers of the organization. This includes both quantitative considerations related to the return on investment (ROI) combined with qualitative considerations focusing on the progress and depth of the relationship. This list is driven by the following considerations:

- What are the costs associated with management of the relationship?
- What are the benefits that the organization has thanks to this relationship?
- How did the engagement start? And how did the relationship evolve?
- What are the measurable benefits from this engagement?
- Is there a room to deepen the engagement?

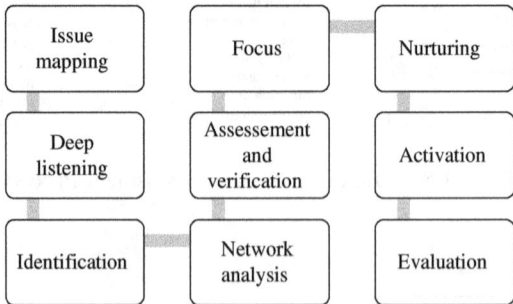

Figure 4.6.   Steps in Influencer Management Process.

Table 4.2. Conceptual Model for Influencer Management.

Phase	Step	Actions	Key Considerations
Discovery	Issue mapping	Definition of the issues impacting the organization	Organizational reputation
		Definition of the key issues where organization wants to lead the dialogue and narrative	Sentiment around organization and issue
			Comparison between traditional media and digital representation
		Large-scale research on the digital and media performance of these issues	Impact of the discourse on the content
		Analysis of the interconnectivity and international or local spread of the issue	
		Discourse analysis and definition of the common themes	
	Deep listening	Analysis of the flows and changes in the discourse	Tools used for monitoring and listening
		Comparison of the statements given by the different actors	Discourse and narrative around the key issues
		Benchmark of the discourse and discourse evolution against identified interests of the actors	Global agenda and global frameworks beyond the core of the issue
		Identification of the interconnections between various issues surrounding organization and its agenda	SDG mapping and digital overview (if relevant)
	Identification	Mapping of the most quoted individuals in the discourse	Difference between reach and relevance
		Check of their reach and relevance for organization and for issue	Identification of the engagement touch points

Table 4.2. (*Continued*)

Phase	Step	Actions	Key Considerations
		Review of interconnectivity between the key actors	Foresight to a potential of future engagement and impact
		Identification of the actors with the highest influencing potential	
		Verification of the likelihood of willingness to partner	
Analysis	Network analysis	Posing the influencers and decision-makers on the interconnection between the issues	Interconnectivity between the issues and actors
		Historical overview of the changes and developments in an issue network	Reasons for inter-actor connections
			Strength of the network and central actors
		Analysis of the resilience of the influence network	Visual representation of the network including both the actors and the issues
		Mapping of the flow of information within the network	
		Design of a network map	
	Assessment and verification	Analysis of the costs and benefits of a prospective influencer program	Personal and organizational reputation of the influencers
		Check of the past statement of the selected influencers	Potential for backlash from influencer engagement
		Verification of the agenda of influencers	Cultural fit between influencer and organization
		Benchmark of personal and organizational priorities of the influencers against organizational agenda	
	Focus	Ranking of the influencers according to	Best potential ROI and ROE from an influencer engagement

Table 4.2. (*Continued*)

Phase	Step	Actions	Key Considerations
		the four criteria of influencer engagement	Social capital of the influencers
		Development of the list of influencers and ranking of the influencers in terms of priority	
		Prioritization of the influencers according to a projected campaign timeline	
Engagement	Nurturing	Development of an exclusive content for influencer engagement	Content formats to reach influencers
		Multi-touchpoint distribution across the channels	Multi-channel influencing landscape
		Listening to the influencer content and engagement	Listening protocol
		Monitoring of engagement and touch points	
	Activation	Definition of the influencer incentive program	Incentive type for influencer
		Distribution of the rewards	Alignment between organic and paid activities
		Alignment of the content (organization-driven vs. organic and influencer-driven)	Amplification of the influencer content
	Evaluation	Analysis of the output, outtake and outcome measures of the influencer engagement program	Ares of improvement in the campaign
		Calculation of the Return on Investment (ROI) and Return on Engagement (ROE)	Changes and evolution of the issue landscape
			Changes in sentiment around an issue and organization

Table 4.2. (*Continued*)

Phase	Step	Actions	Key Considerations
		Identification of improvements of the campaign and approach	
		Implementation of the changes in approach	

The health check list of questions provides a step-by-step guide to assess the quality of influencer marketing and influencer advocacy relationships. This check list aims to provide a practical guidance for the advocacy professionals and help them focus their activities and engage with the meaningful influencer strategies.

4.3.   Conclusions

Digital engagement opened up new opportunities for organizations to engage with their stakeholders and communities. It allowed them to build relationships beyond their regular circle of influence. It also helped several individuals to gain influence beyond their "real-life" networks by creating virtual communities of impact. This double shift created a fertile ground for the new campaigning models including influencer campaigns. Companies and organizations embarked on these new engagement strategies with a high level of enthusiasm and sometimes low levels of criticism toward the value of these relationships. After an initial period of enthusiasm came a period of an increased critical view toward influencer marketing and influencers in general. This led to the raise of the concept of micro-influence and nano-influence – the influencer campaigns using individuals with small followership and focused networks.

There are unquestionable benefits coming from the influencer campaigns and engagement in the digital advocacy strategies:

- The individuals are in general trusted more than the organizations by the general public. Therefore, the impact of messages shared by the individuals is higher compared to the ones shared by the organizations.
- Digital posts shared by the individuals gather better engagement results (in terms of comments, shares and other types of interaction).
- Real social media engagement happens between the individuals. The role of organizations is to animate and orchestrate this engagement.
- Companies can enhance their influence beyond their regular subjects of focus and engage broader audiences.

At the same time, it is important to look at the social capital of the individuals and organizations and remember about their real decision-making influencing power. The proposed model for influencer strategies seeks to integrate these strategic dimensions for organizations to take full benefit from the opportunities offered by influencer engagement.

4.4. Discussion and Further Research

According to statistics, digital channels will continue to be important advocacy and engagement channels (Communication Monitor, 2019). With a growing application of augmented and virtual reality the engagement is re-defined and driven much more by the experiences individuals have with the brands and organizations. This long-term change will require a continuous focus on delivering the best approaches to deliver on the advocacy campaigns' objectives. At the same time, we observe an increased focus of social media strategies on individuals (Communication Monitor, 2019). As a result, the digital advocacy strategies need to take these landscape requirements into account to stay effective. From an advocacy professional perspective this means constantly challenging the status quo and looking for new and creative ways to drive influence.

From a research perspective, it would be interesting to see more research around digital influence with a special focus on micro-influence. Some of the professionals suggest that the influencer marketing is one of the myths of the modern marketing. However, there is a contrary evidence that sets it as one of the most effective means to influence behaviors of the target audiences. It is also applicable beyond social media (Brown & Hayes, 2008). A large sample study looking at the channel and approach effectiveness would provide the insights and evidence to validate or reject this hypothesis.

It would be also interesting to analyze the relationships between the brands and influencers from an ethnographic perspective. What are the main perceptions of each other, how do they find their cooperation, what are the main issues and benefits coming from these relationships – the answers to these questions would allow us to validate further the approaches toward influencer marketing as well as provide more insights into its working model.

Key Takeaways

- *Digital engagement is more and more focused on individuals and individual engagement. Effective strategies need to bring a personalized dimension to keep delivering on relevance. This personalization means changing the way content is thought through and created. It also means building connections with those who matter the most.*
- *Social media and digital influence are both dynamic. They are also dependent on the context. There is no universal influence. Some individuals and organizations are very influential in one subject but have no influence in others. This requires constant research and questioning of the status quo and deep-listening to the landscape.*

- *Effective digital strategies require looking beyond digital. It is crucial to consider a social and cultural capital of an organization or individual while assessing their influencing power. For global advocacy strategies it is important to build relationships that happen not only in the virtual context, but also offline. This multi-touch, multi-channel approach delivers best long-term results.*
- *Micro-influencer campaigns can be a very effective way for organizations to enhance their influencing scope. However, looking at four levels of digital influence provides a necessary verification to get the most out of the advocacy efforts. It also calls for an ongoing monitoring of performance of the efforts.*
- *Digital shift will continue, and future relationships will be further based on personal relationships and experiences created by the brands and individuals. This means that advocacy will be relying even more on personal and individual relationships.*

Chapter 5

Defining a Conceptual Model for Advocacy Strategy Development

5.1. Introduction

Every day, we hear about organizations, companies, NGOs, and individuals trying to influence a global agenda. More messages, more agenda points, more influencers – the landscape of advocacy has long been busy and crowded. Now it becomes even more complex. Almost every year statistics prove that there were more data (content and information) produced in that particular year compared with all the previous years together (Forbes, 2019). Stakeholders, audiences, and publics at large are confronted with a permanent cacophony of messages, ideas, and needs. This creates an environment where it is very difficult to cut through the noise and reach the ones that matter for a particular cause or business.

Many organizations address this challenge by communicating even more. They develop even more messages and use more channels to reach their desired audiences through more channels. As a result, political decision-makers, regulators, and legislators are confronted with immense amounts of content having varying relevance toward their work. Quantity wins over quality and targeting. Permanent production of content and activities build output-driven advocacy approaches. Organizations and advocacy teams reach their KPIs of numbers of contacts made or resources produced. At the same time, this tendency leads to a fatigue of the stakeholders and decision-makers who are permanently confronted with endless number of messages and arguments.

In this busy environment, the success of an advocacy campaign depends a lot on its strategic planning (Patterson & Radtke, 2009; Percy, 2008). Knowing what an organization needs to achieve becomes paramount for the success (or failure) of the advocacy approach. It might sound like a paradox but understanding what an organization wants and needs to achieve is the most difficult part of strategy design. However, there are many more elements that need to be considered while planning the approach. Focusing resources on the activities which bring results (from an outcome-based perspective) and on the stakeholders that matter is crucial in order to design the strategies that are both efficient and effective.

In addition, a strategic approach helps to focus the attention of the organization on what really matters for business. It is not about the number of activities, but about their relevance (Patterson & Radtke, 2009; Percy, 2008). This relevance is rooted in understanding of the socioeconomic context as well as the issues surrounding the organization. The analysis is always supposed to define focus and drive action. However, the idea is not to focus purely on research in advocacy. The insights are gathered in order to inform decisions and provide evidence as the basis for strategic choices. This all has to be paired with creative idea and strong narrative which can bring together various stakeholders around the organization. Finally, all the activities and implementation of the strategy need to be constantly monitored, measured, and evaluated. Evaluation and subsequent innovation in the approach closes the loop (AMEC, 2015).

The model presented in this chapter considers a dynamic character of the advocacy environment. The "status quo" from the planning phase of the campaign will evolve multiple times during the implementation phase. Therefore, foresight into possible scenarios and changes as well as agility to adjust to the changing environment are indispensable elements of the advocacy planning process. The model looks also at the advocacy tools and channels from a broader perspective aiming to force the focus on desired outcomes as opposed to the tools and channels. It seeks to support advocacy practitioners with a simple approach which can help to focus the activities and save the resources by eliminating unnecessary steps. It also provides an analytical framework to review advocacy campaigns and assess the effectiveness of the respective steps.

5.2. Changing Landscape of Advocacy and Communications

The unthinkable becomes a reality – this is a rather frequent observation of the landscape in the recent years. Surprising results of elections; rise of populism in many countries; permanent challenges related to fake news – these are only few examples that have shaped the advocacy landscape in the recent years. These are the trends or rather consequences of the trends shaping advocacy and communications landscapes. While in the past the biggest challenge of advocacy professionals was to get the message across, nowadays they need to ensure that the message is understood, embraced and not considered to be a "fake news." Even defining what "fake news" is becomes a challenge in the multi-channel and multi-message environment.

Low levels of trust toward institutions, organizations, and companies among general public and target audiences amplify these tendencies (see Chapter 3). Concurrently, there is a growing expectation that companies participate in a global discourse through sustainability engagement and more active role in the socioeconomic discourse. Operationalization of the SDG framework is a great example of an engagement platform where companies, government, and nonprofit sector cooperate (Sachs et al., 2017).

Even more dramatic change concerns media and channel landscape. Social media and digital communications change the way information is consumed (Pentina & Tarafdar, 2014). It is not only about the formats and proximity between the senders and receivers of the messages (Pentina & Tarafdar, 2014). The change is much more profound as the social media redefine where and how people consume information. Looking at the current target audiences using mobile phones, jumping between the platforms, it is visible that they have limited attention spans to read/watch the news. This means that the information needs to be presented in a succinct attention-grabbing manner (Ellison & Hardey, 2014; Khan, 2017). For example, studies show that social media users decide within the first six seconds whether they will watch the video or not. This was shaped by the way advertisement was served on YouTube (AdWeek, 2017). As a consequence, content producers need to ensure that they cover their key messages within these first six seconds. This requires an act of balancing between the precision and creativity necessary to grab and keep attention of the target audiences. As stated in the Introduction and Chapter 2 – the confirmation bias shapes the way people interact with information. The target audiences are much more likely to believe the information which reaffirms their pre-existing beliefs (Nickerson, 1998). This makes driving behavioral change and engagement even more challenging.

Social media landscape is considered to be relatively static with the key channels not changing much over the years. However, this view is not necessarily true. There are new channels that appear and gain popularity. There are also new functionalities of the channels, which redefine the engagement patterns. Perishable content such as Instagram Stories is the best example of this tendency. The users need to return to the platform on regular basis in order to keep being engaged. Facebook is still a channel gaining an important number of users in the developing countries and among the older users (Brandwatch, 2019). Twitter on the contrary is the channel that was considered to be sentenced to disappear. Interestingly, while its usage statistics are pretty flat, it has a community of influencers and stakeholders that are loyal to the channel (Brandwatch, 2019). Twitter also redefined the way messages are written. Its initial limit of 140 characters forced organizations and individuals to focus on the essential and write to the point messages. While Twitter itself might not be perceived as the most successful social media channels, it definitely changed the way information is presented. It can be a powerful advocacy tool supporting direct connections with the stakeholders.

Also, social media themselves are evolving into the multimedia platforms based on content and news. The media content consumption on social media is growing (Brandwatch, 2019; Pentina & Tarafdar, 2014). More and more users consider social media as their primary source of news information (Brandwatch, 2019). This tendency is in line with the business interests of the social media platforms. For them keeping users within the platform by satisfying all the media consumption needs means more opportunities to place advertisement messages. On the other hand, it enhances and improves user experience. People don't need to jump between the platforms in order to move from one content piece to another. A current tendency is to provide a holistic experience within one platform.

This provides a great opportunity for advocacy to spread the content across multiple channels and increase the reach among potential target audiences. At the same time, it requires advocacy professionals to think from a user perspective and develop user-centric engagement strategies. For a long time, the advocacy strategies were reflecting organizational structures of those behind them. This did mean moving target audiences from one platform to another. With the current shift in digital platforms design, the user experience should reflect the seamlessness and simplicity.

Channels are changing and target audience expectations are changing. The expectations of decision-makers, legislators and regulators are changing as well. Political stakeholders take a broader view on the organizational contributions in the socioeconomic context (Adler & Jermier, 2005; Zetter, 2014). Also, there are more decision-makers coming from the Millennial generation. It is interesting to see that the narrative around Millennials in many places stopped at the level of talking about "this generation" of young people who are digital natives. Yet Millennials are now the most numerous group in the workplace globally and in many counties biggest group of voters. For instance, study from Pew about the 2020 elections in United States confirms this tendency.[1] Also, there are more and more Millennials in the positions of power. And this is not limited to several highly mediatized individuals. Organizations need to accept that this generation is already there and adjust their engagement strategies accordingly. The companies are required to play a positive constructive role in addressing the issues (Mohr, Webb, & Harris, 2001; Porter & Kramer, 2006, 2011). This goes beyond their statutory requirements and legal obligations (Morsing & Schultz, 2006). As a result, companies become important actors in the international social discourse.

International landscape is changing as well. Well established institutions established by international treaties have difficulty to adjust to the changing landscape of influence (Weiss, 2018). They tend to be slower in adaptation and more conservative in their approach to the global issues. This opens a space for new entrants to the international landscape. The organizations that were not known, or even did not exist make a rapid ascent to power. Moreover, many countries prefer diplomacy at a bilateral level. This increases the role of informal decision-making and direct engagement. Bilateralism and multilateralism co-exist in the international policy making the issues management even more complex. The multilateral platforms gathering entities coming from various sectors gain momentum and become increasingly visible and influential. As a result, we are facing a fragmented and mosaic landscape which is not easy to navigate. Yet it creates multiple opportunities for different engagement approaches and provides more entry-points for advocacy campaigning.

It all impacts the way advocacy strategies are designed. They need to consider the complexity of the landscape and base the recommended actions on evidence coming from research and analysis. Therefore, there is a shift from creativity-driven strategic approach toward an insight-driven one. It requires from advocacy professionals a different skillset and more holistic view of the campaign.

---

[1] https://www.pewsocialtrends.org/essay/an-early-look-at-the-2020-electorate/

5.2.1. Strategic Planning in Advocacy – Role of Multi-step Approach

What does this complexity of external landscape mean for advocacy strategies? How to design evidence-based advocacy approaches? What does it mean to be effective in the current context? These are the basic questions focusing on the "how" of the advocacy strategy development.

First of all, complexity requires focus. The focus on strategic processes is achieved by a clear goal setting. The goals of advocacy need to be developed like any other strategy, and SMART framework is a very useful reference point. As a reminder SMART mnemonic stands for (Specific, Measurable, Achievable, Relevant and Time-Bound) (Doran, 1981).

The goal setting needs to be accompanied by definition of the advocacy objectives and outcomes. This provides the link between organizational needs (expressed by the goals) and what advocacy actually can deliver. It leads in turn to strategic approach and planning process. This process needs to be accompanied by a creative idea and creative development together with definition of the campaign narrative. Strategic campaign narrative in turn is the expression of the DNA of an advocacy campaign. It links together organizational objectives, influence strategy and the delivery mechanism of the campaign. Finally, campaign focus requires a robust measurement and evaluation in order to prove efficiency and effectiveness of the efforts.

Public affairs, corporate communication, and advocacy measurement is one of the "hot topics" in the marketing and communications industries. It is extensively covered in the trade press and magazines. The question of "payback" or ROI has been an emerging research subject for marketing for a long time (Shaw & Merrick, 2005). The similar questions and arguments are now raised in the context of corporate communications. The need to report on the ROI is even a subject of discussion among corporate communications scholars, whereby some argue that the financial framework does not correctly showcase the true value of communication (Ewing, 2009; Gregory & Watson, 2008; Watson, 2011). Nevertheless, there seems to be an agreement among the scholars and practitioners that the current measurement frameworks are too focused on the output measures, channel-specific measures and not enough on the results (outcomes) of communication strategy (Ewing, 2009). Also, recently the subject of measurement and evaluation in communication is becoming important for the communications industry (Association for the Measurement and Evaluation in Communication – AMEC). In fact, measurement association for measurement in communications is the closet structure to advocacy, which delivers best practices and frameworks for measurement of the engagement activities. A more strategic view of corporate communications among senior executives requires more sophisticated procedures of measurement and reporting of the performance (AMEC). The industry itself is trying to define the measurement framework (see below, Barcelona Principles). There is a common agreement that measurement should be linked to overall performance and should include ROI elements. The Barcelona Principles (established in the document post-summit of AMEC) state the following:

- *"Importance of Goal Setting and Measurement*
- *Measuring the Effect on Outcomes is Preferred to Measuring Outputs*
- *The Effect on Business Results Can and Should Be Measured Where Possible*
- *Media Measurement Requires Quantity and Quality*
- *AVEs are not the Value of Public Relations*
- *Social Media Can and Should be Measured*
- *Transparency and Replicability are Paramount to Sound Measurement"*

This list names a desired measurement framework from the perspective of communications executives (AMEC, Global Alliance, ICCO, Institute for Public Relations, Public Relations Society of America, AMEC U.S. & Agency Leaders Chapter). These principles show that communication experts aim to create a tailored framework for measurement based on the outcomes of communications activities. It is stressed that "marketing specific" measures such as AVE (advertising value equivalent) do not show the real value of communications and therefore are not appropriate for corporate communication strategic management. The Barcelona Principles were created from a cross-industry need to structure an approach toward measurement and evaluation in communication. It is worth noting that Barcelona Principles have been updated in 2015 to keep up with the changes in the communication and media landscape. Interestingly, the changes to the principles made them even more relevant from an advocacy perspective:

Barcelona 2.0 Principles are the following:

"Principle 1: Goal Setting and Measurement are Fundamental to Communication and Public Relations

Principle 2: Measuring Communication Outcomes is Recommended Versus Only Measuring Outputs

Principle 3: The Effect on Organizational Performance Can and Should Be Measured Where Possible

Principle 4: Measurement and Evaluation Require Both Qualitative and Quantitative Methods

Principle 5: AVEs are not the Value of Communications

Principle 6: Social Media Can and Should be Measured Consistently with Other Media Channels

Principle 7: Measurement and Evaluation Should be Transparent, Consistent and Valid" (AMEC)[2]

---

[2]https://amecorg.com/how-the-barcelona-principles-have-been-updated/

Quick glance at the principles showcases that they reflect alignment tendencies (measurement of multiple channels in one framework); link with organizational performance as well as focus on the communications outcomes. The same principles of measurement can be applied in the context of advocacy and public affairs activities.

5.2.2. *Influencing Factors in Advocacy Conceptual Planning*

An in-depth understanding of the landscape forms the basis for decision-making and design of a strategic approach. We believe in looking at an issue from a multi-dimensional perspective:

- *Foresight:* looking at the likely and unlikely scenarios of development of the issue helps to bring attention toward the future possibilities of the campaign.
- *Context:* understanding where the issue is at present and which are the interests of the various stakeholders. It also helps to focus on the final decision-making instance.
- *Links with the other issues:* the complexity of the international advocacy landscape requires analysis of the connections between the leading campaign issue with other issues. It helps to enhance the scope of the campaign and ensure its relevance for the various stakeholder groups.
- *Influencers:* identifying those who have an influence and impact over an issue. The influencer research focuses on identifying the individuals and organizations that matter. It also benchmarks the individual organizational agendas with those of the campaign (Figure 5.1).

Spending time and resources on a proper overview of the influencing landscape of an issue is a good investment. It helps to focus the efforts of the

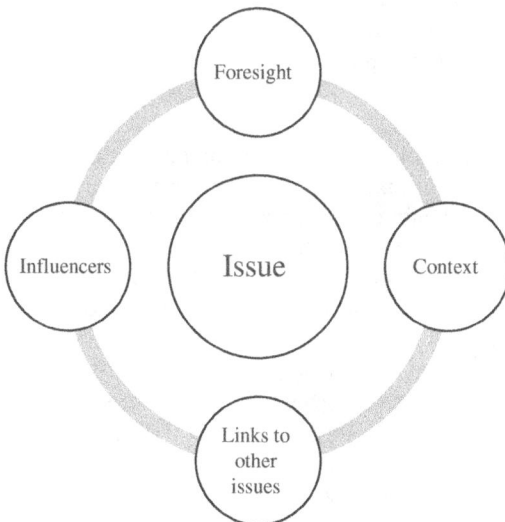

Figure 5.1.   Issue Analysis in a Context of Advocacy Campaign.

campaign and provides organizational readiness for various scenarios. It is worth noting that the advocacy and influence landscape is not static. There are actors and issues that gain momentum and influence, while others lose their impact. Consequently, monitoring the landscape is an ongoing activity in the advocacy strategy development. Otherwise, the campaigners risk to miss on important developments and lose relevance.

5.3. Conceptual Model for Advocacy Campaign Strategic Planning

Advocacy planning requires both focus and appreciation of the changing landscape. In our model we propose to use the tools of project management and strategic planning and apply them to advocacy (Burke, 2013). We also integrate communications and creative elements into the model to ensure that it can be applied in the content of campaigns. Finally, we consider the five basic functions of management and ensure that they are covered throughout the model (see, Chapter 2). Each of the steps of the model is accompanied with the tools that can be directly used in development of the advocacy strategies.

5.3.1. Step 1: Landscape Mapping and Definition of a Unique Point of Engagement (UPE)

We propose the concept of unique point of engagement as an enhancement of the unique selling point/proposition from marketing. We believe that definition of the main value proposition of an organization should be the first step before identification of any campaigns. This should come from an in-depth landscape mapping including competitive benchmarking and organizational foresight. This would allow for any campaign to address not only the known issues, but also the unknown ones that can impact the business or reputation in the future. The landscape mapping is composed from the following steps:

- Materiality analysis looking at organization and its landscape from a perspective of risks and opportunities. Defining and prioritizing of the external issues according to their likelihood and impact on the organization.
- SWOT analysis of the organization in the context of identified issues. Positioning of the organization in its competitive landscape.
- Design thinking exercises and prototyping of the possible likely and unlikely scenarios impacting the organization.
- Definition of the Unique Point of Engagement (UPE). The UPE is the main connection point linking the agenda of the organization with the agendas of its stakeholders and broader target audiences. UPE is created through answering the following questions:
  - What is the issue we need to address?
  - Who has a stake in the issue?
  - Who influences them?

- What do they care about?
- Why would they support us?
- What can we bring to them?

The answer to the last question is critical to define the UPE around which the campaign concept and planning should be developed.

5.3.2. Step 2: Setting Up of the Impact and Ambition Level

This step allows us to define an overall impact of the campaign on an organization and/or business. We believe that clear definition of the desired impact is important in order to link the advocacy campaign with the core of the organizational considerations. It also allows us to align the advocacy and public affairs goals with the organizational goals. It is recommended that the desired impact includes both short- and long-term components.

- *Definition of the advocacy impact.* This step goes beyond the organization, its need, and campaign. It looks at a broader societal or organizational result which is brought by a campaign. This links back to the agenda of the stakeholders as well as identified UPE.
  What change do we want to make?
- *Definition of the advocacy outcomes.* It is important to distinguish between the advocacy outcomes and advocacy outputs. The advocacy outcomes are the final results of the campaigns within the target groups. Many of the advocacy campaigns fail to define their outcomes and as a result the focus is lost, and activities are driving the campaign rather than a strategy.
  What do we need our target audiences to do?
- *Definition of the campaign outtakes* focuses on desired reactions of the target audiences toward the messages. It includes recall of the message, emotional connection with the key messages, and imminent interactions.
  What do our target audiences need to think?
- *Definition of the campaign outputs* looks at the levels of coverage and reach of the campaign messages. This also includes the numbers of meetings, partners aligned with the campaign plan, and members of the coalition.
  How much traction did we get?
- *Definition of the process* looks at the most effective ways of reaching the target audiences. It takes into account the channels they use, the links organization has with them as well as the most effective ways of connecting with them.
  What do we do to convince them?
- *Identification of the inputs* defines the campaign needs in terms of resources, material, research, and collateral. It provides a "reality check" between the desired impact and budgets and resources which are at disposal of the organization.
  What do we need to start our engagement?

In general, this step helps to set the goals that are truly SMART and benchmark organizational ambitions with the resources and structures which are in place.

5.3.3. Step 3: Context Analysis

This step includes further landscape mapping and analysis. It is complemented by the PESTEL analysis. The idea is to have in-depth basis and understanding of the broader landscape. In this step, we look also at potential backlashes and push back related to the campaign (defining the need for defensive advocacy; see Chapter 7 for more details about advocacy defense processes). The idea of this step is to understand a resilience of the campaign and the organization. Finally, at this moment we develop alternative scenarios.

In the context analysis, we also look at defining the links between the issues of the campaign with the broader social context. This helps to define the common points with the other socioeconomic subjects that are related to the advocacy campaign. These analyses help uncover potential additional partnerships and coalitions for the campaign. Several questions can help guiding context analysis.

- What are the influencing factors on the issue of the campaign?
- What is the evolution of the issue in the media and stakeholder landscape?
- Which SDGs are linked with the issue of the campaign?
- How does this issue link with other issues and what are the interconnections?
- What are the facts around the issue? What kind of data and scientific research is available?
- What kind of information/data/scientific research is missing?
- What are the myths and perceptions around the issue and organization?
- Who could be the partners and stakeholders of the campaign?
- Should the organization partner with other organizations, or take the advocacy effort on its own?
- Who has interest in progressing/delaying/stopping development of the campaign?
- Is our organization aligned in terms of the validity of the advocacy approach?

Answering these questions allows us to identify needed corrective actions from the advocacy perspective as well as the focus of the campaign efforts. It also focuses the target audiences and stakeholder research on those who matter the most for the success (or failure) of the campaign.

5.3.4. Step 4: Target Audience Identification and Opinion Tracking

Based on the context analysis we define the primary and secondary target audiences. The primary target audiences are those who have decision power over the issue of the campaign (decision-makers) (Subacchi, 2008). The secondary audiences are those who have leverage over those with decision power (influencers) (Subacchi, 2008).

Having identified all the target audiences we need to understand the sentiment among them toward the campaign theme and toward the organization running the campaign. In addition, it is important to understand the sentiment

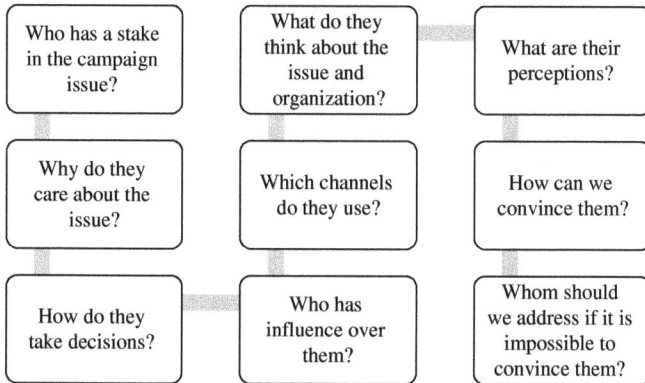

Figure 5.2.   Stakeholder and Influencer Mapping Process.

toward the competing campaigns. The most effective methods for initial opinion tracking include a combination between qualitative and quantitative methods. This analytical process uses both big and small data analytics to define the context holistically (more about influencer mapping in Chapter 4) (Figure 5.2).

The audience mapping process should include also media and social media mapping together with an influencer approach. Finally, depending on the outcomes of the context analysis it can also include market research methodology such as focus groups, pools, omnibus survey. The results of these surveys are useful from an advocacy evaluation perspective as they provide a solid benchmark data point.

5.3.5.   Step 5: Platform Identification

It is important to see the main advocacy platforms that are relevant for the issue of the campaign. Oftentimes, the organizations use the same platforms to advocate on a variety of issues without analyzing their particular effectiveness. In this step, we identify the platforms that are on one hand the most useful to address all the target audiences (both decision-makers and influencers). On the other hand, we look for the most effective media platforms to leverage campaign messaging (including traditional media and digital platforms). There are several questions that can help in taking decisions in terms of the advocacy platforms that organization should use.

- What are the key events, conferences and congresses organized by the key stakeholders in relationship of the issue?
- Are there any initiatives of the stakeholders linked with the issue and identified connected issues?
- Which SDG platforms are relevant for the issue and agenda set by organization?

- Which international days are connected with the campaign issue and how can they be used to leverage the campaign message?
- Which media and social media channels are relevant from the point of view of the target audiences?
- Can organization use its current communications and influence channels, or should it invest in opening new ones?
- How is the issue represented in the key global platforms such as World Economic Forum Annual Meeting (or Regional Meeting) or United Nations General Assembly?

Ultimately the goal of the platform mapping is to focus on the most effective means to reach campaign stakeholders and target audiences. It is important to have a holistic view of the platforms which includes media, social media, and offline.

5.3.6. Step 6: Definition of the Main Communication Tactic

The campaign lever and the main communication tactic are developed based on audience research and selection of the campaign platforms and channels. This lever needs to be in line with an organizational DNA of the one behind the campaign. At the same time, it has to contribute in creating a change among the target audiences. It should also address the issues identified in the PESTEL and SWOT analysis. The main communication tactic refines the strategic approach.

Examples of the key communications tactics include:

- broad coalition;
- individual agenda setting;
- multi-stakeholder alignment;
- singling out global agenda issue;
- broadening up the issue;
- media impact; and
- social coalition.

As per examples above, the key communication tactic links back the advocacy goals with communications and influence delivery mechanism.

5.3.7. Step 7: Development of Strategic Narrative

This is the most defining step for an external view of the campaign. Strategic narrative drives all the engagement of the campaign and provides a guiding point for all content development. It is important to base a campaign narrative on an in-depth understanding of the context of the campaign and of the issue (Denning, 2006). It avoids the campaign being driven by the creative aspects as opposed to strategic considerations. It also puts the target audiences in the center and allows us to focus on the issues and needs identified among them.

Strategic narrative is an expression of the campaign goals in a format which connects with the target audiences. The narrative needs to both define the logic and create an emotional connection with an organization and campaign itself. It is important to see the narrative in the context of organizational goals and overall discourse around an issue (more detail around strategic narrative development is included in Chapter 6).

5.3.8. Step 8: Creative and User-first Content Development

Strategic narrative needs to be translated into the content that has a potential to engage target audiences on an ongoing basis. It is crucial to ensure that the content developed for the campaign resonates with the target audiences. This is executed through testing and analysis of performance in the context of identified audiences.

Finally, the content needs to be focused on the needs of the target audiences and not assumptions from the organization developing a campaign. In order to achieve that the content creation process and planning needs to be based on research among target audiences focusing on the channel preferences.

5.3.9. Step 9: Measurement and Reporting Protocol

Advocacy campaigns need to be measured and evaluated as any other communications and marketing activities (Bochenek & Blili, 2013). Both measurement and evaluation have to be linked with the desired impacts of the campaign (as defined in the step 2). We believe that measurement of the advocacy campaign is used to improve the performance and allow adjustments to the campaign. As such, the reporting needs to be agile and focus on ongoing improvements. The AMEC valid framework is a good starting point for development of the campaign KPIs. Table 5.1 presents suggested operationalization of the campaign measurement:

5.3.10. Step 10: Engagement Calendar and Campaign Plan

The activities of the campaign require proper advanced planning. The calendar of the campaign is the last step of the strategic design. In our view, it should

Table 5.1. Campaign Measurement Framework.

Input	Output	Outtake	Outcome	Impact
Resources produced and costs	Visibility of the campaign	Reactions of the audiences to the message	What change did it make	Long-term societal results of the campaign

combine the team composition (for instance, based on RACI model) with a detailed planning of the activities. This should be aligned with the identified platform and stakeholder agenda (Project Management Institute, 2013; Smith, 2005). Holistic view on advocacy planning allows us to focus the resources in the most effective manner. The campaign timeline should include milestones which can be used as check-in points to adjust the implementation tactics and processes (Table 5.2).

Table 5.2. Model for Advocacy Campaign Strategy Planning.

Steps	Why	What (Tools)
Landscape mapping and definition of the unique point of engagement (UPE)	To understand the position of the issue, gain broad view on the stakeholders and identify main opportunities for the campaign.	Issue mapping and materiality analysis (index) SWOT analysis Design thinking exercises Likely and unlikely scenario development
Setting up impact and ambition level	To define realistic goals for the campaign and identify needed steps and resources at a high level.	Logic model (logical log framework) SMART goal setting Cross-team alignment
Context analysis	To gain in-depth knowledge about the links between the issue and other global issues, define the focus and inform content development.	Foresight and development of the future scenarios PESTEL analysis International policy mapping and analysis
Target audience identification and opinion tracking	To identify those who matter in the issues, their agenda and their positions.	Perception audit Audience survey Omnibus survey Pooling Focus groups Influencer mapping on social and traditional media Media content and discourse analysis

Table 5.2. (*Continued*)

Steps	Why	What (Tools)
Platform identification	To build omni-channel integrated strategy linking offline and online engagement. To decide on the focus of the campaign and inform budget allocation decisions.	Global calendar review and alignment International events and platforms review Channel content analysis
Definition of the main communication tactic	To define key communication approach within the advocacy framework.	Alignment of the activities Creative and design thinking Creative bootcamp
Development of strategic narrative	To ensure close connection between the campaign content and needs to the stakeholders.	Discourse review Messaging house Cross-link between discourse, narrative and organizational objectives Definition of the campaign brand personality (tone, character)
Creative and user-first content development	To put the target audiences in the focus of the campaign and connect with their issues and needs.	One pager White papers Position papers Infographics Video production
Measurement and evaluation protocol	To monitor implementation progress and adjust communications tactics.	Barcelona principles AMEC valid model for communication evaluation
Engagement calendar and campaign plan	To bring focus and accountability positioning campaign in the context of external landscape developments and changes.	GANTT chart RACI model

5.4.   Checklist for Advocacy Strategy Development

There are several considerations which are "must be thought through" elements in campaign design and development.

- Is an overall outcome of the campaign clearly defined? Is it measurable?
- Do we have a Plan B in case the campaign doesn't deliver intended results?
- Who has an influence over decisions critical for campaign success?
- Why our organization embarks on this particular campaign? What is our motivation? Could we achieve our results differently?
- Do we have the resources needed in order to achieve campaign goals?
- What are the perceptions and facts around the issue among general public and key stakeholders?
- Does our narrative provide a platform to influence an overall discourse?
- Where is the issue now and how do we see it evolving?
- Which platforms are the most effective for our campaign?
- What success look like and do we have the means to measure it?
- Is our advocacy team equipped with the skills to embark on this campaign?

5.5.   Discussion and Further Research

This model serves as a toolkit for development of the advocacy campaign concepts and their execution. It aims to help advocacy professionals and researchers to look at strategy development process in a structured manner. It would be interesting to use this systemic approach in further analysis of the advocacy campaign both on a development and conceptual side. The researchers can also look at the different models within the organizations in terms of advocacy strategy development and planning processes. Then it would be fascinating to benchmark different models of strategy and campaign development against their future efficiency and effectiveness. This would allow for the creation of a "best practice" in terms of advocacy strategy design.

At the same time, there is very limited to no research on the design of the advocacy function and its organizational gravity center within the organizations. Which organizational models are most effective? How does advocacy function design impact subsequent performance of the campaigns? What is the best model for advocacy function design: centralized (for alignment and efficiency) or matrix (for cross-organizational involvement)? How does the organizations define their success in advocacy and which measures are used to report on the progress? All these pertinent questions could be answered in the future research helping to understand further the organizational aspects of advocacy profession.

5.6.   Conclusions

Advocacy campaigns run internationally are often very complex projects involving many parties. Having project management discipline and methodology to guide their development can prove itself very effective in ensuring the right focus and alignment of the activities within the organization. Changes in the landscape require new approaches to influence and engagement strategies. Identifying those who matter and engaging them in a meaningful advocacy journey through the channels is paramount to achieve desired outcomes. It is important to remember that the landscape is constantly changing and evolving. The lines of influence are shifting as well as potential impact of the individuals and organizations on an issue. This means that advocacy approaches required flexibility and agility. The power and influence are evolving, and the engagement approach should be evolving as well. Oftentimes, there is a tendency to think about strategy development process from a linear perspective. Yet, advocacy development is circular – we need to have flexibility to come back and adjust tactics all along during the implementation process. The 10-step model for campaign strategy development aims to support structural thinking around campaign planning. It seeks to provide structure and discipline to the engagement process.

Key Takeaways

- *There are more advocacy campaigns than ever. Organizations that were not present in the campaigning seek to enhance their networks of influence and embark on advocacy journeys. It means that the landscape is saturated. In turn, this requires advocacy professionals to be precise in identifying those who matter.*
- *Influence lines are not static. Organizations that are influential might lose their influence, or interest on an issue. As a result, foresight and research into the future possible and unlikely scenarios are effective tools to bring together advocacy strategies.*
- *Campaign strategy development is a fine balance between structure and creativity. Planning and defining of the action steps needs to be paired with a strong creative idea having potential to engage multiple types of stakeholders and influencers.*
- *Cross-connectivity between the various actors means there is even more need for alignment between activities in the advocacy campaigns. The 10-step model for campaign planning is a tool that can be used by the campaign planners to focus planning efforts and create a consistency in the advocacy efforts.*
- *What is not measured, is not getting done. Campaign implementation frameworks need to include strong focus on measurement of the outcomes of the campaign. This goes far beyond reporting on the activities and reach (output). Conversely, it needs looking at what change did the campaign deliver in terms of influencing final decisions.*

Chapter 6

Shaping and (Re-)defining the Discourse: Content Marketing in Advocacy

6.1. Introduction

Advocacy, communications, and marketing management have long been dominated by a channel perspective. The professionals working on external engagement of the organizations were mainly focused on developing channel strategies.
This was accentuated by a rise in importance of the social media. However, the
communications channels are the delivery mechanisms to convey the messages
and positions of the organizations and companies. Therefore, the content posted
or shared at these channels is increasingly important. The focus on the content
means also focus on the target audience's needs. Forcefully, focusing first on the
channels reduces the focus on the end aims of engagement and as a result loses
sight from the business and organizational objectives. Conversely, applying
"channel agnostic" view allows us to get managerial focus where it should be –
what are the aims that we want to achieve and how best to reach the right target
audiences to achieve them. The shift of focus was first personalized by a rise in
the visibility of storytelling techniques and strategies in communications and
marketing. Storytelling techniques are also increasingly used in the advocacy
and lobbying strategies.

Nowadays, the organizations talk more about strategic (or transformative)
narratives while designing their advocacy and communications approaches. This
change is important from a conceptual perspective. It is no longer about the
"what" of communications or about delivery mechanism – stories. The focus
shifts toward the strategic impacts of narratives on the organization. The narratives can have a transformative role for the organizations as they help to shape
the external discourse around the organization. The discourse in turn influences
the views and opinions of the key stakeholders, who have an impact on the business operations. It is interesting to see that while the concept of strategic narratives gains momentum in management science and practice, the discourse still
remains more on a domain of scientific research.

Sociology and cultural anthropology together with the other social sciences
have studied the role of discourse in shaping opinions and behaviors for over
50 years (Charaudeau, 2005; Katz & Lazersfeld, 1955). The discourse is sometimes understood as a combination of all the acts of communication (including
direct and written communications) as well as personal and organizational ones
(Charaudeau, 2005). However, from a social perspective, the post-modernist

view on discourse as expressed by Michel Foucault, for example, seems to be more pertinent from an advocacy perspective. In this view the role of discourse goes beyond the acts of communication and understanding. The discourse is in fact the act of constituting the knowledge (Foucault, 1969). The discourse becomes an invisible force that guides not only perceptions and opinions, but also actions of an organization. In this view, the discourse is seen beyond communications and its impacts are much more overarching. The discourse defines what individuals and organizations know and on a second layer what they think and feel about a given subject or issue. As a result, the discourse has a direct impact on the actions of individuals. It shapes not only their opinions, but also creates the knowledge and perceptions around them. Shaping and influencing the discourse was always one of the main tasks of the communications and engagement professionals (Cornelissen, 2013).

One of the main roles of advocacy is to shape an operating environment of a company or organization (see Chapters 1 and 2). Shaping the discourse is one of the most visible ways engagement disciplines support organizations in achieving their goals. Recently, we observe a growing number of organizations talking about discourse and narratives in the context of their communication strategies. There is a certain level of "fashion" involved where strategic narrative became a trendy term to describe the value communication disciplines bring to the organizations. Before, many organizations were talking about storytelling and story shift. This story shift was supposed to describe the changing role of corporate communications function. The function that evolved from being focuses on disseminating information about the company and its activities to become a function managing and animating engagement with the various stakeholders. However, storytelling was just a delivery mechanism. As a result, a very strong focus on stories makes communication function appear pretty tactical and less linked to an overall business strategy of the company, or organization. Focus on strategic narrative on the contrary is much more strategically driven and focuses external engagement on the value external engagement brings in terms of business and key stakeholder relationship building.

The channels of communication managed by the organizations are the tools that can be used to shape the discourse. At the same time, digital and social media strategies are frequently driven by the channel strategies. The activities and content are then created to "fill" the social media and digital accounts. This tactical usage of the channels limits the relevance of external engagement in influencing the opinions and behaviors of the target audiences. It tends to also focus on communicating the activities and actions of an organization. However, this approach is far from being effective as it hides the "why" of communications. Since Simon Sinek published "Start with why," more and more companies look for their raison d'être and formulate it in the way they engage with internal and external audiences (Sinek, 2009). The need to focus on the "why" is accompanied by a stronger focus of organizations on their purpose. This all follows the shift described in the Chapter 2. Growing expectations toward the companies from a social perspective accentuate the need to communicate more than the information about the products and services. Influencing the discourse is the key for organizational engagement. However, this is not frequently visible in their external communications. Indeed, instead of communicating the organizational "why," companies tend to produce content to fill their channels. As a result, the audiences are confronted with even more information. Information that they have difficulty processing (see Chapter 2 on information overload).

This chapter presents the causes (based on the perceived need of companies to "be out there") and consequences of this challenge, together with a proposed model for content management. This model focuses on the content's relevance to the audiences as opposed to be a mere reflection of the organizational structures. It also provides practical guidelines for content development and approval models that empower organizations to build efficient content strategies.

6.2. Discourse Analysis Research and Impacts on Advocacy

The research on discourse and acts of language as been around for over a century. The semiotic school of De Saussure placed the acts of language in the context of symbolic meaning (1916). Looking at the essence of semiotic theory, it links closely the language and the objects with their cultural meanings (De Saussure, 1916). The other main schools of thought around communications and discourse included:

- structuralism (focusing on the structures of the language and describing acts of language in terms of the interconnection between the elements);
- acts of language (seeing language as a driver of social action and looking for the links between the language and physical events);
- semiotics (looking at the language from a symbolic perspective); and
- post-modernism (seeing language and discourse as the structures driving social behaviors and controlling social meaning).

With all the differences, one thing was common for all these schools of thought. They were placing the language and communication in the center of social integration (Charaudeau, 2005). They all considered communication and engagement acts in a broader social and cultural context. As a result, the language and communication were seen as the transformative tools, which can have far more in-depth organizational impacts. From the perspective of advocacy, it is useful to define the key terms, which are used when talking about development of organizational strategic narratives.

- Discourse − external to the company. Discourse is what is said about an issue in the socioeconomic context. An organization cannot control the discourse but can seek to influence it.
- Narrative − strategic structure designed by a company to communicate with its stakeholders. The narrative needs to link company essence (vision, mission, values) with its purpose and provide a platform for a proactive engagement with the external stakeholders.

- Storytelling – the delivery mechanism for corporate narratives. Stories allow organizations to connect with their target audiences in an engaging manner. They also play an important role in humanizing the brand personality of an organization.

As per the definition above, the discourse is influenced by multiple facts that are beyond control of a company or organization. It is closely linked with the cultural and socioeconomic context in which an organization operates. It is also influenced by the other actors having a stake in the issue (Charaudeau, 2005). Finally, it is also influenced by the other issues which are connected (more on the interconnection between the issues in Chapter 2). This holistic approach ensures that the organization is actually positioned in the center of the influencing factors that impact its ability to shape the discourse. In addition, it is important to remember that public perceptions are heavily influenced by the external events impacting the framing of the issues (Fairhurst & Sarr, 1996). Also, the importance of the issues for stakeholders is dynamic. Priming is a communication technique looking at influencing the relative importance of the issues for the target audiences (Weingarten et al., 2016).

Getting the strategic narrative right requires organizations to look back at their purpose and corporate essence (including vision, mission, and the values). This work brings communication back to the center of the business strategy. In the process, a development of the strategic narrative can also play a transformative role for an organization (Denning, 2006). By focusing on what really matters for an organization from a strategic perspective, the strategic narrative work can spark a need and desire for a change within the organization (Figure 6.1).

Figure 6.1.   Strategic Narrative Components.

6.3.   Social Media Communications – Shaping Opinions in an Ever-changing Environment

The role of social media in communications and marketing has been studied for over 10 years now. There are numerous case studies focusing on how social media delivered to various organizational objectives. The main axis of research around social media can be summarized as following:

- case studies of the social media campaigns (Sashi, 2012);
- inclusion of the social media into overall marketing and communications mix (Couldry, 2012; Perrin, 2015);
- grassroots campaigns and social movements originating from social media (Fenton & Barassi, 2011);
- consumer engagement in digital (Wagner & Hollenbeck, 2015);
- political communications and political campaigning on digital and social channels (Rainie, Smith, Schlozman, Brady, & Verba, 2012; Gil de Zúñiga et al., 2012); and
- organization of social media strategic management within the companies and organizations (Kaplan & Haenlein, 2010; Kietzmann, Hermkens, McCarthy, & Silvestre, 2011).

The last focus area was relatively less studied in the communications and marketing science. There have been some researches from management studies, but they looked at social media and digital from a more content and channel perspective. There is no doubt that social media impact the way advocacy and engagement campaigns are designed and executed. An opportunity for the companies and organizations to reach their audiences directly offers a myriad of possibilities to build resilient relationships with the stakeholders. Not relying on the media and external channels to reach target audiences allows companies and organizations to take ownership of their landscape. At the same time, it increases demand for transparency coming from the stakeholders and general public alike.

6.4.   Digital Advocacy – Concept with a Powerful Potential

Digital advocacy is frequently reduced to the social media engagement and social media campaigning. Yet, digital offers many more opportunities for organizations to shape the agenda of their stakeholders. Effective digital engagement strategies, of course, look at using Facebook, Twitter, Instagram, and other channels. However, they also look at "traditional" websites and other delivery channels in order to effectively reach defined stakeholder groups.

Furthermore, big data offer enormous amounts of insight about opinions and behaviors of the target audiences. For instance, the advocacy campaigns focusing on behavioral change get much better evidence of their actual effectiveness through connected devices than declarations of the target audiences. Yet it poses a question of data privacy and data protection. These define new challenges in terms of engagement that are faced by the international advocacy campaigns. The legal frameworks related to data collection and data usage vary from one market to another. Complying with these oftentimes conflicting regulations complicates further a design of digital advocacy strategies.

It is crucial to look at digital advocacy from a holistic perspective. The role of digital is not limited to running campaigns and channels nor key influencer engagement. It is about creating an architecture in which key messages can be conveyed in a manner that engages target audiences in a meaningful dialog and exchange.

6.4.1. Content Types and Content Performance in Terms of Engagement

Talking about content marketing and storytelling usually brings to mind an image of a written text, which is not necessarily the only vehicle for engagement in digital. Moreover, the current content strategies look at variety of delivery mechanisms to reach the audiences. More and more often we talk about "social-first formats." Several types of content listed below are the basic formats used in the digital campaigns:

- *Visuals* – messages that are accompanied by visual collateral gather higher message retention rate as well as higher engagement. It is important to design the campaign taking into account visual aspect and not only textual storytelling. The campaign thinking process should include the visual aspect and brand personality. Currently, still very few advocacy campaigns are built around mood boards and other advertisement-based implementation methods.
- *Infographics* – advocacy campaigns frequently are based on sharing the knowledge and data. Infographics are a good vehicle to convey these messages. However, with an increased usage of infographics there is a certain level of saturation among the key target audiences. While designing infographics, it is crucial to consider the messages which we want to convey and structure visual aspect accordingly. It is also important to ensure an interactivity for the web-based infographics as static formats limit their usage to mere presentation of the data.
- *Videos* – social media platforms evolve toward multimedia platforms which gather all the content types and all the content needs that the target audiences might have. As such there is a clear preference toward the video that is a great way to attract attention in the short spans of attention that people give toward the content. However, digital videos need to be "made for purpose." The audience decide within the first six seconds whether they will continue watching or not (see, Chapter 5). This means that both the content, but also the structure needs to be thought through and designed in this manner.
- *Stories and "perishable content"* – social media platforms increasingly focus on the content formats that have a limited shelf-life. Starting with Snapchat

and following with Instagram Stories the formats which are supposed to disappear within a given time-frame gain popularity among the users. They also create a need of urgency which in turn is supposed to lead people toward digital platforms and make them return. The usage of perishable content is still limited in advocacy, yet it gives a great possibility to keep audiences engaged and create a daily habit of interaction with the campaign content. In addition, perishable content formats allow for a greater engagement with the message and organization.

- *Live streaming* – social media creates an expectation of "here and now." Therefore, live streaming and live engagement gains popularity. It helps brands and organizations to create direct links with their target audiences. It also focuses the attention and engagement in the moments crucial from an organizational development perspective. However, while using live streaming it is important to bear in mind that not all the formats of events are designed for live streaming. From a digital perspective there is a requirement of the live and novelty component paired with a need to deliver unique content and context not achievable by other means (for instance on-demand watching).

The list of the digital advocacy formats above was focused on those which are ascending and yet frequently forgotten or not taken into consideration while designing advocacy campaigns. From an organizational perspective, the number of available formats and opportunities of engagement means an increased need for focus. The focus allows us to choose the ones which are the most effective and efficient for a defined campaign goal. Content strategy should not be limited to "ticking the box" exercise which in turn leads to usage of all the types of content. Instead, the approach should always be target audience centric and focused on the needs and preferences target audiences have toward respective distribution means.

6.4.2. Building Structure for an Effective Social Media Advocacy

A multiplication of the content formats paired with limited resources of the advocacy teams requires a strong organizational structure to support digital engagement activities. An effective digital engagement team is composed of the professionals with varied backgrounds covering multiple areas of communication and marketing. There are several types of talent needed in order to execute a digital advocacy campaign successfully. Each of the types needs a certain skill-set in order to deliver their set of tasks (Table 6.1).

Of course, not each advocacy campaign team nor each organizational advocacy team will have all of these individuals in-house. However, it is useful to think about the tasks related to a campaign and distribute them accordingly within an existing team. Some of them might end up being outsourced. For this reason, the list of tasks and skills is very practical as it allows us to identify the gaps in the current team structure and act accordingly.

Table 6.1. Digital Advocacy Team Composition.

Function	Tasks	Skills
Strategist	Define campaign goals and objectives	Knowledge of the issue and international landscape
	Analyze target audiences and define the audiences to target	Ability to transform ideas into action
	Define the stakeholders of the campaign and map who influences them	Understanding of the 360° communication and marketing landscape
	Develop high level campaign approach with strategic cornerstones and influence levers	Capacity to structure engagement and oversee implementation
Campaign manager	Develop campaign plan and timeline	Project management
	Coordinate internal and external stakeholders	Knowledge of the channels on tactical level
	Ensure timely development of campaign collateral	Understanding of the landscape and stakeholders
	Post or coordinate posting of campaign content	Quantitative skills related to budget and analytics
	Develop campaign GANTT chart and follow up the execution	Understanding of the reporting best practices
	Monitor results and adjust the campaign accordingly	Ability to translate insights into content
	Report results to both internal and external stakeholders	
	Manage the budgets and approve campaign expenses	
Media planner	Develop media plan and media budget	Knowledge of the trends in digital engagement
	Allocate budgets for paid activities	In-depth knowledge of the channels and paid solution
	Design channel strategy to reach target audiences in the most efficient manner	Understanding of the audiences
	Follow up with the budget spend and adjust campaign tactics accordingly	Agility to adjust the campaign planning in the view of results

Table 6.1. (*Continued*)

Function	Tasks	Skills
Community manager	Listen to the campaign and competitive landscape	Social and engagement skills
	Build listening insights into the daily engagement patters	Focus on detail and understanding of issue escalation
	Engage with the key digital audiences on a daily and on-going basis	Strong writing skills
		Ability to multitask
	Build relationships with the key external and internal stakeholders	Agility to adjust to the changing landscape
	Manage interaction and engagement	
	Analyze the key themes in the discourse in the issues around campaign	
Content manager — digital creative writer	Create campaign content and stories in line with the organizational and campaign narratives	Writing skills for digital content
		Ability to translate facts into the stories
	Develop stories bank for the campaign which would be used in the engagement	Understanding of the link between textual and visual collateral
	Perform story-mining within the organization and among its partners to develop written collateral	Creativity
		Understanding of the strategic narratives and their role in shaping the content
Videographer	Design visual concept for the video collateral of the campaign	Video editing skills
		Ability to distill complex concepts into short formats
	Develop storyboards for the videos	Storytelling skills
	Coordinate filming and development of the campaign videos	Ability to create "social-first" formats
	Cut the videos according to the agreed scenarios	
	Repurpose video content for various types and lengths	

Table 6.1. (*Continued*)

Function	Tasks	Skills
Designer	Design campaign mood board and visual identity	Creativity
	Develop visual collateral to support campaign messaging and campaign material	Ability to create "social-first" formats
	Coordinate development of visual assets such as pictures (coordinate with photographers)	Understanding of the link between visual and storytelling
Analyst	Analyze the campaign and issue landscape and identify risks and opportunities	Knowledge of digital platform and channel analytics
	Identify the influencers and key tactics to reach them	Ability to translate data into insights
	Manage key performance indicators (KPI) framework and monitor campaign results	Understanding of the campaign issue and campaign landscape
	Develop campaign reports focusing on actionable insights	Reporting skills – adaptation of the data into actionable insights

6.4.3.　Social Media Channels – Role and Function in Advocacy

While we argue that the channels should not be the driver of engagement, an understanding of characteristics of each of the main social media channels helps to build an engagement strategy aligned with the expectations of stakeholders. Interestingly, organizations rarely think about their target audiences as the users of certain platforms. Instead, they tend to talk about a stakeholder's audience. This is especially true for international organizations and b2b companies (Cornelissen, 2013). These companies tend to talk about their audiences as "b2b or stakeholder audience." This special audience is supposed to have content and engagement needs that are significantly different to anyone else – expecting long in-depth analysis full of data on every single communication channel including digital. This can have very negative impact on quality and types of content these organizations end up producing.

Also, each of the social media channels has its own characteristics both in terms of its audience and content requirements, which make it unique. Therefore, the advocacy strategy should take these characteristics into account and build an engagement plan accordingly. Of course, there is also a need to be bespoke and to understand well the audiences of a particular organization. However, some of the characteristics and tendencies are almost semi-universal.

Facebook – serves in advocacy campaigns to engage larger audiences. It is a prime channel for raising awareness and driving behavioral change in the wider group. While the usage of Facebook is decreasing in some demographic groups, it is still the most dominant channel. In several developing countries Facebook remains the most used social media channel (Brandwatch, 2019). Thanks to advanced advertisement tools Facebook is also very effective for targeted campaigning in very specific demographic groups.

Twitter – allows connecting directly with the target audiences and having digital conversations. Thanks to its high usage by the journalists, Twitter is a good channel to disseminate the news and support media relations activities.

Instagram – has a younger and more engaged audience. It is also highly based on visual and perishable content. This makes it a good channel for wider audience awareness campaigns. With growing importance of the stories and feedback mechanisms (such as gamification), Instagram is increasingly useful in deepening engagement with the target audiences.

LinkedIn – due to its professional nature it is a great tool to disseminate the knowledge and thought leadership material targeting informed audiences. In addition, LinkedIn is very effective in profiling organizational leaders and campaign experts especially in the niche subjects. In the recent years, LinkedIn started moving toward a multimedia hub allowing individuals to build their thought leadership profiles.

Snapchat – a great channel to engage a wide audience from Generation Z. It is crucial to create the content made for purpose and following the channel requirements in order to generate impact on the key target audiences.

YouTube – for long it was considered by many organizations as an archive and repository of video content. However, YouTube with its own influencers – YouTubers – is considered again as a channel on its own right, which requires proper mapping and content strategy. It can be also used effectively for live streaming events, etc.

Flickr – often used as a repository for the pictures and campaign content for the external stakeholders and journalists (Table 6.2).

6.4.4.   Key Tactics to Leverage Paid Solutions in Digital Advocacy

Advocacy and public affairs professionals have been reluctant toward introduction of the paid solutions in their digital strategies. Growing competition for attention among the audiences paired with social media companies reducing possibilities for an organic reach made paid solutions more widely accepted. There are still some opinions (especially in the NGO and public sector) that using social media paid amplification poses ethical challenges in the relationship between the organization and its audience. It also raises a question about

Table 6.2. Social Media Channel Overview.

Channel	Target Audiences	Content
Facebook	General public	Short videos
	Segmented demographics of general public, or wider stakeholder group	Visuals
		Live videos
Twitter	Journalists	News
	Analysts	Announcements
	Experts	Polls
	Influencers	
LinkedIn	Informed stakeholder public	Thought leadership
		Interviews
		Articles
Instagram	General public	Short videos
	Lifestyle influencers	Pictures
YouTube	General public	Videos
		Live videos
Snapchat	Generation Z General public	Short perishable stories

relationship between an organization and its audience (Lipschultz, 2018). However, an overall acceptance toward using paid amplification on social media is growing across all sectors.

It is perceived to be relatively "easy" to manage social media paid campaigns. The interface is user-friendly and relatively intuitive and targeting tools provided by the social media platforms. Also, the required budgets are comparatively (with other types of advertisement) low. This all gives an impression that everyone can successfully manage digital paid campaigns. However, these campaigns are no different to any other media campaigns and require professional media planning. Even more so, given the depth of analytics about the target audiences that is available.

First of all, it is important to distinguish between boosting of the posts and creating digital advertising campaigns. The first amplifies the messages posted by an organization on its social media channels ensuring impressions among its followers and beyond. The latter means creating specific advertisement formats designed for paid amplification. In this case the targeting options are even more precise. While it would be possible to write a book about the management of paid digital campaigns, there are some considerations that are universal:

A/B testing – best practice doesn't exist or is not necessarily replicable. The organizations need to know what works for them and design the content and targeting which works with their campaign strategy. Checking performance of the call to action and visual aspect in the context of campaign allows to focus the resources better.

Audience building – knowing who the target audiences of the campaign are is crucial for success of any paid activities. Social media platforms also allow to expand these audiences toward their imminent circle. This helps to enhance the reach of the messages.

Cross-channel amplification – as stated above different digital channels help to reach different audiences. Having this consciousness and building the campaign around this helps to ensure the right targeting and enhances audience experience by providing the content that matters.

6.4.5.   *Grassroots Movements and Social Media*

Interconnection between digital engagement and advocacy is visible particularly in the context of grassroots movements which used digital engagement as a leverage to spread their message. One of the recent and most visible examples was the "MeToo" movement which allowed people to raise awareness about the issue of sexual harassment of women in the work space on a global scale. On top of an important number of high-profile men who were denounced and legal action that followed; the movement created a change in perception and led to several changes in the legal systems penalizing further harassment acts. The other example of interconnection between digital mobilization and offline actions are the "climate strikes" in which students communicated through social media in order to organize the protests. Again, this movement put again climate action on the stakeholder agenda and influences the policy discussions on the subject.

The interconnection between the online mobilization and offline action becomes the most effective advocacy vehicle. Digital allows us to reach more people in an unprecedented speed; however, pure digital mobilization doesn't drive behavioral change. This is achieved through action that happens offline. The two need to remain synergetic and feed to each other. Otherwise, digital engagement would be limited solely to the social media discussion.

6.5.   Content Marketing – Applying Theory into Practice

Content marketing has become a sort of a buzz word used for any marketing activities, which include creation of the collateral (textual or visual). When managed properly, the content marketing can be a very effective tool in engaging diverse target audiences. To manage content marketing properly, the organizations need to create structures supporting these activities (Holliman & Rowley, 2014; Pulizzi & Barrett, 2009; Rowley, 2008). In fact, focus on the content marketing and thought leadership brings external engagement functions of the organization closer together. In some organizations this closer link is supported by creation of a dedicated structure focusing on driving external engagement.

6.5.1. Organizations as Broadcasters

Direct access to the target audiences means that the organizations don't need to rely on traditional media and journalists. However, they still need to create the content that is attractive and engaging from the point of view of those who they target. Consequently, the organizations become broadcasters on their own and create channels, which would be traditionally developed by the media organizations (European Communication Monitor, 2018). Some of the organizations go a step further and create thought leadership platforms open for external contributions. This approach requires editorial skills beyond creation of the content and coming closer to actual journalistic work.

6.5.2. Content Hubs and New Ways of Perceiving Corporate Communications Channels

Many organizations struggle in attracting the audiences to return to their channels and website in particular. The solution for that could be creation of the content hub. The most known and considered for several years as the example is the one developed by General Electric. Their approach put thought leadership and engagement in the center of content marketing strategy. The content has been developed on a regular basis and repurposed across the channels. Yet, the company kept the central website hub which combined the contributions and linked to the social media channels. Several other global organizations followed similar pattern. As stated, before this fundamentally changes the role and function of those who manage communications in the organizations. They no longer create the content to pitch to the external channels. Quite the contrary, they produce and disseminate content on the channels they manage. The content published on the hub is then disseminated and promoted through other organizational channels such as social media.

6.5.3. Newsroom Concept

The other model for managing engagement from an organizational perspective is based on a newsroom concept. In this model an organization creates a structure for listening, content development and engagement (Working, 2018). Basically, the role of communications department is translated into the media organization. Therefore, the communications professionals act as journalists working in the medium which is their company's digital presence (Working, 2018). This model requires commitment from the organization both in terms of resources and openness to go beyond traditional framework of corporate engagement. The company and organizational newsrooms gain in popularity, and they are a very effective means to manage advocacy campaigns through engagement with multiple stakeholders.

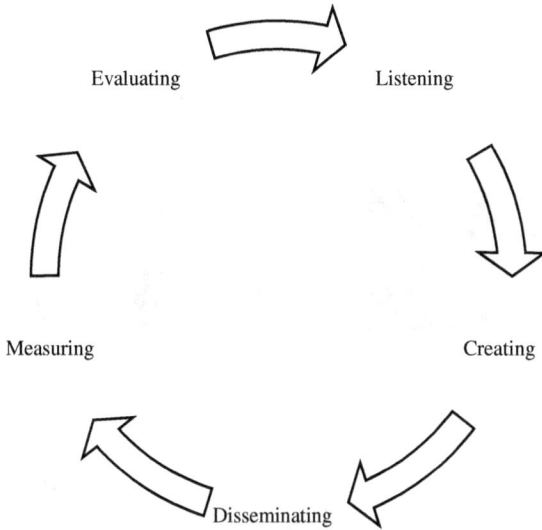

Figure 6.2.   Circular Model of Content Management.

6.5.4. *Structural Model in Content Management*

The content management can be summarized in three phases – listening, development, dissemination. We could also add measurement and evaluation which link back to listening (Figure 6.2).

From an organizational perspective this should be a permanent cycle in which insights from measurement and evaluation fuel the focus of listening, which in turn impacts creation of the content. In reality the organizations have to be constantly active and seek new opportunities of engagement. If not, they risk losing connection with their target audiences and relevance for their agenda.

6.6.   Model for Content-based Advocacy

Organizations build their strategic narratives in order to shape their operating environment. The narrative is in the center of what the organization does in order to build relationships with its stakeholders and influencers. At the same time, there is a need to recognize that the discourse is also shaped by the socio-economic context and general societal trends. It is also shaped by the political agenda and the influencers. Yet the relationship between external discourse and organizational narrative is complex. It is a two-way street where both influence each other and build on each other. The narrative is shaped by the discourse and external environment in the same way as it seeks to influence it. It is also important to recognize that the narrative needs to be anchored in the organizational DNA. This means vision and mission together with the purpose of the organization and the thought leadership positioning of the organization. The delivery mechanism of a corporate narrative is storytelling. This reinforces the

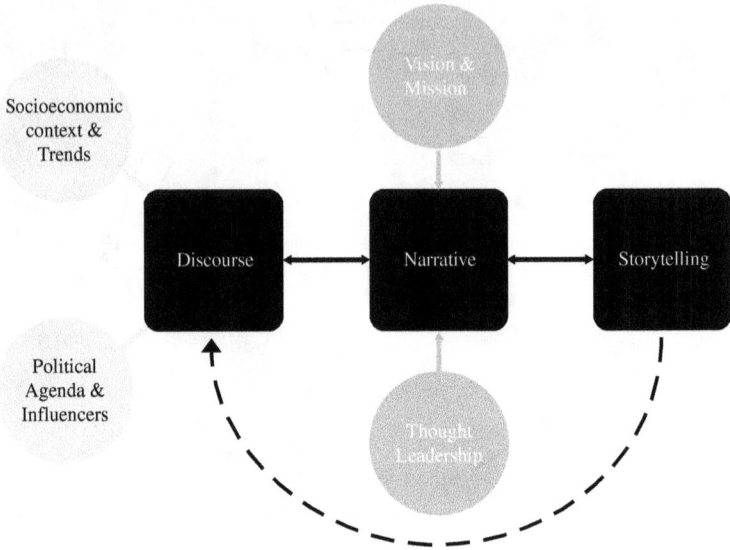

Figure 6.3.   Model for Strategic Narrative Development.

role of the content marketing in the delivery of engagement strategies of the companies and organizations (Figure 6.3).

6.6.1. *Influencing the Discourse*

Influencing external discourse is one of the critical functions of the advocacy strategies. The companies can shape their operating environments by focusing attention of the stakeholders on the elements that are important for them. They also use thought leadership strategies to position themselves as the "go to" organizations for the issues that are impacting their business. This tendency can be seen even more in the case of NGOs and international organizations. They build strategic narratives that become the main tactic to build their unique positioning in the issues they are seeking to address. On top of becoming more influential in their "core business" they also build profile and credibility to strengthen their fundraising efforts. We described before several techniques used to shape the discourse. All of them require organizations to be seen as the knowledge sources by the external actors. In order to achieve that, the organizations need to produce their own and unique content and develop platforms for sharing of this content.

The content in the context of corporate communications was for a long time and still is in many cases reduced to the written content. When communications professionals think about the content, they often associate it with articles, press releases, social media messages, etc. – the written formats. However, with the social media and web 2.0 "re-evolution," it is necessary for organizations to adapt the formats which work best with their audiences. In the current multi-media environment, it is the video that generates the most interaction and engagement (Brandwatch, 2019). Therefore, the thinking about content and content marketing needs to evolve. The organizations which are the most successful in terms of engagement are the ones which become content and news producers.

6.7.   ABCDE for Content Advocacy Strategy

In this chapter we looked already at the various models for content management within an organization as well as a structure of the corporate function responsible for the process. The model we are looking at below seeks to define the process for content advocacy strategy development. We see five stages of the process each feeding into each other and building on each other. In simplistic terms the stages below sum up as following:

Analysis – defining the landscape and looking at what is being said about an issue and an organization.

Benchmark – seeking to define the key difference between our organization and its competitors or similar organizations. This allows us to define a unique point of engagement.

Creativity – building strong story and visual concept encompassing contribution of the organization in the format which is attractive from a stakeholder perspective.

Development – production of the content in the formats which are fitting requirements of the platforms identified as the most effective means to reach target audiences.

Execution – disseminating the assets through organizational and external channels. It is important to always seek new and creative ways of reaching target audiences (Figure 6.4).

6.7.1.   Measurement of Engagement – How to Define the Outcomes

The focus on the content doesn't mean that the measurement of the activities should be output driven. Indeed, this is one of the biggest challenges of the content marketing strategies – focus on produced material and reach as opposed to engagement and added value to the organizational and campaign goals. Referring to the measurement and evaluation model presented in Chapter 1; the ultimate goal of content-driven advocacy remains the same as for any other type of advocacy. It is driving the change and behaviors among stakeholders that ultimately support the organizational goals of the organization. This requires looking at the outcomes of the strategy – what change of perception and consecutive action did the campaign content create (AMEC 2015; Macnamara, 2012).

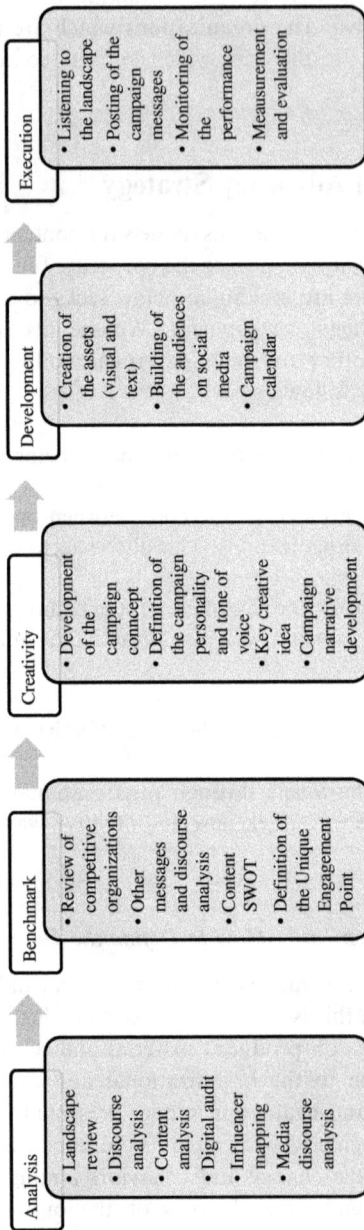

Figure 6.4.   ABCDE Model for Digital Content Marketing.

6.8.   Conclusions

Organizations and companies rethink the way they structure their external engagement. Thanks to social media and digital they increasingly play the role of broadcasters reaching their target audiences directly. This creates a great opportunity to build stronger and more resilient relationships with those who matter for business or organizational success. This also creates a challenge for focus. How to define the audiences that matter? How to build structures which support organizational engagement? Who are the ones that have highest impact on the organizational goals? These questions need to be permanently answered by advocacy and communications professionals. As a result, the external engagement functions of an organization are more and more often grouped under one leadership (Communication Monitor, 2019). This helps to align the priorities, streamline resources, and ensure focus on the organizational outcomes.

At the same time, the organizations need to review the way they manage their channels. Perceived simplicity of usage of digital platforms means that many organizations embark on social media engagement strategies. This means that even more content circulates and targets, oftentimes, the same stakeholders. As a result, it is imperative to use the content formats that are developed for purpose and structure engagement around unique value proposition.

In the future, it will be interesting to see how virtual reality and augmented reality developed content impacts the way organizations structure their content strategies. This will pose new challenges that will need to be addressed both at content and organizational levels.

Key Takeaways

- *Influencing discourse means developing the narratives which have potential to engage various groups of stakeholders. At the same time, it requires a good understanding of the content preferences among the target audiences. ABCDE (analysis, benchmark, creativity, development, execution) approach allows us to get full benefit from these changes.*
- *External engagement strategies of the organizations used to be built around communications and influence channels. This reduced their influencing potential as organizations focused on "how to use the channels" and not "which channels are the most effective for the goals they have."*
- *Narrative shift in corporate communications raises awareness about an importance of shaping and influencing the discourse by the companies and organizations. Linking communications structure with the organizational objectives helps to create a strategic link and elevate the role of engagement within the organizational structures.*
- *Focusing on content marketing requires from organizations to build appropriate structures for developing ideas and transferring them into engaging collateral. This redefines the role of communication department*

which becomes a producer of the content as opposed to being a broker of
information pitching the content ideas to media.
* As attention spans of the target audiences are shorter, the requirements
  toward content formats are changing. Nowadays, effective content marketing is based on visual and video content as opposed to purely written
  communications is the past. This requires new skills from communications
  and advocacy professionals. It also means that holistic 360° strategies are
  more effective in achieving desired organizational outcomes.

Chapter 7

Doing Good and Being Good or Simply Getting It Right – Corporate Crisis and Defensive Advocacy

7.1. Introduction

Managing reputation becomes a key function of corporate communications, marketing, and public affairs departments for many organizations (Bochenek & Blili, 2013). Corporate reputation can be considered as one of the most important intangible corporate assets (Forman & Argenti, 2005). There are several studies that draw parallels between the "good" corporate reputation and overall performance of an organization (De la Fuente Sabate & de Quevedo Puente, 2003). The benefits of good corporate reputation are relatively obvious – from employee attraction and retention to stakeholder support and consumer preference. Frequently, the studies focused on the moment when reputation is lost during the crisis (Coombs, 2007, 2014). Several studies analyzed a positive correlation between "good" reputation and overall performance of the company in financial terms (De Quevedo Puente, de la Fuente-Sabate, & Delegado-Gracia, 2007). This was especially visible during the crisis when good reputation allows companies to activate external support for an organization (Schnietz & Epstein, 2005). Often these studies were non-conclusive, or presented conflicting results depending on geographical context and definition of what reputation stands for. This on its own shows the challenge related to reputation management from an organizational perspective. If it is impossible to prove beyond any doubt that a positive corporate reputation contributes to the business results, then some executive might say "why to bother at the end?"

Ethics in communications has become increasingly important (Crane, 2008; Wood, 2010). Organizations are judged by whether they do what they say they will (Helm, Garnefeld, & Tolsdorf, 2009; Melo & Garrido-Morgado, 2011). With the ultimate transparency quest amplified by social media sharing culture, it is nearly impossible to hide anything from the public eye. Past corporate crises were often triggered by events (accidents, terrorist attacks, closures of the plants, etc.). Nowadays, the causes of the crises are frequently internal (corporate misconduct, labor issues, etc.). For instance, the organizational culture and internal systems can be a root cause of reputational issues like it was in the case of Uber. Moreover, external events and incidents play the role of triggers, uncovering the practices that existed within the organization long before the crises occurred (Fearn-Banks, 2011).

This chapter looks at the nature of communications and reputational crises. It also looks at the impacts that corporate crises have on the organizations. It compares the spread of the crises both on social and traditional media. This comparison brings to light the changing dynamics of the communications/ reputational crises and the way they need to be managed.

We also develop a concept of defensive advocacy and showcase the difference between crisis communications and defensive advocacy. The two are very similar in terms of the tools used but differ in the final aims. The aim of crisis communications is to bring organization to the recovery phase and "move on." Defensive advocacy is much more complex as it deals with the long-term issues. As a consequence, defensive advocacy requires much a more analytical approach and in-depth understanding of the operating environment.

7.2.   Crisis Communications – State of Research

Crisis management has been studied for a long time; there are several scientific journals that focus on crisis studies. Crisis communications and reputation management have also been subject of research from multiple perspectives (Coombs, 2014; Fearn-Banks, 2011; Regester & Larkin, 2005). There were more studies focusing on actual crisis management including the communication aspects than the studies looking at the crisis communications management per se. At the same time, for a communications profession crisis management and readiness are some of the key functions in any organization (Coombs, 2014). In addition, the moment when crisis hits an organization is when the corporate communications department becomes the center of gravity for the executive and senior management.

There have been multiple studies focusing on the role and function of the corporate reputation (Melo & Garrido-Morgado, 2011). The loss of reputation is considered to be one of the key risks associated with the corporate crisis or discrepancy between corporate promise and action (Minor & Morgan, 2011; Solomon, 1992; Swoboda & Hirschmann, 2017). Corporate reputation is a multi-variable concept (Argenti, 2004; Barnett et al., 2005; Solomon, 1992).

Understood this way corporate reputation becomes a key corporate asset (Bochenek & Blili, 2013). Also, reputation management becomes an executive C-suite level concern (Agnihotri, 2014; Communication Monitor, 2018). Most importantly, current research looking at key concerns of senior executives showcase that the loss of reputation is one of them (Coombs, 2014). Yet the organizations don't necessarily embrace reputation focused culture in their strategic design.

At the same time, the representation of the corporate reputation in the professional press and publications is frequently reduced to its communications and marketing aspect. This limited view can have very negative impacts on the way reputation is managed within an organization (Agnihotri, 2014). Reduced view on corporate reputation means also reduced investment and in consequence very tactical approach. This tactical approach is often driven by corporate communications. However, as per above definition, the corporate reputation is a multivariable concept and needs to be managed from multiple perspectives and across the organization.

In summary, there are several axes upon which crisis communications have been studied in the past:

- Crisis management and communications aspects of the crisis management – these studies focused on the crisis itself and how organizations managed it. The crisis communications aspect was linked to the recovery phase and business continuity.
- Crisis communications per se as a part of corporate communications portfolio from an organizational perspective – in this case during the crisis the role of communications and connection with stakeholders is crucial.
- Corporate reputation management and the impact of the loss of reputation during the crisis situations – these studies looked at the long-term consequences of the reputational crisis and how they impacted brand perceptions in the long run.

There are several studies that focused on crisis communication. On the contrary, the number of studies focusing on defensive advocacy is very limited. There were also several studies focusing on the impact of a crisis on the actors of the not-for-profit sector. However, very few researchers looked at long-term impact of the issues on the organizational performance and crisis potential from a perspective of proactive advocacy campaign strategy.

7.2.1. Key Concepts and Tools in Crisis Management

Crisis communications and crisis management in general are based around several concepts that are worth defining and clarifying. They range from the pre-crisis, during crisis, and post-crisis communications management. The list below is not exhaustive but provides a good overview of the key concepts impacting the strategic thinking about crisis communications management.

- *Crisis mitigation* – work that an organization does in order to prevent the crisis from happening. This can include materiality analysis, reputation surveys, internal and external issues monitoring. From a managerial perspective, crisis mitigation focuses on the changes that organization does in its operations to solve the issues before they become a crisis.
- *Crisis preparedness* – steps that an organization undertakes in order to respond to the crisis in an effective manner. This includes crisis potential reviews, training, crisis processes development, and internal crisis awareness raising. Again, preparedness processes if managed well can support crisis mitigation and create an internal culture making an organization ready to respond to the inevitable crises.

- *Crisis communications protocol* – collection of material and processes related to crisis management. It frequently takes form of a handbook focusing on scenarios and organizational response to the various types of crisis. It can include hands on response examples. However, more importantly it describes the roles and responsibilities in the crisis and processes that need to be followed. Frequently, crisis communications protocol includes also classification of the crisis according to its severity.
- *Issues management* – actions an organization takes in order to prevent the issues to become the crises. This includes issue identification, monitoring, listening, and reporting. Issues management needs to include internal stakeholders from various functions from across the organization. Oftentimes organizations prepare issue positions, which serve as a guidance to answer stakeholder questions, doubts, and concerns before issues escalate to the crisis level.
- *Reputation management* – strategies and tactics that an organization takes in order to increase its positive reputation among the key stakeholders (including employees) and customers. This includes issues management, crisis mitigation as well as proactive advocacy programs. Often organizations focus their reputation management activities only on the crisis prevention. Yet, proactive advocacy and organizational engagement can positively contribute to the reputation building.
- *Issues monitoring* – series of steps that organization does internally and externally to identify the issues which have a potentially negative impact on the organizational reputation. It also includes monitoring of the regulatory and media developments as well as listening to the landscape. Proactive issues management includes also steps that organization takes to minimize the potential impacts of the identified issues.
- *Materiality index* – tool allowing organizations to prioritize the issues. Typically, materiality index looks at the issues from a perspective of their potential severity for an organization and the likelihood that they can occur. It is a very simple and effective tool helping to focus an organization's attention on the issues that matter the most.
- *Crisis toolkit* – sets of tools that are used by the organization during the crisis. It often includes crisis communications flowchart, composition of the crisis team, roles and responsibilities in terms of external communication. It should also have "ready to go" communications materials such as "dark website," holding statements, Q&As around key issues, and key positions of an organization.
- *Crisis communications* – series of communications steps taken by an organization in management of the crisis. It includes external communications, internal communications, advocacy, and stakeholder management. It is important to strive for an alignment of all the types of communication. Any lack of alignment in the messaging can have damaging impact on the crisis management.
- *Crisis response* – the first reaction of the organization to a crisis. In the social media and digital context, the first response is often the only one that is

remembered by the public. Therefore, it is the most critical moment in the crisis communications management. Again, the crisis response includes the elements that are beyond the remit of corporate communications. For instance, it can include the recall of the product, which obviously has to be communicated properly. However, this business decision cannot be taken by the communications function.

- *Crisis team* – the group of individuals from across the organization who manages the crisis. It needs to include representatives from various business functions: communications, product management, external affairs, legal, human resources, finance. The crisis team takes tactical decisions related to crisis management and communicates them to the organizational senior leadership.
- *Crisis room* – place where the crisis team meets and from which it manages the crisis. Traditionally, it was a physical room. Nowadays, the crisis room might be set up virtually for the teams working across a geographical area. However, a physical place where all crisis management material is printed can prove very useful in the case of cybersecurity-related crises.
- *Stakeholder management* – actions and steps taken during the crisis in order to address the key external stakeholders of the organization. It includes opening of the direct communications channels, in-depth updates, and joint initiatives. In reality, crisis stakeholder management begins well before any crisis.
- *Crisis review* – post-crisis review; of all the steps that were undertaken during the crisis management process. It includes also the lessons learnt and provides recommendations on how to mitigate further crises and improve the processes of crisis management. The documentation of the crisis management is crucial for organizational learning (Coombs, 2014; Regester & Larkin, 2005; Stead & Smallman, 1999). Several researches showcase that the organizations that don't follow proper learning protocols are much more likely to be the subjects of repeated crises (Regester & Larkin, 2005).
- *Crisis learning* – documentation which documents what the organization has learnt during the crisis (Coombs, 2014) This step of post-crisis management is crucial from an organizational learning perspective. The strategic approach to crisis learning supports future crisis mitigation (Coombs, 2014; Regester & Larkin, 2005).

These key tools showcase two main tendencies which need to be taken into account in a communication crisis management. The first one is the importance of preparation and pre-crisis work paired with organizational learning post-crisis. The second is the importance of involvement of all organizational functions in the crisis management process. Effective management of the complex crises requires input from across the organization.

7.2.2. Crisis Communications and Reputation Management

There are several researchers that claim there is a link between crisis communications and reputation management. For example, Coombs points out an importance of communications during crisis management for the recovery phase (Coombs, 2014). At the same time, it is crisis preparedness that defines to what extent an organization is ready to manage a crisis. As seen in several examples of recent crises the reputational damage can be very significant. Looking at the drop of share price of United, BP during their recent crises showcases the correlation between crisis communications and overall view of the company by investors in a short-term perspective.

The way an organization responds in the crisis situation defines its recovery as well as long-term effects of the crisis. Usually, companies and organizations face a similar dilemma while dealing with the crisis. The legal teams push the organization not to take responsibility and protect itself from the court action and risks of paying damages. Therefore, the legal professionals tend to recommend relatively dry and short statements and limited communications and engagement during the crisis. Legal approach to crisis management tends also to be clean of emotions and not necessarily connecting with those who are impacted. Communications professionals tend to present the contrary view and focus more on building and maintaining relationships with the key stakeholders and affected individuals. They would push for a more emotional reaction and are more prone to accept organizational responsibility for an issue.

Several researches show an importance of learning from the crisis situations (Regester & Larkin, 2005; Stead & Smallman, 1999). The organizations learn from crises by documenting the processes and actions and benchmarking them against the procedures. In case the procedures were followed, this might be the point of reflection about the procedures themselves. In case they were not followed, this allows them to review the training and implementation processes within the organization. This learning can only happen if an organization has a clear protocol for documentation of the crises and reporting procedure (Regester & Larkin, 2005). Crisis debrief and lessons learned constitute an internal part of crisis management within the organization (Regester & Larkin, 2005).

7.2.3. Crisis Management in Advocacy Campaigning

Advocacy campaigns are equally impacted by the organizational and communication crises. A busy landscape and multiple stakeholders voicing their opinions and positions mean that the attention spans are limited. Many organizations respond to this challenge by boldness of their positions. Strong messages and bold statements can be a very effective tool to grab attention and connect with the external stakeholders. However, at the same time there is an increased risk of creating conflicts with other organizations. In addition, advocacy campaigns by their nature attract conflicting and competing ideas and campaigns. Some would claim that advocacy campaigning is a permanent crisis management.

The reputation of an organization is what defines whether an advocacy campaign effort will be successful or not. Looking at the recent reputational issues of WWF or Oxfam we can observe that nonprofit sector is under increased scrutiny and therefore crisis readiness is even more crucial. For a long time, there was a perception that NGOs don't need to work on their brand and image as a positive connotation comes from the fact that they "are NGOs." However, with an increased scrutiny the NGOs and international organizations need to work on building and maintaining their corporate image in order to keep a license to operate.

7.3.   Conceptual Model of Crisis Management

All crisis communications management models present a set of commonalities. In principle, they focus on three phases: pre-crisis, actual crisis, post-crisis (Fearn-Banks, 2011; Palttala, Boano, Lund, & Vos, 2012). This is a very good way to structure the thinking about a crisis as it helps to focus on the message that the crisis begins much earlier than when a trigger happens. Issue mapping and identification is the first step in crisis mitigation. Many organizations focus only on the issues directly linked with their operations. However, the crises are much more complex and tend to originate from issues seemingly not linked with the organization directly. As a result, the risk factor identification needs to focus on a broader array of subjects as well as the subjects which are interconnected. Only after in-depth issue mapping can the organization move on to the further stages of crisis preparedness including training and design of the crisis protocols.

Preparedness means also installing a culture of reputation across the organization. The reputation needs to be a concern of everyone in the organization from line employee to the senior executives and CEO. It also includes crisis and issues awareness paired with organizational process of response (Palttala et al., 2012). Defining clear roles and processes allows an organization to be more efficient in the initial response to the crisis. It is important to distinguish between two types of crises sources:

- *Internal* – coming from organizational procedures, culture, or internal incidents. The internal crisis is usually triggered by an event. However, the signs of the issues can be visible well in advance to the crisis. The internally sourced crises present an important risk for organization's reputation as they trigger stakeholder thinking of "they could have done more to avoid it."
- *External* – coming from the external environment of the company. The organization has to respond to external circumstances and manage their impact. These crises are less predictable and require a lot more work in mapping in preparedness to be mitigated. Some external crises might be unavoidable (i.e., natural disasters) and organization can only try to minimize their impacts.

In both cases of the crises the trigger can be related to an issue or incident. The main difference related to the two types of triggers is the speed of spread and long-term impact. The issue-driven crises tend to have more lasting impacts, as the crisis response needs to lead to a deep organizational change beyond working procedures. In some cases, it leads to a questioning of the corporate culture and values. The change of corporate culture requires a concentrated effort from across the organization and has to be seen as a long-term investment.

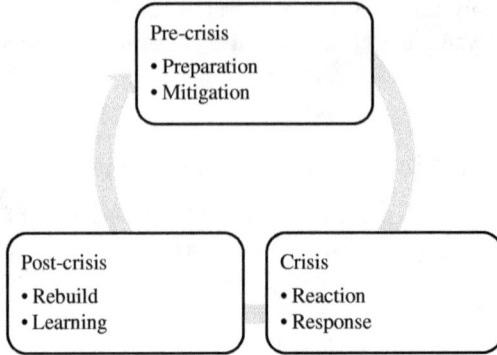

Figure 7.1.   Crisis Communications Management Phases.

There are several distinct phases identified in the crisis management process (Figure 7.1).

During the actual crisis management, the initial reaction is crucial to the way it will unfold and to its long-term consequences. It is also important to recognize the role of preparation and mitigation in the crisis management. When the monitoring protocols work, it is often possible to recognize the early warning signs linked to the issues surrounding an organization.

The role of advocacy in crisis management is not to be underestimated. The stakeholder support and third-party endorsement can help organization go through the crisis and facilitate rebuild of the trust. This support is also important from a business continuity perspective as it helps gain support to continue business operations.

There are several ways in which companies respond to the crisis. Below we present a model which is inspired by an organizational learning theory and looks at how different types of organizations according to their advocacy profiles manage their crisis communications. We look at the five archetypes and types of actions taken for each of the stages in crisis management (see Chapter 2) (Table 7.1).

7.3.1.   Social Media and Crisis – Toward New Cycle

Social media and digital media changed the nature of crisis management by shortening the news cycle. In the past organizations benefited from time to prepare a crisis response. This time got shorter and shorter with advancement of technology.

- Several hours: when organizations needed to respond before the next newspaper edition went into print.
- Some hours: when organizations needed to respond before the next after dinner TV news report.

Table 7.1. Conceptual Model of Crisis Preparedness and Response.

		Sleeping	Delegative	Following	Shaping	Leading
Pre-crisis	Preparation	Limited crisis awareness No training for the teams Lack of crisis procedures in place Ad-hoc and event driven focus and managerial attention toward crisis	Crisis awareness within communications and external relations teams Some crisis processes in place Executive focus on mitigation of the crisis	Crisis awareness within business units both at HQ and regional levels Crisis manual and process in place Training of spokespeople Executive focus on protecting reputation	Crisis awareness at all levels of organization Crisis tools and processes in place Multi-layer training across the organization Executive focus on reputation as business opportunity	Crisis awareness as part of organizational strategy Training at all levels of the organization Management leading by example reputation-driven culture
	Mitigation	Lack of issues mapping Internal awareness of issues driven by incidents No process to map and monitors the issues	Mapping of business-critical issues Internal awareness driven by risk factors Outsourced monitoring of the issues	Mapping of the issues surrounding organization Internal awareness driven by business opportunities Outsources crisis mitigation function	Materiality index developed Internal and external monitoring in place for crisis Regular updates on the issues' developments and risks	Materiality index permanently updated Tools and external support in place to monitor issues from a business intelligence and public affairs perspectives

Table 7.1. (*Continued*)

		Sleeping	Delegative	Following	Shaping	Leading
Crisis	Reaction	Delayed reaction Externally driven messaging Ad-hoc approach Low engagement with stakeholders Blocking statements	Limited reaction Conservative reaction Approach driven by the events Low engagement with stakeholders Protective statements	Fast reaction and holding statements Approach driven by crisis process Engagement limited to the key stakeholders Statements tailored to external developments	Immediate reaction and holding statement Crisis team in place High level of engagement with stakeholders Proactive statements tailored to various stakeholder groups	Immediate acknowledgment of the crisis Strategically driven approach Empathetic messaging connecting with key stakeholder groups
	Response	Ad-hoc developed messaging Not coordinated replies to stakeholders Lack of internal alignment Conflicting messages sent to	Prepared off-the-shelf messaging Centralized and HQ controlled reply to stakeholders Full alignment by centralization	Prepared messages tailored to different scenarios Centralized reply HQ driven with local sensitivities taken into account High degree of centralization	Reply and tone adjusted to the events Centralized reply with coordination across the organization High degree of central coordination	Messaging based on mapped scenarios permanently updated Coordinated reply managed by a crisis team Aligned messages across organizational departments and locations

		Full alignment between communication and legal aspects	Management through crisis team Alignment between legal protection and communication management	Internal management through crisis team Response driven by the events and prospects of reputation rebuild	Internal control through central crisis team Response driven by legal risk mitigation	different stakeholders Internal confusion Legally driven limited response
Post-crisis	Rebuild	Activation programs for external ambassadors Brand recovery supported by the third-party endorsement	Activation programs deigned before the crisis begins Activation of the networks and ambassadors	Activities involving wide selection of stakeholders Activation of organization's influencers and ambassadors	Activities limited to the core stakeholders Activation of networks and external support	Ad-hoc activities Activation of philanthropy or CSR project Activities driven by external events
	Learning	Full documentation of all the steps and events Revision of all processes based on the learnings	Extensive documentation of all the crisis developments and actions Review of the processes and procedures post-crisis	Documentation of the crisis and crisis communications Adjustments to the crisis communications management processes	Documentation of the crisis Debrief and revision of the crisis and mitigation protocol	Limited learning and acknowledgment of the events Lack of debrief and re-alignment of the activities

- Some minutes: when organizations needed to respond before next 24/7 news station report.
- Few minutes: when organizations needed to respond to the social media messages.
- Immediately: when organizations need to respond to the users requiring immediate acknowledgment of the issue and reply.

The cycle is even more shortened by the fact that social media are increasingly consumed on mobile devices. Mobile devices have a high recoding capability meaning that people can share interactive content imminently. Yet, it is traditional media that have the furthest reach both in traditional media landscape and on social media. Therefore, the interconnection between the two is important. United crisis example of offloading a passenger from the plane ("Dr. Dao crisis") is a good proof of this. The social media messages including videos of the passenger dragged off an aircraft were posted on social media (Twitter), but immediately tagging traditional media TV stations to gather their attention. The crisis was then amplified by them and spread further across all the channels.[1]

Social media crisis spreads much faster than on traditional media. This means that the organizations have much less time to respond. However, it also means that the social media crisis tails off much sooner as social media moves to another subject. As a result, the organization's initial reaction will be the one that will be remembered by the stakeholders and audience. In addition, postcrisis and recovery actions tend to gather much less attention on social media than the crisis itself.

7.3.2.   Difference between Communications Crisis and Actual Crisis

In the crisis situation, there are actually two crises: an actual crisis and communications crisis. Obviously, they are both tied together and influence each other. However, there is a difference between the two. In fact, if not managed properly the communication crisis can last longer than actual crisis. It can also have very long-term reputational impacts on an organization. Therefore, it is important to consider crisis management as both management of the process (dealing with actual crisis) and management of reputation (connecting with the right stakeholders and building organizational image). For some executives the distinction and relationship between communications and actual crisis is not obvious. This leads to pure focus on operational aspects, which might have negative impact on the organization in a long run (Nätti, Rahkolin, & Saraniemi, 2014; Palttala et al., 2012) (Figure 7.2).

---

[1]https://www.forbes.com/sites/michaelgoldstein/2017/12/20/biggest-travel-story-of-2017-the-bumping-and-beating-of-doctor-david-dao/#28b54b2ef61f

Crisis management	Crisis communications management
• Solving the issue • Ensuring business continuity	• Managing perceptions • Building corporate reputation

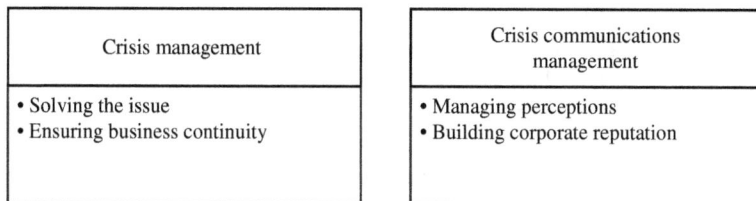

Figure 7.2.   Difference between Crisis Management and Crisis Communications Management.

Dual approach to crisis management looking at both operational and communication aspects is necessary to avoid long-term reputational risks. It considers losses in terms of reputation as equally important to the operational issues.

7.3.3.   *Crisis Recovery and Organizational Learning*

After the crisis is over there is an obvious question imposing itself: "what is next?". As stated before in this chapter, the extent to which an organization embraces the lessons from the crisis will define its future readiness to deal with the issues and crises. It will also shape the future reputation of the organization. There are several elements that need to be considered:

- Documenting crisis learnings and benchmarking the process during the crisis against the organizational processes.
- Debriefing and lessons learned – comparing the processes and actual events and their consequences.
- Integration of the lessons learned into crisis documentation and possible update or change of the crisis procedures and processes.
- Knowledge management systems and internal crisis awareness – review of who should be involved and/or trained within the organization.

Finally, crisis communications management is a cycle. Once the actions and crisis learning are integrated, the organization is again on a pre-crisis mode of preparedness.

7.4.   Defensive Advocacy – Key Parameters

Defensive advocacy supports an organization's advocacy activities in the situation of external rejection of the messages or stakeholder backlash. It is frequent that the advocacy strategies are designed with desired outcomes in mind, but without considering a possibility of rejection of the message. This is due partially to the fact that advocacy professionals tend to be emotionally connected with the causes they defend. Moreover, for a long time advocacy, was considered to be a tool for proactive issues management, while crisis communications focused on reactive issues management (Fearn-Banks, 2011; Gonzalez-Herrero & Smith, 2008).

In the current context of increased stakeholder expectations and interconnectivity between the issues this distinction becomes slightly obsolete.

Defensive advocacy shares almost all tools with crisis communications management. The main difference is that it is much more issue driven. Therefore, issue mapping and stakeholder identification are even more crucial. The defensive advocacy element needs to be embedded in the design of the advocacy campaign since its earliest conceptualization. In fact, part of the strategy development and mapping consists in reviewing the context from a perspective of potential push back and negative reaction. This allows us to further tailor the approach and messaging together with alignment of the tools and stakeholders to mitigate reputational risks.

While crisis communication looks at the issues and landscape from an organizational perceptive, defensive advocacy looks at it from a campaign perspective. Of course, the two are interconnected and organizational processes and procedures impact advocacy response. However, they are also structurally different as defensive advocacy is much more focused and tailored. We believe there are six steps that support organizational response to negative reaction to the advocacy campaign (DEFEND model):

- *Define* – focusing on mapping the landscape and looking for the conflict points with the other stakeholders around the issue of advocacy.
- *Explore* – linking the issue with the surrounding issues and understanding crosslinking points and associated risks.
- *Find* – looking for the potential opponents of the advocacy campaign or the organization. The finding exercise should look both at the interests of the groups as well as emotional (negative) connections with the organization.
- *Engage* – when the backlash happens it is important to engage both supporters as well as those who present a negative view. The organizations often forget to seek third-party endorsement focusing on discussing the issues as opposed to solutions.
- *Neutralize* – imposing a positive and forward-looking narrative which overrides arguments of the opponents in an implicit manner.
- *Debrief* – including the lessons from the defensive advocacy process in the subsequent development and planning of the future campaigns and activities.

7.5.   Conclusions

There are more crises than ever, and they gain more and faster visibility. Mobile technology and universal connectivity mean that the crises can happen whenever and wherever. Citizen reporters can share their videos and images on a global scale. At the same time, they frequently address traditional media channels in order to gain additional reach. This interconnection between social (spontaneous and uncontrollable) and organizational (media channels) makes crisis management much more complex.

Corporate reputation is important for all types of organizations. Crises can have long lasting impacts on reputation and organizational results. The sources of crises are much more complex. This means that organizations need to focus on crisis preparedness and mitigation. In addition, organizations need to monitor and understand the surrounding landscape. Issues management, advocacy, and crisis communications are at the same nexus of influencing factors for an organization.

Crisis communications needs to reach far beyond communications and public affairs professionals. Proactive advocacy builds the ground for crisis response and constructs the links with the stakeholders that matter. Defensive advocacy aims to mitigate long-term impacts of the crises and build organizational resilience around the issues.

7.5.1. *Discussion and Future of Corporate Reputation Management*

The channels continue evolving and the experience of crisis already visual (through videos developed on mobile devices) can become even more personal through augmented and virtual reality. This means that the crisis response will need to be adapted and address more and deeper emotions. There are also other types of crises that organizations will face in the future. Already, cybersecurity and data protection have become one of the key concerns and fears among the executives. This is paired with the concerns around privacy.

One of the key questions is about the future role and impact of corporate reputation on the business results. The studies already showcase an attachment of Millennials and Generation Z toward ethical values and role the organizations play within society. Some companies already respond to these requirements – for instance Patagonia in the quest against climate change. Other companies adopt more reactive approaches and respond to the pressures, drive sustainability programs but are yet to integrate the reputation into their whole chain of operations.

Some questions and considerations remain valid and would be interesting subjects of further research and considerations:

- *Who will be defining the rules in crisis management* – to what extent will the organizations be able to "manage" their crises?
- *How will the structures and crisis preparedness processes change to adjust* – what will be the best practice of crisis management and how reputation management will be integrated vertically and horizontally across an organization?
- *What will be the causes of crises* – future crises will be increasingly issue driven. How will the issues management be integrated into the organizational design?

Finally, it would be interesting to see a multi-sector, multi-country study analyzing the link between corporate reputation and business results both short and long term.

Key Takeaways

- *Organizational reputation is equally important for companies, international organizations, and NGOs. Therefore, reputation management is one of the core functions for advocacy. It is also where advocacy brings the most tangible benefits for the organization.*
- *Crises impact both organizations and companies. There is no industry or organization that would be "safe" from a crisis. Mapping of the issues and stakeholders is crucial for reputation management of all the entities.*
- *The issues impacting organizations are much more complex. They are also more interlinked between themselves. This means that the "unlikely" scenarios happen more and more often, and organizations need to be ready for crises coming from the unexpected sources.*
- *Each cause or organization will inevitably attract criticism and contrary views. Defensive advocacy and crisis management share the same toolkit. Defending the cause is very similar to protecting organizational reputation.*
- *Management of the crisis starts before the crisis. The need for imminent reaction requires that the organizations need to be prepared for a crisis and activate their response as soon as a trigger happen. They do not benefit from any "golden hour" anymore.*
- *Crisis management and crisis communications management need to be interlinked and aligned. A disconnection between the two can lead to negative ripple effects on an organization and long-term negative operational impacts.*
- *Effective crisis management requires involvement of executives from across the organization. Team approach mitigates the risk related to the silos and triggers holistic view on all aspects of the crisis.*
- *Reputation management and crisis communications need to be seen as a circle. The organizations learn from the incidents and issues that occur. These learnings should be integrated in the revision of preparation and management processes.*

Chapter 8

New Frontier for Advocacy – Toward an Experience-based Model of Engagement

8.1. Introduction

Social and digital media allow companies to become broadcasters of their own messages without a need to pass through traditional media channels (see Chapter 6). They eliminated the imperative of a middle man (media) between the corporates and their audiences. This has shifted the focus of communication from channel management to content management (see Chapters 2 and 6). This new focus requires also new types of skills from communication and advocacy professionals. All externally facing functions of an organizations merge closer together. It means more alignment, but also requires professionals who did not use to work together to adjust working styles and practices. Moreover, the media landscape is not static. Social media channels evolve – they move from static content format toward dynamic content delivery with an increase in the role of live and perishable content. Also, technology evolves. Virtual reality, augmented reality, connected devices – all these developments – provide new ways to connect and engage with the target audiences.

The following questions arise: How will the changes in the landscape and new technologies influence the way advocacy is managed and perceived? Will there be a fundamental shift, or will new means of communication and engagement simply be embedded into the engagement strategy mix? Will these changes make new entrants become key stakeholders and influencers? Our foresight analysis suggests that communication paradigm will move from engagement to experience. This means organizations will need to rethink the content formats as well as the ways of connecting with their target audiences. It will also change the nature of relationships organizations have with their stakeholders – the relationships will become deeper and more rooted in the core of the organization. Responding to this challenge will require more than just inclusion of the new means of communication. It will call for more agility, better alignment, and another skillset within advocacy teams. The main managerial question is how to design organizations to respond to these challenges?

The answer to this question is far from being obvious. For instance, is agility and matrix organization an answer? Or increased centrality? Or cross-functional advocacy team? Or a mix between all of the above? In addition, do we talk only about advocacy and communication, or do we talk about the whole external engagement mix?

This chapter proposes a model describing how marketing, communication, and public affairs functions should merge and become central to the business decision-making processes.

According to We Are Social, 45% of the global population are social media users. Fifty-seven percent of the population has access to the Internet globally. Nine percent is the growth rate of the active Internet users annually. While the differences between the continents and countries are still significant the trend is clear. Also, more and more social media communication is happening on mobile devices (42% and growth of 10%).[1] This is the fastest growing group of users of new technologies and social media. It means that the future of technology and social communication will be mobile. This trend is especially relevant for developing countries. There, a majority of users will use mobile as the first and primary source of communication on the digital channels. On the one hand, it is a great opportunity as it enhances the number of people potentially reached and on the other hand, it creates completely different expectations in terms of content formats and content types.

Meanwhile, the trust level toward these channels of communication is constantly shifting. Recently, the highest growth of trust globally was attributed to the traditional and local media (Edelman Trust Barometer, 2019). However, is this trend stable and set to stay? In this sense, we are facing a paradoxical situation in which the technology is available to more and more people. However, at the same time these people don't necessarily trust the messages they see, nor the technology behind them. This trend is even more accentuated by the debates around privacy, privacy laws and general data protection regulation (GDPR) in the European Union. If advocacy is about creating trust and organizations, products and solutions, then management of advocacy in this climate of general distrust is extremely complex. It requires the organizations to look beyond their operating environment and provide a broader range of solutions.

For many new users, the mobile will be the first technology to deliver social and digital media content. However, mobile technology itself is not static either. It evolves to accommodate for a broader range of connected devices, services, and solutions as well. 5G Technology is out there not without controversy, and its impact on advocacy is generally underestimated. While the majority of the 5G discourse focused on technology, privacy, and health effects, there were very few reflections looking at how 5G will change the way organizations engage with their target audiences. At the same time, the power of change embedded in 5G technology is huge. It can change the way we consume information, the way we perceive information, and the way information is managed by multiple stakeholders and actors in the system:

> Set to arrive within the next three years, 5G could account for as many as 1.2 billion connections by 2025. By then, 5G networks

---

[1]https://wearesocial.com/blog/2019/01/digital-2019-global-internet-use-accelerates

are likely to cover one-third of the world's population. The impact on the mobile industry and its customers will be profound. 5G is more than a new generation of technologies; it denotes a new era in which connectivity will become increasingly fluid and flexible. 5G Networks will adapt to applications and performance will be tailored precisely to the needs of the user. (GSMA Understanding 5G)[2]

Indeed, 5G applications will be far above the speed of connection – the subjects that dominated an initial discourse and reflection about this technology. It will allow further integration of the data and predictive analytics analyzing user behaviors and anticipating the landscape developments. It will also allow a much deeper customization of messages for the individuals. Finally, it will provide much more data with many more data points to analyze and embrace the behaviors of the users and publics. An integration of the technology in the mix of solutions shaping implementation of the Sustainable Development Goals is critical. It will allow better and evidence-based decision-making across issues and stakeholders. The view below from the International Telecommunication Union showcases further the opportunities that 5G brings to advocacy strategies:

5G is expected to support applications such as smart homes and buildings, smart cities, 3D video, work and play in the cloud, remote medical surgery, virtual and augmented reality, and massive machine-to-machine communications for industry automation and self-driving cars. 3G and 4G networks currently face challenges in supporting these services.

Due to its sheer scale and scope, 5G is expected to accelerate the achievement of all 17 Sustainable Development Goals (SDGs), from affordable and clean energy to zero hunger. (ITU 5th Generation of Mobile Technologies)[3]

Majority of the reflection about new technologies in advocacy focuses on virtual and augmented reality. These are the most visible and tangible change factors for the way organizational engagement is thought through and executed. Without a doubt the integration of the new emerging technologies into the advocacy strategies will define their efficiency and effectiveness. It will also require rethinking the "long-term view" in the planning process. The "long-term" view has to be based on the overall desired impacts and the processes have to allow for agility and flexibility in order to integrate the new engagement channels and

---

[2]https://www.gsma.com/futurenetworks/technology/understanding-5g/5g-innovation/
[3]https://www.itu.int/en/mediacentre/backgrounders/Pages/5G-fifth-generation-of-mobile-technologies.aspx

platforms. In this perspective, VR and AI could be just the most visible external signs of a profound change driven by a holistic connectivity of devices and new ways of perceiving technology.

8.2.   New Challenges for Advocacy Management

Beyond changes in the technology and influencing landscape, a global advocacy is set to face multiple challenges in the future. Not only the channels of communication and ways of conveying messages will change, but also an external landscape is set to evolve and change. Some claim that the relationships of power will revolutionize. The most fundamental questions remain the same for all advocacy efforts: *who is making the rules and who will be making the rules?*

Traditionally the rules were anchored in the laws that were set by the legislators and regulators operating in the political systems at country, regional, and international levels. However, the developments of the stakeholder landscape and international landscape give more power to industry and self-regulatory bodies. The so-called soft laws and industry standards have a growing impact on business (Guzman & Meyer, 2010). In some cases, self-regulation and soft laws can have higher impact on industry practices than the traditional laws and regulations. The example of ISO 14000 family standards that became the reference point for sustainability management and recognition:

> The ISO 14000 family of standards provides practical tools for companies and organizations of all kinds looking to manage their environmental responsibilities.
>
> ISO 14001:2015 and its supporting standards such as ISO 14006:2011 focus on environmental systems to achieve this. The other standards in the family focus on specific approaches such as audits, communications, labelling and life cycle analysis, as well as environmental challenges such as climate change. (ISO 14001 Environmental Management)[4]

In the international context, we observe a growing influence of non-traditional multilateral forums on the global agenda setting. For instance, G7, G20, and bilateral summits rise in influence over the established forums which leads to a new definition of power (Subacchi, 2008). The bilateral agreements or even arrangements between the countries challenge the status quo of the international system. It also means that the international organizations need to adapt to this new reality and search for their own relevance. For example, with discourse around Brexit we see this dichotomy. On the one hand, Brexiteers claimed that United Kingdom after Brexit would benefit from better deals

---

[4]https://www.iso.org/iso-14001-environmental-management.html

directly with the other countries. On the other hand, they called WTO rules as a guiding principle in case a deal with the EU could be not reached.

Conversely, private sector companies become very active around the events where they were not present in the past. They are seen and act as the actors of discourse in the international arena, in some instances, equal to the international organizations and governments. A good example is UN General Assembly where multiple companies and industries organize side events and host discussions in relationship with the event's agenda. As a result, advocacy professionals will need to adapt and seek innovative entry points to influence the global agenda through targeted multi-channel approaches. These platforms provide a leverage for the organizational messaging and positioning of the corporate contributions in a broader context.

There are multiple changes in the influencing landscape which include:

- *Growing requirements on transparency* (there is a growing tendency to regulate the lobbying and advocacy sector and set the rules that all actors need to follow – EU Transparency Register is a good example). This allows advocacy professionals coming from organizations and companies to play on an equal field, where no matter who they represent, they are subject to the same rules and regulations.
- *Higher focus on ethics in advocacy and lobbying* (advocacy and lobbying professionals are subject of a higher public scrutiny). This paired with transparency requirements means that advocacy professionals need to follow the strictest ethical rules and ensure alignment between what they communicate and their actions.
- *Changes in the models of advocacy and influence* (nonprofit actors and private sector companies using similar tools and techniques in their advocacy strategies). It enhances the scope of advocacy and allows actors not used to working together to build relationships and drive a common agenda.
- *Blurring lines between communications, marketing, and advocacy* (the same channels are used for different aims almost interchangeably). Advocacy becomes a key concern and building block of external activities of the organizations. It supports alignment between the functions and focus of organizations on the activities delivering best influencing results.

These tendencies can have a very positive impact on advocacy as a profession. A growing complexity of the landscape paired with ever-changing communication and influence channels and platforms means that advocacy will be increasingly complex. In parallel, the organizations are expected to play an important role in multiple issues where they were not necessarily present in the past. As a result, advocacy will need to reinvent itself to better serve the organizations.

There might be an impression that all was said about the impact of new technologies on advocacy and public affairs. Or not? Frequently, when talking about emerging technologies in advocacy we think about social media and digital communications. The reality is that these tools become legacy technologies that have been used for at least 10 years. New technologies include predictive analytics, big data, artificial intelligence, virtual reality, and 5G mobile technology. They will all change the way advocacy strategies are executed. It will be not enough to build attractive form for messages and narratives – it will be necessary to design experiences for the users and targets of campaigns. The campaigns will be also increasingly focused and targeted. Big data and predictive analytics provide a great insight into user behaviors and user preferences. Being tailored and bespoke means being analytical. This requires an important shift of focus and skillset. Those who design influence campaigns will need to become more tech-savvy and master the new technologies. There will be also a growing demand for analytical and research skills in advocacy. Creativity will need to be strongly supported by data and insights.

At the same time, it is important not to forget that new technologies created some controversies among the general public and stakeholders alike. The fears about privacy and security are growing. GDPR application in the European Union is a good example. At the beginning, an introduction of the regulation was accompanied by a certain level of fear from professionals with regard to the types of information and stakeholder data they will be able to collect. Also, a relevance of the big data analytics was questioned – to what extent the information collected via big data will be usable. The controversies around stakeholder lists created by a public affairs consultancy for Monsanto and subsequently leaked to the media in France aggravated this discussion. Some of the politicians called for further regulation of what "lobbyists" can collect in terms of data and information. However, looking closely at the regulation itself and the types of data usages it specifies, it doesn't really impact to a great extent the work of public affairs and advocacy professionals. In fact, it supports focusing on the information and data that matter and that are relevant from an organizational perspective.

Personal data shall be:

- processed lawfully, fairly and in a transparent manner in relation to the data subject ("lawfulness, fairness and transparency");
- collected for specified, explicit and legitimate purposes and not further processed in a manner that is incompatible with those purposes; further processing for archiving purposes in the public interest, scientific or historical research purposes or statistical purposes shall, in accordance with Article 89 (1), not be considered to be incompatible with the initial purposes ("purpose limitation");
- adequate, relevant and limited to what is necessary in relation to the purposes for which they are processed ("data minimization");

- accurate and, where necessary, kept up to date; every reasonable step must be taken to ensure that personal data that are inaccurate, having regard to the purposes for which they are processed, are erased or rectified without delay ("accuracy");
- kept in a form which permits identification of data subjects for no longer than is necessary for the purposes for which the personal data are processed; personal data may be stored for longer periods insofar as the personal data will be processed solely for archiving purposes in the public interest, scientific or historical research purposes or statistical purposes in accordance with Article 89 (1) subject to implementation of the appropriate technical and organizational measures required by this Regulation in order to safeguard the rights and freedoms of the data subject ("storage limitation");
- processed in a manner that ensures appropriate security of the personal data, including protection against unauthorized or unlawful processing and against accidental loss, destruction or damage, using appropriate technical or organizational measures ("integrity and confidentiality").
- The controller shall be responsible for, and be able to demonstrate compliance with, paragraph 1 ("accountability"). (GDPR, 2018)[5]

8.2.1. Advocacy for New Technology

Also, some of the new technologies are in need of advocacy themselves. Set to challenge the ways of doing and perceiving things they also suffer from high level of stakeholder scrutiny, if things don't go as planned. The accidents of Tesla cars in a self-driving mode are a good example. After enthusiasm related to what self-driving technology can mean, there was a general reflection and concern related to risks posed by this technology. It also raises questions from a regulatory perspective – who would be responsible for casualties and damages caused by autonomous technology. Another example, in case of an unavoidable accident – who should be the victim? The driver (owner of the car and the technology), or for example a pedestrian (external person)? Also, who has the authority to decide on it – is it car manufacturers, regulators? What is the moral legitimacy of a technology producer, or supplier, to take these decisions on behalf of its users and society at large? And if regulators should be providing a framework for this kind of decision: why should they have more power over individuals' lives than a judge in court? All these deliberations illustrate the complexities that new technologies bring to advocacy. They also showcase a growing need of advocacy needed by the new technology producers and suppliers. There

---

[5]https://ec.europa.eu/info/sites/info/files/eag_draft_guidelines_1_11_0.pdf

is no doubt that the technologies need to be accompanied by regulations, but is the regulatory framework ready to address all the issues posed by the recent developments? And if not, then again there is a question – who should be regulating the usage of these new technologies ad interim?

Another example of a similar tendency is 5G technology mentioned earlier in this chapter. After an initial enthusiasm around the opportunities that 5G brings in terms of both the speed and interconnectivity of the devices, the questions around the ownership of the data and control of the data started to appear. This was aggravated by the conflict between the US government and Huawei company.[6] At the same time, several health concerns have been brought to the public attention. As a result, at the time of writing of this book several cities put a moratorium on the installation of 5G antennas (e.g., Brussels).

8.2.2.   Generational Shift and Demographic Challenges

New generations enter the citizen life. Millennial generation (digital natives) was already described as the generation that changes all the paradigms of citizen involvement (Hanks et al., 2008; Lippincott, 2012). It engages more with the causes directly, frequently ignoring existing parties and other actors from the traditional political system. Another level of citizen engagement can be observed among the Z generation (people born after 2000). It starts with a mobilization aspect – digital natives can mobilize themselves globally in an unprecedented speed. Good example would be Marches for Climate and Climate Strikes that spread globally within couple of weeks. This mobilization accompanied with a distance toward traditional democratic institutions and political system.

Social media make people used to the shorter forms of communications (see Chapter 6). The attention spans are shorter, and people tend to take decisions before knowing the facts. If we think that average decision time on consumption of the content is as low as eight seconds, this creates an environment in which narratives become the headlines.[7] Therefore, advocacy narratives will need to be further simplified and thought from a slogan/headline perspective. This can mean losing out on the depth, but at the same time it helps advocates to focus on the essence of their call to action.

For a long time, a lower middle class was a "forgotten part" of the society not addressed by any traditional political parties. This is changing now in many countries where populist movements claimed the space and appealed to those frequently forgotten and left aside from the social system group. Without a doubt the rise of populism and shaking of the traditional political systems impact the construction of the advocacy strategies. Previously, the political and socioeconomic elites of many countries were coming from the same background and benefited from the same or similar education (see example of France where a

---

[6]https://www.ft.com/content/0214a4e4-8158-11e9-b592-5fe435b57a3b
[7]https://www.cision.com/us/2018/01/declining-attention-killing-content-marketing-strategy/

good proportion of the legislators and regulators graduated from the same school – ENA). With the new elites and shake-up of the political scene (especially visible in Europe), these systems of power are disrupted. New political elites come from various backgrounds and frequently did not benefit from a privileged upbringing.[8] This means that advocacy has to be even more agile and permanently questioning the status quo. It also requires in-depth research to understand the agenda and connections between those in power.

8.2.3.   *Need for an Integrated Research Approach*

Advocacy strategies shouldn't base themselves on the assumptions. For instance, infamous Brexit campaign managed to appeal with the simple messaging to the groups that felt left out and not included in sharing the benefits from the political system.[9] The vote "Leave" came as a surprise to many, but from a pure advocacy perspective the campaign to leave the EU offered more targeted messaging and appealed to the human (often negative) sentiments. Future advocacy campaigns need to be even more targeted and data-driven. This will ensure their relevance toward their target audiences.

The complexity of the issues and complexity of the political systems means that even more individuals and institutions will be considered as organizational stakeholders. In fact, more individuals feel that they are concerned by the issues even if they are quite remote from their daily areas of activities (Alniacik et al., 2011). As stated above, the growing role of self-regulations and soft laws means more decision-makers on the issues (Abbott & Snidal, 2000). Both together mean that advocacy strategies will need to address more individuals and institutions in a targeted manner. It also requires an extra level of agility in permanent review of the landscape and its influencing factors.

For a long time, we have talked about decreasing levels of trust toward media and institutions (Edelman Trust Barometer, 2010–2019). However, recent trust studies indicate a certain growth of trust toward the traditional media and institutions (Edelman, 2019) This is accompanied with lowering trusts toward social media and "individual like myself" (ibid.). Since these are relatively new results there is a question for how long the tendency will persist. However, it might be an early indication of the social shift toward more traditional institutions based on social capital. It could be seen as a reaction to the results of the recent rise of populism. In any case this is a tendency that if transformed into trend might revolutionize further advocacy approaches. The return of traditional influence channels will need to be accompanied by further embracement of the new tools.

Finally, advocacy messaging is frequently based on a negative messaging painting a sober vision of the state of the world (Rosling, 2019). The campaigns are often alarmistic in tone and create a sentiment of "feeling bad" in order to mobilize the target audiences to act. However, as Rosling argues, this negative

---

[8]https://www.ft.com/content/0d864f88-81a0-11e9-9935-ad75bb96c849
[9]https://www.bbc.com/news/uk-politics-eu-referendum-36574526

vision of the world is often based on the wrong assumptions and ignoring the facts (Rosling, 2019). Moreover, positive connotations and positive messaging can have a positive impact on efficiency of the advocacy campaigns. As a result, there is a room for advocacy strategies to appeal more to the positive emotions.

8.2.4.   *Using Big Data to Shape Public Opinion and Influence*

Without a doubt big data applications are not yet used to their full potential in advocacy campaigns. Their usage is frequently limited to social media listening and high-level landscape scanning. However, there are several campaigns which analyzed digital behaviors of social media users and adjusted messaging accordingly. The scandal around the data usage and privacy violations by Cambridge Analytica shed light on both dangers and also possibilities that insights from big data bring to advocacy strategies. It allows very precise targeting of the messages and creation of the cognitive connections among target audiences. This can have a direct positive impact on absorption of the call to action. At the same time, there are growing concerns related to cybersecurity (constant data breaches even in the most respected companies) and privacy (who owns the data and who controls the data).

There is still a lack of a global standard that would define the ownership and usage of the data. The regulators and legislators tend to react ad-hoc based on the media coverage of the data breaches, etc. Some of the regulations are very far reaching – for instance General Data Protection Directive from the European Union. The GDPR principles have already inspired local regulations in other parts of the world, for example, in California (Privacy Act).[10] The question of data control also requires the analysis to whom data belong. Is it the subject of data collection? The platform that is collecting the data. Or any other entity? The answer to these questions will define future possibilities of big data relevance for advocacy. It will shape data accessibility and usability.

Despite all the concerns and reservations related to the data collecting, processing, and cybersecurity; big data and data in general will become increasingly important for advocacy strategies. Data focus also means that the future advocacy strategies will be more and more evidence-based as opposed to being assumption-based. There are several conditions making data-centric advocacy successful:

- *Clearly defined goals and desired outcomes of engagement.* This helps to define what kind of data is needed or useful from an advocacy campaign perspective.
- *Understanding of the stakeholder landscape and its changes.* Who shapes the agenda and who are those who shape the opinions of those shaping the agenda? The answer to these questions brings further relevance to the advocacy efforts.

---

[10]https://www.law.com/njlawjournal/2018/12/01/the-california-consumer-privacy-act-what-you-need-to-know/?slreturn=20190506005705

- *Clarity of the target audiences and their agenda.* Knowing what is important for those who we influence allows us to further target the messaging and call to action.
- *Development of the maps of influence and understanding who influences whom in the decision-making processes.* The influence is a dynamic process, so it is important to recognize its dynamic character and shape the organizational strategy accordingly. It is also crucial to follow all the landscape developments and permanently integrate the changes of the approach into the campaign development and roll-out.

8.2.5.   *Virtual Reality, Artificial Intelligence – Moving toward Brand and Organizational Experiences*

Making people experience the lives of the others is in brief what virtual reality brings to advocacy. The applications of VR allow people to feel the concerns and joys of the others. It also brings new ways of interacting with the target audiences. VR redefines what storytelling is. It is no longer about using the words and images to draw the landscape. It is about creating the experiences that are real and can be felt by others. There are some initial examples of the usage of augmented reality for advocacy. For instance, *New York Times* created VR experience 360° movie *The Displaced* to showcase the daily difficulties and struggles of the refugees.[11]

Predictive analytics and artificial intelligence are already used in the CRM and contact management applications. For instance, chatbots use the learnings from the questions and previous interactions with the users to perfect the answers they are serving to the future users. Defining the potential future questions and possible answers is one of the key functions predictive analytics can play. Analyzing the patterns and behaviors of interactions and engagement can also help to understand better the expectations of the target audiences and therefore tailor the content a message better.

8.2.6.   *Toward a Future Advocacy Management Model*

We discussed the composition of an advocacy team as well as potential learning patterns of advocacy within the organization (see Chapters 1 and 2). However, how will advocacy be managed in the future? What will be its relationship with other functions within the organization? There is always a risk in presenting possible future managerial models and predictions about the landscape changes. However, taking the risks into account, we propose an organizational model of advocacy structure and management. The model includes organization of the advocacy function as well as its role in the broader organizational engagement agenda.

---

[11] https://www.nytimes.com/2015/11/08/magazine/the-displaced-introduction.html

8.3.   Conceptual Model for Organizational Advocacy

This model assumes an integration of all engagement functions of an organization under one umbrella and one leadership (Figure 8.1).

- *Corporate communication* will remain a key function managing reputation of the organization.
- *Marketing and marketing communications* will continue being responsible for building brand and managing brand equity.
- *External relations and public affairs* will be responsible for engagement with larger group of stakeholders.
- *Internal engagement and communication* will continue shifting toward higher involvement in employee advocacy.

All these functions will continue playing an important role. However, bringing them together under one leadership will foster collaboration and internal understanding of the value of advocacy and benefits of organizational engagement with the key stakeholders.

8.3.1.   Key Considerations for Advocacy Integration

The changes and future scenarios described in this chapter will require further changes in the way advocacy campaigns are planned and executed both on a local and global scale. Tools will change, audiences will change, stakeholders will change making the reality even more complex for the advocacy professionals. However, several of the key principles guiding advocacy strategy development are set to remain valid, or become even more important:

- Advocacy needs to be clearly linked and interconnected with the business objectives. Growing expectations from stakeholders and consumers mean that the organizations willing to be successful and impactful need to integrate advocacy in all levels of their activities. It can mean that the organizations will move away from developing advocacy strategies. Instead, advocacy will

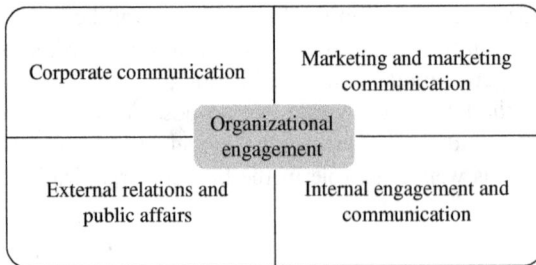

Corporate communication	Marketing and marketing communication
Organizational engagement	
External relations and public affairs	Internal engagement and communication

Figure 8.1.   Conceptual Model for Future Advocacy Management.

be integrated at multiple levels of their organizational planning. So, advocacy will be a part of various business strategies.

- Advocacy needs to be vertically and horizontally integrated within the organization. It is paramount to align advocacy positions between the organizational leadership, the experts and employees. The agenda and organizational priorities need to be clear to all involved in the advocacy activities. As the employees of the company are considered to be the most credible source of information about its activities – there is an additional need for a horizontal integration of the advocacy.

- Advocacy has to be considered as a business discipline that delivers the value for the organization and is considered as a profit line as opposed to being an expense line. The costs associated with a lack of advocacy action, in the majority of the cases, far exceed the costs of advocacy strategies. Therefore, the considerations of return on investment need to be part of advocacy design. Advocacy (if measured and evaluated properly) has the power to become a profit line for an organization as opposed to an expense line. This will further elevate its cross-organizational and business relevance from an internal stakeholder perspective.

- Advocacy needs to be considered as a profession – growing popularity of the term "advocacy" leads a multiplication of the number of individuals calling themselves advocacy professionals. While we claim that vertical integration of advocacy means that "advocacy is the job of everyone within the organization," at the same time we see a need for advocacy to be managed by a designated job function. However, this professionalization need goes beyond an individual organization. It also requires creation of the professional structures (associations), rules (codes of conduct), and skillset (training) for those who work in advocacy.

- Advocacy activities have to be monitored, measured, and evaluated in line with the other organizational activities. Advocacy still suffers from perception created by the lobbying professionals that were averse to performance measurements. As a result, there was an impression that lobbying activities were limited to "wining and dining," which in turn limited the recognition of the business value lobbying brought. Enhanced measurement and evaluation standard will address this issue. The good starting point would be a global agreement on principles of advocacy measurement. It would mirror an approach of communication profession and AMEC Barcelona Principles first introduced in 2009. However, to introduce the principles, there is a need for an organization to drive the agenda of advocacy profession.

These principles underlie a model which combines advocacy trends considerations with an organizational learning theory. It proposes a simple model for advocacy strategic management from a managerial perspective. It includes also proposed engagement patterns that organizations can undertake depending on their advocacy management profiles.

8.4.   Discussion and Future Research Paths

New approaches to advocacy, new definitions of influence, new ways of looking at stakeholders. There are many subjects and paths the researchers can explore further new advocacy strategies and tactics. It would be really interesting to see comparative studies from different cultural contexts exploring the adoption of new technologies in advocacy execution. It would be also fascinating to explore how the organizations are being perceived by their key stakeholders' groups. These perception studies could reach far beyond just looking at organizational attributes by looking at relationships individuals have with the organizations and institutions. It would be also interesting to develop case-study research comparing different advocacy campaign delivery mechanisms. It could benchmark the results of "traditional" advocacy approaches vs. usages of virtual and augmented reality. Finally, there is a real need for an in-depth research on the evolution of an internal perception of advocacy within the international businesses and international organizations.

8.5.   Conclusions

Advocacy is an evolving discipline. There are multiple external factors that impact the way advocacy strategies are managed and executed. However, the ultimate goal of advocacy, which is to shape a favorable external environment for an organization, remains the same. Advocacy of the future will become more research and evidence-based. This will enhance further the types of skillsets needed in the international advocacy teams. Integration of the insight and direct delivery mechanisms will change the way organizations define their strategic narratives. The emotional element will become increasingly important. The storytelling is already based on videos and visuals and this trend toward stronger involvement of the target audiences is set to stay relevant. It is certainly a great time for advocacy professionals as the organizations facing changes in the landscape will look to them to for support in navigating this challenge.

Key Takeaways

- *New technologies such as virtual reality and augmented reality are set to change the way advocacy campaigns are thought through. The paradigm shifts from engaging the users to creating experience-based communication. This requires new skills from the advocacy professionals. In addition to the new skills, it requires a radical shift in thinking about advocacy strategies.*
- *Big data and predictive analytics give an unprecedented insight into the agendas and ways of thinking of the advocacy target audiences and stakeholders. The campaigners need to embrace the opportunities provided by data to best tailor and target their messages.*

- *New technologies come also with some controversy and requirements for a greater transparency and respect of privacy. The professionals working on advocacy strategies for the organizations and companies need to be mindful of these requirements and adjust their strategic approaches accordingly.*
- *Professionalization of advocacy in the companies and organizations requires professional structures and rules of engagement to support the activities. A codification of who an advocacy professional is as well as a dedicated networking and knowledge sharing platform would be an important contributor to a further integration of the function in the corporate design.*
- *In the context of growing importance of advocacy for an organizational success, measurement and evaluation of advocacy become a mission critical for advocacy professionals. There is a need to establish a common framework for measurement and evaluation of advocacy. With the lack of common framework, the organizations need to define the indicators internally and create a consistent understanding what is the success and how the success looks like.*
- *There will be definitely a room for further development of advocacy as a profession. The complexity of the international landscape is set to grow further. It will create an environment in which organizational engagement plays an even more important role.*

Epilogue – What's Next for Advocacy

The expectations from stakeholders, consumers, and general public toward companies and organizations are evolving. This evolution is accelerated and accentuated by the expectations of the Millennial and Z generations (Hanks et al., 2008; Taylor & Keeter, 2010). The Millennial generation is still frequently presented in the corporate material as a "generation of the future." Meanwhile, the "oldest millennials" approach 40 years of age and frequently are the decision-makers and/or subjects of advocacy strategies. It increases the need for more comprehensive approaches of the companies toward their engagement and advocacy strategies.

However, this evolution of relationships between the organizations and individuals doesn't stop there. "Generation Z" grows up in the context where the consciousness around global issues such as climate change become a norm (World Economic Forum [WEF]). The middle class represents the highest percentage of the population (WEF). More and more people live in the cities (especially in the developing countries) (WEF). The WEF showcases the changes in the society, economy, and business as the Fourth Industrial Revolution:

> The First Industrial Revolution used water and steam power to mechanize production. The Second used electric power to create mass production. The Third used electronics and information technology to automate production. Now a Fourth Industrial Revolution is building on the Third, the digital revolution that has been occurring since the middle of the last century. It is characterized by a fusion of technologies that is blurring the lines between the physical, digital, and biological spheres. (WEF, 2016)[1]

Globally operating businesses, but also SMEs, need to adapt to this changing landscape and develop relationships with those who matter for their businesses (WEF, 2016). This need is accentuated by the fact of blurring barriers between physical and digital sphere (WEF). The need to adapt the communications and engagement strategies is clear.

---

[1] https://www.weforum.org/agenda/2016/01/the-fourth-industrial-revolution-what-it-means-and-how-to-respond/

Advocacy becomes the best way for organizations and companies to build their relationships with those who matter for their business and operations. At the very core of advocacy is duality of relationships. Indeed, advocacy stands in opposition to a traditional broadcasting communications model based on a one-to-many principle. In contrary advocacy seeks to build and animate relationships of a bidirectional nature.

However, the advocacy professionals need to keep up with the changing landscape. As advocacy becomes core to the business as it helps to build and maintain corporate reputation, the expectations toward advocacy professionals are ever growing. For a long time, advocacy used to be considered as a "nice to have" activity performed without a clear strategy and with limited (to zero) measurement of the performance.

Measurement and evaluation of advocacy will define its future place in organizational structures. In fact, advocacy should become a business line with its proper targets and should report on return on investment of its activities. The advocacy professionals will also need to adopt the language that is understood and appreciated by the senior management of the organizations. This means definitely moving away from input- and output-based measurement and reporting toward outcome- and impact-based models.

The model for measurement and evaluation of advocacy proposed in this book can help to build a culture of measuring and reporting the results as opposed to the activities. For too long, advocacy and lobbying professionals created a certain level of mystery around their activities. Measurement frameworks that were based on the input and output measures such as the number of meetings held and the number of people reached contributed to a certain skepticism around the profession.

The new generation of advocacy professionals comes well equipped to challenge the status quo of the profession. Firstly, the newcomers can benefit from the professional training, which means creation of the advocacy professionals as opposed to individuals reconverted by the circumstances to work on advocacy. Secondly, there is a broader understanding by the senior managers of organizations of the need to build reputation through relationships with those who matter for the business. Finally, thanks to the social media and digital channels, the organizations are in position to build direct relationships with their key stakeholders (Couldry, 2012). This opens further opportunities for employment for advocacy professionals.

Virtual reality, augmented reality, artificial intelligence will challenge further the status quo of advocacy profession. While digital communications allowed us to engage the groups of stakeholders that were in the past non-reachable by companies and organizations (Kaplan & Haenlein, 2010; Kietzmann et al., 2011), these technologies bring an opportunity to create experiences for the target audiences. We claim that we are at the edge of paradigm shift of communications and advocacy. This shift toward experiences will allow to create deeper relationships with the stakeholders and create new emotional connections between the organizations and individuals.

Some of the new technologies are feared by the advocacy professionals, yet they create a remarkable opportunity to rethink the way strategies are being conceptualized and executed. Below we present a snapshot of opportunities/ considerations for advocacy strategies and tactics:

Virtual reality – will allow us to create the applications connecting the target audiences through experiences. It will also help to build the visual narrative beyond words and images and bring closer the stakeholders and target audiences to the organizations. Finally, VR applications will help to bring advocacy into more daily usages of technology (message placement).

Augmented reality – having a lower entry point than virtual reality (no need for additional equipment), it will help to visualize further the impact of the advocacy campaigns and impact of the messages. This will permit us to focus advocacy efforts further on the final outcomes of campaigning.

Gamification – will help to connect broader groups of stakeholders with the global issues. Oftentimes, the issues and advocacy messages might appear as somewhat far from the daily reality of target audiences. Having the opportunity to create the engagement through games will simplify absorption of the messages and lower the entry point to engage.

Big data – already helps us to understand the connections between the target audiences. It also allows us to understand how influencers and stakeholders are connected and who is influencing whom. In the future, big data applications will allow for a very precise targeting of the advocacy campaigns and sophisticated selection of the stakeholders that need to be convinced in order to achieve the desired outcomes.

Artificial intelligence (AI) – predictive analytics and applications of AI will definitely impact advocacy targeting. It will be easier to create the campaigns that anticipate the reactions from target audiences. AI will also help to create the scenarios for risk anticipation and mitigation in the advocacy strategies.

At a strategic level all these changes mean a shift toward integrated approach which requires more alignment throughout the organizations. As highlighted multiple times in this book, advocacy cannot be managed in a silo. It has to respond to the needs and capacities of the internal stakeholders within the organization. It needs to also seek to engage the internal actors.

There are several future paths for research around advocacy that can be suggested. First of all, further research on managerial perceptions of advocacy would bring additional insights to the development of advocacy governance model. It would require qualitative and quantitative methodology, addressing senior managers of the international companies and organizations. This research would allow further development and validation of the models proposed in this book.

An ethnographic research among the advocacy professionals would bring insights to the daily operation of the multi-stakeholder initiatives. This study could also focus on the change management and internal communications aspects of the advocacy initiatives.

Virtual reality and other technologies described above surely represent an opportunity for advocacy campaigning. However, it would be pertinent to study a broader data sample in order to determinate the real effectiveness in achieving the set goals in terms of the outcomes.

Finally, it would be interesting to compare the advocacy models based on intercultural differences. This study would focus on comparing the adoption and management of advocacy based on the location of an organization. We believe that this insight would be necessary to develop further thinking around advocacy modeling. It could also focus on comparison of effectiveness between locally developed strategies and adaptations of the global approaches.

The field of advocacy is definitely set to grow. There are more and more professionals who have job titles with "advocacy" in. This is a good moment for further reflection on the profession. We believe that it is also the time to ensure that advocacy is managed as a business line which can prove its positive contribution to the corporate results and/or organizational performance.

References

Abbott, K., & Snidal, D. (2000). Hard and soft law in international governance. *International Organization, 54*(3), 421–456. doi:10.1162/002081800551280

Adler, P., & Jermier, J. (2005). Developing a field with more soul: Standpoint theory and public policy research for management scholars reviewed. *The Academy of Management Journal, 48*(6), 941–944.

Agnihotri, A. (2014). Corporate reputation based theory of choice between organic, hybrid and inorganic growth strategies. *Corporate Communications: An International Journal, 19*(3), 247–259. doi:10.1108/CCIJ-11-2012-0080

Alniacik, U., Alniacik, E., & Genc, N. (2011). How corporate social responsibility information influences stakeholders' intentions. *Corporate Social Responsibility and Environmental Management, 18*, 234–245.

Amaladoss, M.-X., & Manohar, H. L. (2011). Communicating corporate social responsibility – A case of CSR communications in emerging economies. *Corporate Social Responsibility and Environmental Management, 20*, 65–80. doi:10.1002/csr287.

AMEC. (2009). Barcelona Principles. Retrieved from https://amecorg.com/how-the-barcelona-principles-have-been-updated/

AMEC. (2015). Barcelona Principles 2.0. Retrieved from https://amecorg.com/how-the-barcelona-principles-have-been-updated/

AMEC. (2019). How the Barcelona Principles have been updated? Retrieved from https://amecorg.com/how-the-barcelona-principles-have-been-updated/

Andonova, L. B. (2010). Public-private partnerships for the Earth: Politics and patterns of hybrid authority in the multilateral system. *Global Environmental Politics, 10*(2), 25–53..

Angel, R., & Sexsmith, J. (2011). Social networking: The corporate value proposition. *Ivey Business Journal*. Retrieved from http://www.iveybusinessjournal.com/topics/leadership/social-networking-the-corporate-value-proposition

Argenti, P. A. (1996). Corporate communication as a discipline: Towards a definition. *Management Communication Quarterly, 10*(1), 73–97.

Argenti, P. A. (1997). Reputation: Realizing value from the corporate image. *Management Communication Quarterly, 11*(2), 310–313.

Argenti, P. A. (1998). Strategic employee communication. *Human Resource Management, 37*(3–4), 199–206.

Argenti, P. A. (2004). The employee care revolution. *Leader to Leader, 33*, 45–52.

Argenti, P. A., & Druckenmiller, B. (2004). Reputation and the corporate brand. *Corporate Reputation Review, 6*(4), 368–374.

Argenti, P. A. (2006a). How technology has influenced the field of corporate communication. *Journal of Business and Technical Communication, 20*(3), 357–370.

Argenti, P. A. (2006b). Communications and business value: Measuring the link. *Journal of Business Strategy, 27*(6), 29–40.

Argyris, C., & Schon, D. (1978). *Organizational learning: A theory of action perspective.* New York, NY: Addison-Wesley.

Arora, P., & Dharwadkar, R. (2011). Corporate governance and corporate social responsibility (CSR): The moderating roles of attainment discrepancy and organization slack. *Corporate Governance: An International Review, 19*(2), 136–152.

Attaran, A. (2006). Correction: An immeasurable crisis? A criticism of the millennium development goals and why they cannot be measured. *PLOS Medicine, 3*(5), e224. doi:10.1371/journal.pmed.0030224

Balmer, J. M. T., & Greyser, S. A. (2006). Corporate marketing: Integrating corporate identity, corporate branding, corporate communications, corporate image and corporate reputation. *European Journal of Marketing, 40*(7/8), 730–741. doi:10.1108/03090560610669964

Barbier, E. (2011, August). The policy challenges for green economy and sustainable economic development. In *Natural resources forum* (Vol. 35, No. 3, pp. 233–245). Oxford: Blackwell Publishing.

Barnett, B., Lafferty, B., & Jermier, J. (2005). Corporate reputation: The definitional landscape. *Corporate Reputation Review, 9,* 26–38.

Bastien, F., & Neveu, E. (1999). *Espaces publics mosaiques. Acteurs, arenes et rhetoriques, des debats publics contemporains.* Rennes: PU Rennes.

Bateson, G. (1972a). *Steps to an ecology of mind: Collected essays in anthropology, psychiatry, evolution, and epistemology.* Chicago, IL: University of Chicago Press.

Bateson, G. (1972b). *Steps to an ecology of mind.* San Francisco, CA: Chandler Publishing Company.

Baumgartner, R. J., & Ebner, D. (2010). Corporate sustainability strategies: Sustainability profiles and maturity levels. *Sustainable Development, 18,* 76–89.

Benoit, W. L. (1997). Image repair discourse and crisis communication. *Public Relations Review, 23*(2), 177–186.

Berens, G., & Van Riel, C. (2004). Corporate associations in the academic literature: Three main stream of thought in the reputation measurement literature. *Corporate Reputation Review, 8*(1), 161–187.

Berthon, P. R., Pitt, L. F., Plangger, K., & Shapiro, D. (2012). Marketing meets Web 2.0, social media, and creative consumers: Implications for international marketing strategy. *Business Horizons, 55*(3), 261–271.

Beuker, R., & Abbing, E. R. (2010). Two faces of social media: Brand communication and brand research. *Design Management Review, 21*(1), 54–60.

Black, L. D., & Hartel, C. E. J. (2004). The five capabilities of socially responsible companies. *Journal of Public Affairs, 4*(2), 125–144.

Bochenek, L. M., & Blili, S. (2013). Profiling corporate communications strategy: Mastering organisational learning – A dynamic maturity model for corporate communications strategic management. *The Marketing Review, 13*(2), 143–165.

Bochenek, L. M., & Blili, S. (2014). Social media champions—Drivers and sophistication process of social media strategic management. In M. R. Olivas-Luján & T. Bondarouk (Eds.), *Social media in strategic management* (pp. 143–167). Bingley: Emerald Publishing Limited.

Boddewyn, J. J. (2012). Beyond the evolving discipline of public affairs. *Journal of Public Affairs, 12*(1), 98–104.

Booth, N., & Matic, J. A. (2011). Mapping and leveraging influencers in social media to shape corporate brand perceptions. *Corporate Communications: An International Journal, 16*(3), 184–191.

Borgatti, S., & Halgin, D. S. (2011). On network theory. *Organization Science, 22*, 5. doi:10.1287/orsc.1100.0641

Bowen, H. R. (1953). *Social responsibilities of a businessman.* New York, NY: Harper & Row.

Boyd, C. (1996). Ethics and corporate governance: The issues raised by the Cadbury Report in the United Kingdom. *Journal of Business Ethics, 15*(2), 167–182.

Brandwatch. (2019). Retrieved from https://www.brandwatch.com/blog/facebook-statistics/. Accessed on May 31, 2019.

Breen, J. M. (2017). Leadership resilience in a VUCA world. In *Visionary leadership in a turbulent world: Thriving in the new VUCA context* (pp. 39–58). Bingley: Emerald Publishing Limited.

Brinkmann, J., & Ims, K. (2003). Good intentions aside: Drafting a functionalist look at codes of conduct. *Business Ethics: A European Review, 12*(3), 265–274.

Brown, D., & Hayes, N. (2008). *Influencer marketing.* London: Routledge.

Bruni, A., & Teli, M. (2007). Reassembling the Social – An introduction to actor network theory. *Management Learning, 38*(1), 121–125. doi:10.1177/13505076070 73032

Burchelll, J., & Cook, J. (2006). Assessing the impact of stakeholder dialogue: Changing relationships between NGOs and companies. *Journal of Public Affairs, 6*, 210–227.

Burke, R. (2013). *Project management: Planning and control techniques.* Hoboken, NJ: Wiley.

Burrell, M. (2012). A decade of change and continuity in public affairs. *Journal of Public Affairs, 12*(1), 74–76.

Cai, L., Cui, J., & Jo, H. (2016). Corporate environmental responsibility and firm risk. *Journal of Business Ethics, 139*(3), 563–594.

Calk, R., & Patrick, A. (2017). Millennials through the looking glass: Workplace motivating factors. *The Journal of Business Inquiry, 16*(2), 131–139.

Carbonara, N., Costantino, N., & Pellegrino, R. (2014). Concession period for PPPs: A win–win model for a fair risk sharing. *International Journal of Project Management, 32*, 1223–1232.

Carroll, A. (1979). A three-dimensional conceptual model of corporate social performance. *Academy of Management Review, 4*(4), 497–505.

Carroll, A. B. (1999). Corporate social responsibility. Evolution of a definitional construct. *Business and Society, 38*(3), 268–295.

Chan, M., Kazatchkine, M., Lob-Levyt, J., Obaid, T., Schweizer, J., Sidibe, M., ... Yamada, T. (2010). Meeting the demand for results and accountability: A call for action on health data from eight global health agencies. *PLoS Medicine, 7*(1), e1000223.

Charaudeau, P. (2005). *Les medias et l'information.* Paris: De Boeck.

Christiano, A., & Neimand, A. (2017). Stop raising awareness already. *Stanford Social Innovation Review*, (Spring), 34–41.

Chun, R. (2005). Corporate reputation: Meaning and measurement. *International Journal of Management Reviews, 7*(2), 91–109.

CMS Wire. (2018). *Social media influencers: Mega, macro, micro or nano*. Retrieved from https://www.cmswire.com/digital-marketing/social-media-influencers-mega-macro-micro-or-nano/. Accessed on May 05, 2019.

Cochran, P. L., & Wood, R. A. (1984). Corporate social responsibility and financial performance. *The Academy of Management Journal, 27*(1), 42–56.

Cohen, B. (1963). *The press and foreign policy*. Princeton. NJ: Princeton University Press.

Coombs, W. (2007). Protecting organization reputations during a crisis: The development and application of situational crisis communication theory. *Corporate Reputation Review, 10*, 163. doi:10.1057/palgrave.crr.1550049

Coombs, W. T. (2014). *Ongoing crisis communication: Planning, managing, and responding*. Thousand Oaks, CA: Sage Publications.

Cornelissen, J. (2011). *Corporate communication* (3rd ed.), Thousand Oaks, CA: Sage Publications.

Cornelissen, J. P. (2013). Corporate communication. In W. Donsbach (Ed.) *The international encyclopedia of communication*. Retrieved from http://doi.org/10.1002/9781405186407.wbiecc143.pub2

Cornelissen, J., Thøger Christensen, L., & Kinuthia, K. (2012). Corporate brands and identity: Developing stronger theory and a call for shifting the debate. *European Journal of Marketing, 46*(7/8), 1093–1102.

Couldry, N. (2012). *Media, society, world: Social theory and digital media practice*. Cambridge: Polity.

Crane, A. (Ed.). (2008). *The Oxford handbook of corporate social responsibility*. Oxford: Oxford University Press.

Crane, A., & Matten, D. (2005). Corporate citizenship: Missing the point or missing the boat? A reply to van Oosterhout. *The Academy of Management Review, 30*(4), 681–684.

Crossan, M., & Guatto, T. (1996). Organizational learning research profile. *Journal of Organizational Change Management, 9*(1), 107–112.

Dahlsrud, A. (2008). How corporate social responsibility is defined: An analysis of 37 definitions. *Corporate Social Responsibility and Environmental Management, 15*(1), 1–13.

Dasgupta, S. A., Suar, D., & Singh, S. (2014). Managerial communication practices and employees' attitudes and behaviours: A qualitative study. *Corporate Communications: An International Journal, 19*(3), 287–302. doi:10.1108/CCIJ-04-2013-0023

Davis, K., & Blomstrom, R. L. (1966). *Business and its environment*. New York, NY: McGraw-Hill.

Dayan, D., & Katz, E. (1992). *Media events: The live broadcasting of history*. Cambridge, MA: Harvard University Press.

De la Fuente Sabate, M., & de Quevedo Puente, M. (2003). Empirical analysis of the relationship between coporate reputation and financial performance: A survey of literature. *Corporate Reputation Review, 6*(2), 161–177.

De Quevedo Puente, E., de la Fuente-Sabate, J. M., & Delegado-Gracia, J. B. (2007). Corporate social performance and corporate reputation: Two intervowen perspectives. *Corporate Reputation Review, 10*(1), 60–72.

Deaton, A., & Heston, A. (2010). Understanding PPPs and PPP-based national accounts. *American Economic Journal: Macroeconomics, 2*(4), 1–35.

Denning, S. (2006). Effective storytelling: Strategic business narrative techniques. *Strategy & Leadership, 34*(1), 42−48. doi:10.1108/10878570610637885

Doran, G. T. (1981). There's a S.M.A.R.T. way to write management's goals and objectives. *Management Review, 70*(11), 35−36.

Du, S., Bhattacharya, C. B., & Sen, S. (2010). Maximizing business returns to corporate social responsibility (CSR): The role of CSR communication. *International Journal of Management Reviews, 12*(1), 8−19.

Duncan, T., & Caywood, C. (1996). The concept, process, and evolution of integrated marketing communication. *Integrated Communication: Synergy of Persuasive Voices, 13024*, 13−34.

Edelman Trust Barometer. (2012). Retrieved from https://www.edelman.com/research/2012-edelman-trust-barometer

Edelman Trust Barometer. (2019). Retrieved from https://www.edelman.com/trust-barometer

Egri, C. P., & Herman, S. (2000). Leadership in the North American environmental sector: Values, leadership styles, and contexts of environmental leaders and their organizations. *The Academy of Management Journal, 43*(4), 571−604.

Ellison, N., & Hardey, M. (2014). Social media and local government: Citizenship, consumption and democracy. *Local Government Studies, 40*(1), 21−40. doi:10.1080/03003930.2013.799066

Englander, E., & Kaufman, A. (2004). The end of managerial ideology from corporate social responsibility to corporate social indifference. *Enterprise and Society, 5*(3), 404−450.

EPACA. (2019). Retrieved from https://epaca.org/about-lobbying/

Etizoni, A. (1998). A communitarian note on stakeholder theory. *Business Ethics Quarterly, 8*(4), 679−691. ISSN 1052-150X.

European Communication Monitor. (2018). *Challenges and competencies for strategic communication, results of an empirical survey in 42 countries.* Brussels: EACD/EUPRERA.

European Communication Monitor. (2012). Retrieved from http://www.communication-monitor.eu/2012/06/14/ecm-european-communication-monitor-2012-ethics-operational-strategic-tasks-social-media-qualifications-recruiting-integrated-communication/

European Communication Monitor. (2013). Retrieved from http://www.communicationmonitor.eu/2013/06/13/ecm-european-communication-monitor-2013-ceo-communication-social-media-skills-digital-gatekeepers-international-crisis-communication-status/

European Communication Monitor. (2014). Retrieved from http://www.communicationmonitor.eu/2014/06/13/ecm-european-communication-monitor-2014-social-mobile-communication-media-technologies-job-satisfaction-gender-excellence/

European Communication Monitor. (2015). Retrieved from http://www.communicationmonitor.eu/2015/06/13/ecm-european-communication-monitor-2015-communication-value-listening-messaging-measurement-content-marketing-excellence-strategic-communication/

European Communication Monitor. (2016). Retrieved from http://www.communicationmonitor.eu/2016/06/13/ecm-european-communication-monitor-2016-big-data-algorithms-social-media-influencer-strategic-communication-automated-pr/

European Communication Monitor. (2017). Retrieved from http://www.communica-tionmonitor.eu/2017/06/04/ecm-european-communication-monitor-2017-social-bo ts-visualisation-hypermodernity-benchmarking-strategic-communication/

European Communication Monitor. (2018). Retrieved from http://www.communica-tionmonitor.eu/2018/06/13/ecm-european-communication-monitor-2018/

European Communication Monitor. (2019). Retrieved from http://www.communica-tionmonitor.eu/2019/05/23/ecm-european-communication-monitor-2019/

Evans, N., & Elphick, S. (2005). Models of crisis management: An evaluation of their value for strategic planning in the international travel industry. *International Journal of Tourism Research, 7*, 135–150.

Ewing, M. T. (2009). Integrated marketing communication measurement and evalua-tion. *Journal of Marketing Communication, 15*(2–3), 103–117.

Fairhurst, G., & Sarr, R. (1996). *The art of framing.* San Francisco, CA: Jossey-Bass.

Fan, W., & Gordon, M. D. (2014). The power of social media analytics. *Communications of the ACM, 57*(6), 74–81.

Fearn-Banks, K. (2011). *Crisis communications: A case studies approach.* New York, NY: Routledge.

Fenton, N., & Barassi, V. (2011). Alternative media and social networking sites: The politics of individuation and political participation. *The Communication Review, 14*(3), 179–196.

Ferguson, R. (2008). Word of mouth and viral marketing: Taking the temperature of the hottest trends in marketing. *Journal of Consumer Marketing, 25*(3), 179–182. doi:10.1108/07363760810870671

Ferrell, O. C., & Krugman, D. M. (1978). The role of consumers in the public policy process. *Journal of the Academy of Marketing Science, 6*(2), 167–175.

Ferrier, W. J. (2001). Navigating the competitive landscape: The drivers and conse-quences of competitive aggressiveness. *The Academy of Management Journal, 44*(4), 858–877.

Fieseler, C. (2011). On the corporate social responsibility Perceptions of equity ana-lysts. *Business Ethics: A European Review, 20*(2), 131–147.

Fiol, M. (1999). Corporate communication: Comparing top executives private and public statements. *The Academy of Management Journal, 38*(2), 522–536.

Fisher, T. (2009). ROI in social media: A look at the arguments. *Database Marketing and Customer Strategy, 16*(3), 189–195.

Fiss, P. C., & Zajac, E. J. (2006). The symbolic management of strategic change sen-segiving via framing and decupling. *The Academy of Management Journal, 49*(6), 1175–1193.

Forbes. (2019). Retrieved from https://www.forbes.com/sites/bernardmarr/2015/09/ 30/big-data-20-mind-boggling-facts-everyone-must-read/#17f715f617b1. Accessed on May 30, 2019.

Forman, J., & Argenti, P. A. (2005). How corporate communication influences strat-egy implementation, reputation and corporate brand. An exploratory qualitative study. *Corporate Reputation Review, 8*(1), 245–264.

Fornell, C., & Bookstein, F. L. (1982). Two structural equation models: LISREL and PLS appliead to consumer exit-voice theory. *Journal of Marketing Research, 19*, 440–452.

Foucault, M. (2002). *The archaeology of knowledge [1969]* (p. 198). A. M. Sheridan Smith (Trans.). Abingdon: Routledge.

Fox, J. A., & Brown, L. D. (Eds.). (1998). *The struggle for accountability: The World Bank, NGOs, and grassroots movements.* Cambridge, MA: MIT Press.

Freberg, K., Graham, K., McGaughey, K., & Freberg, L. A. (2011). Who are the social media influencers? A study of public perceptions of personality. *Public Relations Review, 37*(1), 90–92.

Freeman, R. (1994). The politics of stakeholder theory: Some future directions. *Business Ethics Quarterly, 4*(4), 409–421. doi:10.2307/3857340

Gil de Zúñiga, H., Jung, N., & Valenzuela, S. (2012). Social media use for news and individuals' social capital, civic engagement and political participation. *Journal of Computer-mediated Communication, 17*(3), 319–336.

Goodpaster, K. E. (1991). Business ethics and stakeholder analysis. *Business Ethics Quarterly, 1*, 53–73.

Gonzalez-Herrero, A., & Smith, S. (2008). Crisis communications management on the web: How internet-based technologies are changing the way public relations handle business crises. *Journal of Contingencies and Crisis Management, 1*(3), 143–153.

Gotsi, M., & Wilson, A. M. (2001). Corporate reputation: Seeking a definition. *Corporate Communications: An International Journal, 6*(1), 24–30. doi:10.1108/13563280110381189

Gregory, A., & Watson, T. (2008). Defining the gap between research and practice in public relations programme evaluation – Towards a research agenda. *Journaal of Marketing Communication, 14*(5), 337–350.

Gunningham, N., & Rees, J. (1997, October). Industry self-regulation: An institutional perspective. *Law & Policy, 19*(4), 363–414.

Guzman, A. T., & Meyer, T. L. (2010, Spring). International soft law. *Journal of Legal Analysis, 2*(1), 171–225. doi:10.1093/jla/2.1.171

Hall, R. B., & Biersteker, T. J. (2002). *The emergence of private authority in global governence.* Cambridge: Cambridge University Press.

Hall, S. (1980[1972]). Encoding/decoding. Centre for Contemporary Cultural Studies (Ed.) *Culture, media, language: Working papers in cultural studies, 79*, 128–138.

Hancock, C. (2010). You are connected. Now, what are you going to do about it? *The Design Management Institute, 21*(1), 62–67.

Hanks, K., Odom, W., Roedl, D., & Blevis, E. (2008, April). Sustainable millennials: Attitudes towards sustainability and the material effects of interactive technologies. In Proceedings of the SIGCHI Conference on Human Factors in Computing Systems (pp. 333–342). Florence, Italy: ACM.

Heinonen, K. (2011). Consumer activity in social media: Managerial approaches to consumers' social media behavior. *Journal of Consumer Behavior, 10*(6), 356–364.

Heinrichs, J. H., Lim, J.-S., & Lim, K.-S. (2011). Influence of social networking site and user access method on social media evaluation. *Journal of Consumer Behavior, 10*(6), 347–355.

Helm, S., Garnefeld, I., & Tolsdorf, J. (2009). Perceived corporate reputation and customer satisfaction an experimental of casual relationships. *Australasian Marketing Journal, 17*, 69–74.

Henriques, I., & Sadorsky, P. (1999). The relationship between environmental commitment and managerial perceptions of stakeholder importance. *The Academy of Management Journal, 42*(1), 87–95.

Hofstede, G. (2001). *Culture's consequences: Comparing alues, behaviors, institutions, and organizations across nations* (2nd ed.). Thousand Oaks, CA: Sage Publications.

Hollebeek, L. D. (2018). Individual-level cultural consumer engagement styles: Conceptualization, propositions and implications. *International Marketing Review, 35*(1), 42−71. doi:10.1108/IMR-07-2016-0140

Holliman, G., & Rowley, J. (2014). Business to business digital content marketing: Marketers' perceptions of best practice. *Journal of Research in Interactive Marketing, 8*(4), 269−293.

Huber, G. (1991, March). Organizational learning: The contributing processes and the literatures. *Organization Science (Special Issue: Organizational Learning: Papers in Honor of (and by) James G), 2*, 1, . 88−115.

Husted, B. W., & Allen, D. B. (2006). Corporate social responsibility in the multinational enterprise: Strategic and institutional approaches. *Journal of International Business Studies, 37*(6), 838−849.

Influencer Marketing Hub. (2019). Retrieved from https://influencermarketinghub.com/influencer-marketing-2019-benchmark-report/. Accessed on May 28, 2019.

Iyengar, S., Peters, M., & Kinder, D. (1982). Experimental demonstrations of the "not-so-minimal" consequences of television news programs. *American Political Science, 76*(4), 848−858.

Jacoby, J. (1984). Perspectives on information overload. *Journal of Consumer Research, 10*(4), 432−435.

Johnstone, L., & Lindh, C. (2018). The sustainability-age dilemma: A theory of (un) planned behaviour via influencers. *Journal of Consumer Behaviour, 17*(1), e127−e139.

Jordan, L., & Van Tuijl, P. (2000). Political responsibility in transnational NGO advocacy. *World Development, 28*(12), 2051−2065.

Kaplan, A. M., & Haenlein, M. (2010). Users of the world, unite! The challenges and opportunities of social media. *Business Horizons, 53*(1), 59−68.

Katz, E., & Lazersfeld, P. (1955). *Personal influence. The part played by people in the flow of mass communications.* A report of the Bureau of Applied Social Research, Columbia University. Glencoe, IL: The Free Press.

Kietzmann, J. H., Hermkens, K., McCarthy, I. P., & Silvestre, B. S. (2011). Social media? Get serious! Understanding the functional building blocks of social media. *Business Horizons, 54*(3), 241−251.

Kilgour, M., Sasser, S. L., & Larke, R. (2015). The social media transformation process: curating content into strategy. *Corporate Communications: An International Journal, 20*(3), 326−343.

Klayman, J. (1995). Varieties of confirmation bias. In *Psychology of Learning and Motivation* (Vol. 32, pp. 385−418). Academic Press.

Knobloch-Westerwick, S., Johnson, B. K., & Westerwick, A. (2015). Confirmation bias in online searches: Impacts of selective exposure before an election on political attitude strength and shifts. *Journal of Computer-mediated Communication, 20*, 171−187.

Koontz, H., & O'donnell, C. (1972). *Principles of management: An Analysis of managerial functions (No. HD31 K6 1972).* New York, NY: McGraw-Hill.

Lacey, R., Kennett-Hensel, P., & Manolis, C. (2015). Is corporate social responsibility a motivator or hygiene factor? Insights into its bivalent nature. *Journal of the Academy of Marketing Science, 43*, 315–332.

Lasswell, H. (1948). *Power and personality.* New York, NY: W. W. Norton & Company.

Lawrence, A. T. (2010). Managing disputes with nonmarket stakeholders: Wage a fight, withdraw, wait, or work it out? *California Management Review, 53*(1), 90–113.

Le Pennec, M., & Raufflet, E. (2018). Value creation in inter-organizational collaboration: An empirical study. *Journal of Business Ethics, 148*(4), 817–834.

Lee, N. R., & Kotler, P. (2015). *Social marketing changing behaviors for good.* Thousand Oaks: Sage Publications.

Lee, Y., Mazzei, A., & Kim, J. N. (2018). Looking for motivational routes for employee-generated innovation: Employees' scouting behavior. *Journal of Business Research, 91*, 286–294.

Leidar. (2016). Little talk, little action. Retrieved from https://www.leidar.com/wp-content/uploads/2016/11/Leidar-Insight-nov-2016-SDGs.pdf

Lin, N. (2017). Building a network theory of social capital. In R. Dubos (Ed.), *Social capital.* (pp. 3–28). New York, NY: Routledge.

Lippincott, J. K. (2012). Information commons: Meeting millennials' needs. *Journal of Library Administration, 52*(6–7), 538–548.

Lipschultz, J. (2018). *Social media communication.* New York, NY: Routledge.

Liu, W., Sidhu, A., Beacom, A., & Valente, T. (2017). Social network theory. In P. Rossler, C. A. Hoffner, & L. van Zoonen (Eds.), *The International Encyclopedia of Media Effects.* John Wiley & Sons, Inc. Retrieved from https://doi.org/10.1002/9781118783764.wbieme0092

Mack, O. Khare, A. Krämer, A., & Burgartz, T. (Eds.). (2015). *Managing in a VUCA world.* Switzerland: Springer.

Macnamara, J. (2012). Corporate and organisational diplomacy: An alternative paradigm to PR. *Journal of Communication Management, 16*(3), 312–325.

Maigret, E. (2007). *Sociologie de la communication et des médias* (2e éd.). Paris: Armand Colin.

Malaval, P., & Decaudin, J.-M. (2005). *Pentacom: Communication: Théorie et pratique.* Paris: Pearson.

Maltz, E., Thompson, F., & Jones Ringold, D. (2011). Assessing and maximizing corporate social initiatives: A strategic view of corporate social responsibility. *Journal of Public Affairs, 11*(4), 344–352.

Maon, F., Lindgreen, A., & Swaen, V. (2010). Organizational stages and cultural phases: A critical review and a consolidative model of corporate social responsibility development. *International Journal of Management Reviews, 12*(1), 20–38.

Matten, D., & Crane, A. (2005). Corporate citizenship: toward an extended theoretical conceptualization. *The Academy of Management Review, 30*(1), 166–179.

Mavis, C. P., Richter, A., Landau, C., Schmidt, S. L., Simons, T., & Steinbock, K. (2018). What happens when companies (don't) do what they said they would? Stock market reactions to strategic integrity. *European Management Review.* doi:10.1111/emre.12175.

Mazzei, A. (2014). A multidisciplinary approach for a new understanding of corporate communication. *Corporate Communications: An International Journal, 19*(2), 216–230. doi:10.1108/CCIJ-12-2011-0073. Retrieved from https://doi.org/10.1108/CCIJ-12-2011-0073

McCombs, M., & Shaw, D. (1972). The agenda-setting function of mass media. *Public Opinion Quarterly, 36*(2), 176–187.

Meek, D. (2011). YouTube and social movements: A phenomenological analysis of participation, events and cyberplace. *Antipode, 44*(4), 1429–1448. doi:10.1111/j.1467-8330.2011.00942.x

Melo, T., & Garrido-Morgado, A. (2011). Corporate reputation: A combination of social responsibility and industry. *Corporate Social Responsibility and Environmental Management, 19*(1), 19–31.

Meraz, S. (2009, April 1). Is there an elite hold? Traditional media to social media agenda setting influence in blog networks. *Journal of Computer-mediated Communication, 14*(3), 682–707. doi:10.1111/j.1083-6101.2009.01458.x

Merchant, G. (2012). Unravelling the social network: Theory and research. *Learning, Media and Technology, 37*(1), 4–19.

Merriam-Webster. (2019). Retrieved from https://www.merriam-webster.com/dictionary/advocacy

Miller, K. D., Fabian, F., & Lin, S.-J. (2009). Strategies for online communities. *Strategic Management Journal, 30*(3), 305–322.

Mills, A. J. (2012). Virality in social media: The SPIN framework. *Journal of Public Affairs, 12*(2), 162–169.

Minor, D., & Morgan, J. (2011). CSR as reputation insurance: Primum non nocere. *California Management Review, 53*(3), 40–59.

Missika, J. (2006). *La fin de la télévision*. Paris: Seuil.

Mohr, L. A., Webb, D. J., & Harris, K. (2001). Do consumers expect companies to be socially responsible? The impact of corporate social responsibility on buying behavior. *The Journal of Consumer Affairs, 35*(1), 45–72.

Moon, B.-J., Lee, L. W., & Oh, C. H. (2015). The impact of CSR on consumer corporate connection and brand loyalty: A cross cultural investigation. *International Marketing Review, 32*(5), 518–539. doi:10.1108/IMR-03-2014-0089

Moon, J., Crane, A., & Matten, D. (2005). Can corporations be citizens? Corporate citizenship as a metaphor for business participation in society. *Business Ethics Quarterly, 15*(3), 429–453. ISSN 1052-150X.

Morsing, M., & Schultz, M. (2006). Corporate social responsibility communication: Stakeholder information response and involvement strategies. *Business Ethics: A European Review, 15*(4), 323–338.

Mouchon, J. (Ed.). (2005). *Les mutations de l'espace public*. Paris: L'esprit du livre éditions.

Nätti, S., Rahkolin, S., & Saraniemi, S. (2014). Crisis communication in key account relationships. *Corporate Communications: An International Journal, 19*(3), 234–246. doi:10.1108/CCIJ-08-2012-0056

Nelson, P. (2000). Heroism and ambiguity: NGO advocacy in international policy. *Development in Practice, 10*(3–4), 478–490.

Nickerson, R. S. (1998). Confirmation bias: A ubiquitous phenomenon in many guises. *Review of General Psychology, 2*(2), 175–220.

Norman, W., & MacDonald, C. (2004). Getting to the bottom of "triple bottom line". *Business Ethics Quarterly, 14*(2), 243–262. doi:10.5840/beq200414211

Orlitzky, M. (2008). Corporate social performance and financial performance: A research synthesis. In A. Crane A. McWilliams D. Matten J. Moon, & D. S. Siegel (Eds.), *The Oxford Handbook of CSR*. Oxford: Oxford University Press.

OXFAM. (2016). Retrieved from https://oxfamilibrary.openrepository.com/bit-stream/handle/10546/620550/dp-walking-the-talk-business-sdgs-240918-en.pdf

Palttala, P., Boano, C., Lund, R., & Vos, M. (2012). Communications gaps in disaster management: Perceptions by experts from governmental and non-governmental organizations. *Journal of Contingencies and Crisis Management, 20*(1), 2–12.

Parkhe, A. (1991). Interfirm diversity, organizational learning and longevity in global strategic alliances. *Journal of International Business Studies, 22*, 579–600.

Patagonia. (2018). Corporate website. Retrieved from https://www.patagonia.com/corporate-responsibility.html

Patterson, S. J., & Radtke, J. M. (2009). *Strategic communications for nonprofit organizations: seven steps to creating a successful plan.* Hoboken, NJ: John Wiley & Sons.

Pentina, I., & Tarafdar, M. (2014). From "information" to "knowing": Exploring the role of social media in contemporary news consumption. *Computers in Human Behavior, 35*, 211–223.

Percy, L. (2008). *Strategic integrated marketing communications.* London: Routledge.

Perrin, A. (2015). *Social media usage: 2005–2015.* Washington, DC: Pew Internet & American Life Project. Retrieved from http://www.pewinternet.org/2015/10/08/social-networking-usage-2005-2015/. Accessed on October 12, 2015.

Pew Research Center. (2019). Retrieved from https://www.pewinternet.org/2019/04/24/sizing-up-twitter-users/. Accessed on May 20, 2019.

Phillips, R. (1997). Stakeholder theory and a principle of fairness. *Business Ethics Quarterly, 7*(1), 51–66. doi:10.2307/3857232

Phillips, R. (2003). Stakeholder legitimacy. *Business Ethics Quarterly, 13*(1), 25–41. doi:10.5840/beq20031312

Phillips, R., Freeman, R., & Wicks, A. (2003). What stakeholder theory is not. *Business Ethics Quarterly, 13*(4), 479–502. doi:10.5840/beq200313434

Plangger, K. (2012). The power of popularity: How the size of a virtual community adds to firm value. *Journal of Public Affairs, 12*(2), 145–153.

Porter, C. E., Donthu, N., MacElroy, W. H., & Wydra, D. (2011). How to foster and sustain engagement in virtual communities. *California Management Review, 53*(4), 80–110.

Porter, M., & Kramer, M. (2006). The link between competitive advantage and corporate social responsibility. *Harvard Business Review, 84*(12), 78–93.

Porter, M., & Kramer, M. (2011). Creating shared value. *Harvard Business Review, 89*(1/2), 62–77.

PR Council. (2019). Retrieved from https://prcouncil.net/about/. Accessed on March 05, 2019.

Prakash Sethi, S. (1978). Advocacy advertising – The American experience. *Journal of Marketing, 21*(1), 55–68.

Preuss, L., Haunschild, A., & Matten, D. (2006). Trade unions and CSR: A European research agenda. *Journal of Public Affairs, 6*, 256–268.

Pulizzi, J., & Barrett, N. (2009). "Get content get customers" – Turn prospects into buyers with content marketing. *Management Case, 98*, 55–68.

PwC. (2018). From promise to reality: Does business really care about the SDGs? Retrieved from www.pwc.com/sdgreportingchallenge. Accessed on March 11, 2019.

Quéré, B. P., Nouyrigat, G., & Baker, C. R. (2018). A bi-directional examination of the relationship between corporate social responsibility ratings and company financial performance in the European context. *Journal of Business Ethics, 148,* 527. doi:10.1007/s10551-015-2998-1

Rainie, L., Smith, A., Schlozman, K. L., Brady, H., & Verba, S. (2012). Social media and political engagement. *Pew Internet & American Life Project, 19,* 2–13.

Rasche, A., Waddock, S., & McIntosh, M. (2013). The United Nations global compact: Retrospect and prospect. *Business & Society, 52*(1), 6–30. doi:10.1177/0007650312459999

Regester, M., & Larkin, J. (2005). *Risk issues and crisis management in public relations: A casebook of best practice.* London: Kogan Page Publishers.

Reputation Institute. (2019). Retrieved from https://www.reputationinstitute.com/about-us

Roberts, P., & Dawling, G. R. (2002). Corporate reputation and sustained superior financial performance. Strategic management. *Journal Strategic Management Journal, 23,* 1077–1093.

Romani, S., Grappi, S., & Bagozzi, R. P. (2016). Corporate socially responsible initiatives and their effects on consumption of green products. *Journal of Business Ethics, 135*(2), 253–264.

Romero, D. M., Galuba, W., Asur, S., & Huberman, B. A. (2011). Influence and passivity in social media. In D. Gunopulos, T. Hofmann, D. Malerba, & M. Vazirgiannis (Eds.), *Machine learning and knowledge discovery in databases.* ECML PKDD 2011. Lecture Notes in Computer Science (Vol. 6913). Berlin, Heidelberg: Springer.

Rosling, H. (2018). *Factfulness.* New York, NY: Flatiron Books.

Rowley, J. (2008). Understanding digital content marketing. *Journal of Marketing Management, 24*(5–6), 517–540.

Sachs, J. D. (2012). From millennium development goals to sustainable development goals. *Lancet, 2012*(379), 2206–2211.

Sachs, J. D. (2015). Goal-based development and the SDGS: Implications for development finance. *Oxford Review of Economic Policy, 31*(3–4), 268–278.

Sachs, J., Schmidt-Traub, G., Kroll, C., Durand-Delacre, D., & Teksoz, K. (2017). *SDG index and dashboards report 2017.* New York, NY: Bertelsmann Stiftung and Sustainable Development Solutions Network (SDSN).

Salmon, C. (2007). *Storytelling.* Paris: La Découverte.

Sashi, C. M. (2012). Customer engagement, buyer-seller relationships, and social media. *Management Decision, 50*(2), 253–272. doi:10.1108/00251741211203551

Scherer, A. G., & Palazzo, G. (2011). The new political role of business in a globalized world: A review of a new perspective on csr and its implications for the firm, governance, and democracy. *Journal of Management Studies, 48*(4), 899–931.

Scheyvens, R., Banks, G., & Hughes, E. (2016). The private sector and the SDGs: The need to move beyond "business as usual". *Sustainable Development, 24,* 371–382. doi:10.1002/sd.1623.

Schnietz, K., & Epstein, M. J. (2005). Exploring the financial value of a reputation for corporate social responsibility during a crisis. *Corporate Reputation Review, 7*(4), 327–345.

Schwartz, M., & Carroll, A. (2003). Corporate social responsibility: A three-domain approach. *Business Ethics Quarterly, 13*(4), 503–530. doi:10.5840/beq200313435

Seitanidi, M. M., & Ryan, A. A. (2007). Critical review of forms of corporate community involvement: From philanthropy to partnerships. *International Journal of Non-profit and Voluntary Sector Marketing, 12*, 247–266.

Sethi, S. P., & Schepers, D. H. (2014). United Nations global compact: The promise–performance gap. *Journal of Business Ethics, 122*, 193. doi:10.1007/s10551-013-1629-y

Shaw, R., & Merrick, D. (2005). *Marketing payback: Is your marketing profitable?* London: Pearson Education.

Shumate, M., & O'Connor, A. (2010). The symbiotic sustainability model: Conceptualizing NGO-corporate alliance communication. *Journal of Communication, 60*(3), 577–609.

Sinek, S. (2009). *Start with why: How great leaders inspire everyone to take action.* London: Penguin.

Smith, E. A., & Malone, R. E. (2003). Thinking the "unthinkable". Why Philipp Morris considered quitting. *Tobacco Control, 12*(2), 208–213.

Smith, J. L., Bohner, S. A., & McCrickard, D. S. (2005, March). Project management for the 21st century: Supporting collaborative design through risk analysis. In *Proceedings of the 43rd annual Southeast regional conference, Volume 2* (pp. 300–305). ACM.

Solomon, R. C. (1992, July). Corporate reputation, personal values: An Aristotelean approach to business ethics. *Business Ethics Quarterly, 2*(3), 317–339.

Stead, E., & Smallman, C. (1999). Understanding business failure: Learning and unlearning lessons from industrial crises. *Journal of Contingences and Crisis Management, 7*(1), 1–18.

Strike, V., Gao, J., & Bansal, P. (2006). Being good while being bad: Social responsibility and the international diversification of US. *Journal of International Business Studies, 37*(6), 850–862.

Stroup, S. S., & Murdie, A. (2012). There's no place like home: Explaining international NGO advocacy. *The Review of International Organizations, 7*, 425. doi:10.1007/s11558-012-9145-x

Subacchi, P. (2008). New power centres and new power brokers: Are they shaping a new economic order? *International Affairs, 84*(3), 485–498.

Sustein, C. (2007). *Republic.com.2.0.* Princeton, NJ: Princeton University Press.

Sweetser, K. D. (2010). A loosing strategy: The impact of nondisclosure in social media on relationships. *Journal of Public Relations Research, 22*(3), 288–310.

Swoboda, B., & Hirschmann, J. (2017). Perceptions and effects of cross-national corporate reputation: The role of Hofstede's cultural value approach. *International Marketing Review, 34*(6), 909–944. doi:10.1108/IMR-08-2016-0154

Tapscott, D. (2008). *Grown up digital.* New York, NY: McGraw-Hill.

Taylor, P., & Keeter, S. (2010). *Millennials: Confident. Connected. Open to change.* Washington, DC: Pew Research Center.

Tench, R., Verhoeven, P., & Zerfass, A. (2009). Institutionalizing strategic communication in Europe – An ideal home or a mad house? Evidence from a survey in 37 countries. *International Journal of Strategic Communication, 3*, 147–164.

Transparency Register. (2019). http://ec.europa.eu/transparencyregister/public/staticPage/displayStaticPage.do;TRPUBLICID-prod=lqSoH7yfjHjvNIPRreU0A kglIM4zOKQ-gZ-kFa-A_49cG2_BMIis!-1240251725?locale=en&reference=WHY_ TRANSPARENCY_REGISTER

UN Global Compact. (2019). Retrieved from https://www.unglobalcompact.org/what-is-gc/our-work/sustainable-development. Accessed on May 29, 2019.

UN Global Compact Guide to Corporate Sustainability. Retrieved from https://www.unglobalcompact.org/library/1151. Accessed on May 12, 2019.

UNICEF. (2015). Advocacy toolkit. Retrieved from https://www.unicef.org/evaluation/files/Advocacy_Toolkit.pdf

United Nations. (2015). Retrieved from https://sustainabledevelopment.un.org/?menu=1300

Urban, G. L. (2005). Customer advocacy: A new era in marketing? *Journal of Public Policy & Marketing, 24*(1), 155–159. doi:10.1509/jppm.24.1.155.63887

Veil, S. R., Buehner, T., & Pakenchar, M. J. (2011). A work-in-process literature review: Incorporating social media in risk and crisis communication. *Journal of Contingencies and Crisis Management, 19*(2), 110–122.

Waddock, S., & Mcintosh, M. (2011). Business unusual: Corporate responsibility in a 2.0 world. *Business and Society Review, 116*(3), 303–330.

Wagner, J., III. & Hollenbeck, J. (2015). *Organizational behavior*. New York, NY: Routledge. Retrieved from https://doi.org/10.4324/9780203385418

Watson, T. (2011). An initial integration of the use of return on investment in public relations practice. *Public Relations Review, 37*, 314–317.

Weingarten, E., Chen, Q., McAdams, M., Yi, J., Hepler, J., & Albarracín, D. (2016). From primed concepts to action: A meta-analysis of the behavioral effects of incidentally presented words. *Psychological Bulletin, 142*(5), 472–497. doi:10.1037/bul0000030

Weiss, T. G. (2000). Governance, good governance and global governance: Conceptual and actual challenges. *Third World Quarterly, 21*(5), 795–814. doi:10.1080/713701075

Weiss, L. (2018). *The myth of the powerless state*. Ithaca, New York, NY: Cornell University Press.

Wettstein, F. (2012). CSR and the debate on business and human rights: Bridging the great divide. *Business Ethics Quarterly, 22*(4), 739–770.

White, J. (1994). *Strategic communications management: Making public relations work*. London: Wokingham.

WHO. (2015). Health in 2015. From MDGs to SDGs. Retrieved from https://www.who.int/gho/publications/mdgs-sdgs/en/

Winkin, Y. (1996). *Anthropologie de la communication: De la théorie au terrain*. Paris: De Boeck & Larcier/Seuil.

Wood, D. J. (2010). Measuring corporate social performance: A review. *International Journal of Management Reviews, 12*(1), 50–84.

Working, R. (2018). PR Daily. How to create a highly shared newsroom. Retrieved from https://www.prdaily.com/6-ways-to-create-a-highly-shared-newsroom/

World Business Council of Sustainable Development. (2019). Retrieved from https://www.wbcsd.org/. Accessed on May 31, 2019.

Wright, D. K. (1999). Perceptions of corporate communication as public relations. *Corporate Communications, 2*(4), 143–154.

Yin, H., Hu, Z., Zhou, X., Wang, H., Zheng, K., Nguyen, Q. V. H., & Sadiq, S. (2016, May). *Discovering interpretable geo-social communities for user behavior prediction*. In 2016 IEEE 32nd International Conference on Data Engineering (ICDE) (pp. 942–953). IEEE.

Zellweger, T. M., Nason, R. S., Nordqvist, M., & Brush, C. G. (2013). Why do family firms strive for nonfinancial goals? An organizational identity perspective. *Entrepreneurship Theory and Practice, 37*(2), 229–248

Zerfass, A., Verčič, D., Verhoeven, P., Moreno, A., & Tench, R. (2012). European communication monitor 2012. In *Challenges and competencies for strategic communication, results of an empirical survey in 42 countries.* Brussels: EACD.

Zetter, L. (2014). *Lobbying3e: The art of political persuasion.* Petersfield: Harriman House Limited.

Ziek, P. (2009). Making sense of CSR communication. *Corporate Social Responsibility and Environmental Management, 16*(3), 137–145.

Zyglidopoulos, S. C. (2004). The impact of downsizing on the corporate reputation for social performance. *Journal of Public Affairs, 4*(1), 11–25.

Index

www.ingramcontent.com/pod-product-compliance
Lightning Source LLC
Chambersburg PA
CBHW062347300326
41947CB00013B/1549